Japanese Confucianism

For more than 1500 years Confucianism has played a major role in shaping Japan's history – from the formation of the first Japanese states during the first millennium CE, to Japan's modernization in the nineteenth century, to WWII and its still unresolved legacies across East Asia today. In an illuminating and provocative new study, Kiri Paramore analyzes the dynamic history of Japanese Confucianism, revealing its many cultural manifestations as religion and as political tool, as social capital and public discourse, as well as its role in international relations and statecraft. The book demonstrates the processes through which Confucianism was historically linked to other phenomenon, such as the rise of modern science and East Asian liberalism. In doing so it offers new perspectives on the sociology of Confucianism and its impact on society, culture, and politics across East Asia, past and present.

KIRI PARAMORE teaches History and Asian Studies at Leiden University.

New Approaches to Asian History

This dynamic new series publishes books on the milestones in Asian history, those that have come to define particular periods or to mark turning points in the political, cultural and social evolution of the region. The books in this series are intended as introductions for students to be used in the classroom. They are written by scholars whose credentials are well-established in their particular fields and who have, in many cases, taught the subject across a number of years.

Books in the series

Japanese Confucianism

A Cultural History

Kiri Paramore

Leiden University, the Netherlands

CAMBRIDGE
UNIVERSITY PRESS

CAMBRIDGE
UNIVERSITY PRESS

University Printing House, Cambridge CB2 8BS, United Kingdom

Cambridge University Press is part of the University of Cambridge.

It furthers the University's mission by disseminating knowledge in the pursuit of education, learning and research at the highest international levels of excellence.

www.cambridge.org
Information on this title: www.cambridge.org/9781107635685

© Kiri Paramore 2016

First published 2016
Reprinted 2017

Printed in the United Kingdom by Clays, St Ives plc

A catalogue record for this publication is available from the British Library

Library of Congress Cataloguing in Publication data
Paramore, Kiri, author.
Japanese Confucianism : a cultural history / Kiri Paramore.
Cambridge ; New York : Cambridge University Press, 2016. | Series: Asian connections | Includes bibliographical references and index.
LCCN 2016004898| ISBN 9781107058651 (hardback) |
ISBN 9781107635685 (paperback)
LCSH: Confucianism – Japan | Japan – Civilization.
LCC BL1843 .P37 2016 | DDC 181/.12–dc23
LC record available at http://lccn.loc.gov/2016004898

ISBN 978-1-107-05865-1 Hardback
ISBN 978-1-107-63568-5 Paperback

自我作古

Antiquity is constructed by us.

Liu Zhiji (661–721), Historian and Confucian, Tang China.
Kagawa Shūan (1683–1755), Confucian and Medical doctor, Tokugawa Japan.
Fukuzawa Yukichi (1835–1901), Liberal public intellectual and educator, Meiji Japan.

Antiquity is constructed by us.

Contents

Figures

Maps

Acknowledgments

This book tries to engage Confucianism not as dead tradition, but as history alive in the contemporary politics of East Asia. This approach is influenced by my time as a student at the University of Tokyo, where Confucianism was engaged in seminars on politics, history, philosophy and social studies taught by professors like Kurozumi Makoto, Mitani Hiroshi, Watanabe Hiroshi, Karube Tadashi, Kojima Yasunori, Kojima Tsuyoshi and Hiraishi Naoaki, in an intellectual environment which encouraged cross-disciplinary and socially engaged analysis. I thank them for creating that environment and my fellow graduate students who enriched it with a multi-cultural breadth of experience and opinion. Among fellow students, Lan Hung-Yueh, Ōta Hideaki, and Kōno Yūri have been steadfast comrades; Koh Heetak, Sekiguchi Sumiko, Nakada Yoshikazu, Han Dongyu, and many others inspiring examples. The book's outlook has since been enriched by conversations with Milinda Banerjee, Benjamin Elman, Matsuda Kōichirō, Sugawara Hikaru, Ōkubo Takeharu, Chen-Tao Shih, Barak Kushner, Hans Martin Krämer, Mark Teeuwen, Fuyuko Matsukata, Patrick O'Brien, David Mervart, James McMullen, Hung-Yueh Lan, David Ambaras, Mark Driscoll, Morgan Pitelka, and Barbara Ambros. For invaluable criticism on late-stage drafts, I would particularly like to thank Bill Callahan, Barend ter Haar, Yuan-Kang Wang, and Hans van Leeuwen. I also thank Machi Senjurō and Karube Tadashi for important ideas as I was finishing the book. At Leiden I thank colleagues who discussed the project with me - Wim Boot, Marc Buijnsters, Oliver Moore, Anna Yeadell, Alice de Jong, Daan Kok, Nadia Kreeft, Paul Wijsman and Jeroen Wiedenhof – others who even read sections – Ethan Mark and Ivo Smits – and particularly, Joep Smorenburg who drafted the maps and tables. Research for this book was assisted by the awarding of visiting fellowship grants from Academia Sinica, Taipei, and Rikkyo University, Tokyo. I thank both institutions and particularly Chen Weifen and Matsuda Kōichirō. I also acknowledge the assistance of the Shibunkai in provision of access to Yushima Seidō and material for illustrations. The cover image of the book was supplied courtesy of the Chapman University, Orange, California. The early conceptualization of this book was greatly aided by discussions with Roger Malcolm Haydon of Cornell University Press, Emily Andrew of UBC Press, Anne Routen of Columbia University Press, and Marigold Acland of Cambridge University Press. Others at CUP, notably Lucy Rhymer, have helped immensely through the whole project. Last but not least, I am immensely grateful for the intellectual acumen and relentlessly critical nature brought to bear on discussion of this book, as on everything else, by my daily conversation partner Ya-pei Kuo.

Notes on the text

This book uses Pinyin for the Romanization of Chinese, the Hepburn system for Japanese, and McCune-Reischauer for Korean. Exceptions are made for readings established in English using other systems, or nowadays accepted as English words. For instance, Chiang Kai-shek stays as is, as does KMT, Choson, ronin, etc.

Chinese, Japanese, and Korean names are given with the surname first, except where the name is commonly established in another order in English. When using a single name to refer to an already established figure, the book universally gives the surname. This goes against a common practice of early modern Japanese history writing, both in Japanese and in English, where the *gō* name rather than the *myō* surname is commonly used. Thus, in many publications Ogyū Sorai (1666–1728) is simply referred to as Sorai. But in this book he is referred to by his surname as Ogyū. This method of naming allows us to use the same standard system cross-period (into the modern period), conforming to general English usage, and also reflecting more up-to-date editorial guidelines of major journals in the field, notably the *Journal of Japanese Studies*.

References are given using name and date in in-text bracket citation, with full bibliographical references for each entry in a list at the end of the book. This means that many references to premodern primary sources in modern printed compilations will have a twentieth-century date, even though the actual text is much older. For instance, some quotes from the late eighteenth-century writings of Shibano Ritsuzan (1736–1807) appear referenced as "(Takimoto 1914)," giving the name of the editor who oversaw the modern printed compilation. The referencing system is thus designed primarily to facilitate a reader being able to find the source themselves in the commonly available modern compilations through a library catalog. Abbreviations are used for a number of large compendium series used extensively in the book. The key to abbreviations is at the beginning of the Bibliography.

Timeline

Timeline 1 (500–1600 AD)

Chapter of book	Chapter 1			Chapter 4		Chapter 2 →
Years AD	500	1200	1300	1400	1500	1600
Japanese period name		Nara / Heian	Kamakura		Muromachi	Warring States →
Chinese period name	Sui / Tang	Song	Yuan		Ming →	
Historical period (Jpn)	Early	Medieval				
Events (East Asia)		Shogunate established / Zhu Xi born	Mongols defeated by Japan / Mongols conquer Song China		Wang Yangming born / Yi Toegye born / Chosŏn established	Japan invades Korea
Events (global)	Birth of Islam		Peak of Mongol Empire / Mamluk defeat Mongols		Protestant Reformation / Magellan circles globe / Jesuits established / Galileo born	

Timeline 2 (1600–2000 AD)

Chapter of book	← Chapter 2 / ← Chapter 4	Chapter 5 / Chapter 6			Chapter 7 →
Years AD	1600	1700	1800	1900	2000
Japanese period name	Tokugawa (Edo)			Meiji / Taishō / Shōwa	Heisei
Chinese period name	← Ming	Qing		Republic / People's Republic →	
Historical period (Jpn)	Early Modern			Modern (kindai) / Post-War (gendai) →	
Events (East Asia)	Manchus take Beijing / Ogyū Sorai born		Kang Youwei born / Opium Wars / Meiji Restoration	First Sino-Japanese War / Xinhai Revolution	
Events (global)	Thirty Years War / Peace of Westphalia		Industrial Revolution / American Revolution / French Revolution / Maratha sack Mughal Delhi / Revolutions of 1848 / British Raj	First World War / Bolshevik Revolution / Second World War	

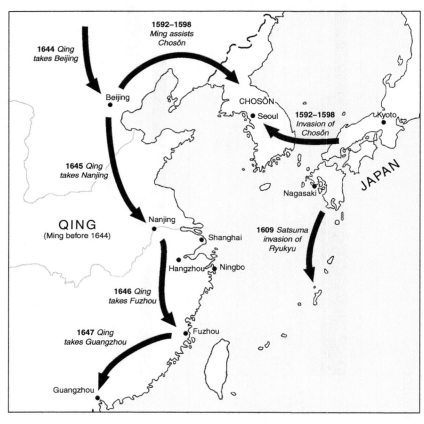

1. East Asia 1590–1650

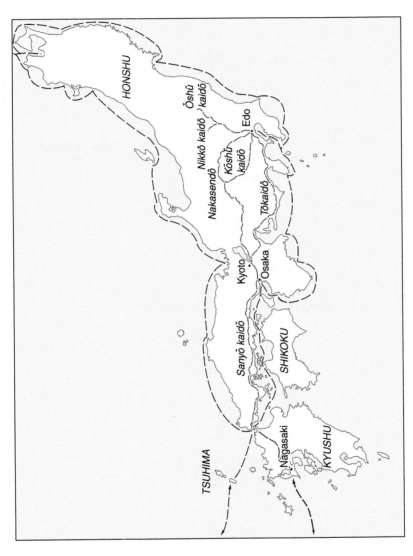

2. Japan 1700

3. East Asian trade connections to Japan 1650–1850

4. Japan in East Asia 1934

5. Japan in East Asia 1942

6. Japan in East Asia 1952

Introduction

Be they pro-Japanese or anti-Japanese, be attentive to everything in their words, deeds, public and private lives. Do not forget the words [from the Confucian Classic, the *Zuozhuan Commentary of the Spring and Autumn Annals*]: "If he is not of our race, then he will of necessity be of a different heart."

Alleged entry referring to Chinese and Manchus in the service handbook of a Japanese official working in the office of Zhang Jinghui, Prime Minister of Manchukuo, 1935–45 (Fogel and Yamamuro 2007: 11)

The cover of this book represents a modern Confucian paradise: the state of Manchukuo (1932–1945). Established by Japan in occupied Northeastern China in the interbellum, it was billed as the apex of both East Asian Confucian tradition and industrial high modernity. The population, made up of Chinese, Koreans, Manchus, Mongolians, and Japanese, lived happily together in this multi-ethnic and multicultural state. Trans-Asian Confucian principles of benevolence and righteousness reigned under a "Kingly Way" of morally virtuous governance led by a paternal sovereign, the Manchu Emperor Pu Yi, aided by his good friend and kingly brother the Japanese Emperor Hirohito. Nations lived happily together, ethnicities united in the nation, tradition and modernity perfectly harmonized through a conservative and indigenous trans-Asian ethic of Confucianism, striving toward the material welfare that only high modernity could offer. This was the Confucian dream.[1]

Of course, it was a lie. Manchukuo was a regime where strict rules of racial discrimination and subjugation, covering everything from bus seats to wages, created a pyramid-like hierarchy, with ethnic Japanese at the top, followed by Manchus and Koreans, and at the bottom the vast majority of Chinese. Life for most of the Chinese majority in this Confucian paradise was at best hard and at worst hellish. They were regularly sacrificed in the thousands, through wages mandated at starvation levels, through lethal forced labor projects, and even occasionally, as in the famous Unit 731, as guinea pigs in biological warfare experiments. Manchukuo is probably one of the most negative examples of

Confucianism in over 2000 years of history. It is certainly not representative of Confucian history nor of modern Japanese history, nor of the long history of Japanese Confucianism. Nonetheless, it is one real example of *a* Confucian history.

Most pertinently, however, it is an attractively counterintuitive example. Common imaginations of Confucianism all over the world perceive it as exclusively "premodern," "traditional," "harmonious," and "Chinese." The Manchukuo example overturns all these stereotypes. Here is Confucianism as the ideology of Japanese occupation in China, in a rhetorical package advancing modernism and modernity, manifested in the midst of bitter guerilla war, all set in the fulcrum of the creation of what historian Prasenjit Duara has described as a new kind of postcolonial modernity which would inform later Cold War norms across the region (Duara 2003).

Confucianism in history has played a much more diverse and active role than most people imagine. It has been a key element in modern history, as well as premodern history, employed to advance liberalism and socialism as well as conservatism and fascism, right up into the late twentieth century. It has been applied and practiced both domestically within states and across state boundaries in international relations, on the individual level, as well as on the social. It has been used on many occasions throughout history both to advance the interests of Chinese states and by outsiders to attack, conquer, and colonize those states. In history, there is no single Confucianism. There are multiple Confucianism*s*, manifested in different places and times.

This book studies multiple manifestations of Confucianism that occurred in Japan and/or under the auspices of Japanese control through the entire history of organized Japanese states. Confucianism has been present in Japan since the beginnings of the first large-scale, organized Japanese (*ritsuryō*) state in the middle of the first millennium CE. It was crucially influential both in the formation of that state and thereafter on multiple aspects of Japanese history through many different periods. Confucianism even played a key facilitating role in Japan's early modernization and Westernization (as discussed in Chapters 4 and 5 of this book), as well as in its drift toward fascism (Chapter 6). This book attempts to provide a history which, although centered on Japan, may provide new ways of looking at Confucianism across East Asia.

One key to that new outlook is to think about the links between premodern and modern history. Most writing on Confucianism simply ignores the influence of modern history. Scholarship on contemporary Confucianism, although usually acknowledging history, concentrates overwhelmingly on continuity at the expense of analyzing change and rupture. Major changes in Confucianism, however, were almost always interlinked with major points of rupture in broader socio-economic history. This is why the major change in East Asian history, the transition to modernity, should be a major element in the history of Confucianism, just as it is in any other facet of global history. The effects of modernity and modernization on religious tradition have been well documented globally (Asad 1993; Casanova 1994). Modernity universally transforms religion, and it usually does that in specific universal ways: religious tradition is individualized, religious organizations are differentiated from and sometimes disengaged from larger social institutions, religion is harnessed to nationalist objectives, religious practice and thinking are constrained into limited realms of life.

This book aims to bring out the significance of that transformation in the history of Confucianism and demonstrate its links with many similar moments of transformation in both premodern and contemporary history. Key here is the history of the early modern period, where in Japan, Confucianism reached its apex of social penetration and cultural and political influence. In this book, I argue that the history of Confucianism in Japan, particularly in the early modern period, but also through modernity right up until the present, offers up new formulations for thinking about the sociology of Confucianism which challenge former understandings of how Confucianism affects society, culture, and politics across East Asia. This book presents highly influential manifestations of Confucianism in early modern and modern history which allow Confucianism to be characterized in terms which for some might be challenging. For instance:

- Confucianism as religion: the manifestation of Confucianism in Japan was primarily religious, in the sense that its capacity to affect politics, culture, education, and other spheres relied on its schemes of religious practice. Throughout the study presented in this book, the more religiously Confucianism was manifested, the greater its wider social impact, including on politics. In this respect, what in Chapter 3 I call the "Confucian public sphere" of late early modern Japan was effected and supported primarily by aspects of Confucian culture which we would today characterize as religious and/or educational (Chapters 1–7).
- Confucianism as subversive politics: This book argues that Confucianism was most popular in Japan when politically critical. Creativity in early modern and modern Confucianism was often the product of political tension between Confucianism's religiosity, on the one hand, and the political order, on the other. The more critical Confucian religiosity was perceived to be, the more successful its

cultural integration and impact on politics (as argued in Chapters 1 and 2 particularly, but also throughout the book). This challenges the common image of Confucianism as inherently politically conservative.

- Confucianism as science: Confucian culture consistently facilitated technical innovation. In the Japanese history argued in this book, Confucianism fed science, including Western science. Confucianism's central role in the private learning spheres of early modern Japanese society directly impacted scientific thought, effecting what I call an "intellectual revolution" comparable to (and interlinked with) the "industrious revolution" in early modern agricultural society described by economic historian Hayami Akira (Chapters 2 and 4).
- Confucianism as ultra-individualism: Confucianism encouraged an at times rampant individualism. As in the case of the "industrious revolution," the Confucian "intellectual revolution" was driven in part by a new extreme individualism which was linked to Neo-Confucianism's development of what Kurozumi Makoto has criticized as a harsh ethic of "unlimited individual responsibility" (Chapter 3).
- Confucianism as relativism: Socially effective manifestations of Confucianism in Japanese history were usually highly relativized rather than doctrinaire in nature. Through most of the history studied in this book, the more culturally relativized and politically diversified the manifestation of Confucianism, the deeper its cultural integration and political impact (Chapters 1–5, but particularly Chapters 2 and 3). This argument challenges the historical applicability and significance of doctrinally centered explanations of Confucianism.
- Confucianism as liberalism: Confucianism was the primary conceptual framework through which liberalism was culturally reproduced in East Asia (Chapter 5). This was facilitated in part by the parallel roles of Confucian and Christian forms of humanist universalism in the politics of both traditions.
- Confucianism as fascism: Representing Confucianism as "philosophy" was a modern invention designed to facilitate an ultra-nationalist employment of the Confucian tradition which was later also adopted by fascists, both in 1930s Japan and throughout post-World War II Asia (Chapter 6).

This book thus presents a Confucianism which is (at key historical junctures) politically subversive, deeply religious, relativistic, and individualistic. These are not typical images of Confucianism. Nor are they attributes that are manifested in all the Confucianisms studied in this book. Notably, however, they are attributes that at times led to particularly deep social and cultural integration and political impact. They are manifestations of Confucianism that were very historically influential, particularly in the transition to modernity. They are also representations which I hope might provide grist for the mill of wider thinking about Confucianism, including in debates on Confucianism's position in contemporary East Asia.

What is Confucianism?

Confucianism is a constellation of ways of thinking, writing, behaving, and practicing brought together and theorized as a single unified tradition closely associated with the imperial state during the Chinese Han dynasty (206BCE–220CE). The word Confucianism today is also commonly used to refer to the intellectual and religious factions active *before* the Han dynasty, identified with the Chinese word "*ru*" and with certain historic personages including Confucius. Han dynasty political thinkers used traces of writings associated with these earlier factions to manufacture a larger, more cohesive textual apparatus and ideology which became Confucian*ism*. Confucianism was then posited post ipso facto as a historical tradition, especially in the official histories of the Han dynasty, the *Books of Han*, edited by Ban Gu (32–92CE). To some extent, Confucianism as it emerged in the common era can thus be seen as the ideological construction of Han officials like Ban Gu (Kojima 2013: 22–4). Its roots then were projected back into the "distant past." The origination of the tradition, although utilizing older textual transmissions, thus began with the launch of a commentarial tradition in the Han. This commentarial tradition continued to transform and take on new manifestations through the course of the rest of history. It is this dense, constantly developing, and changing commentarial tradition, not simply the classic texts, which provides most of the doctrinal basis for Confucianism. This is one reason why Confucianism is in a constant state of historical change.

The "practice" of Confucianism, as we will see later, depended on historical context. It could be a mix of various elements that we today might describe using adjectives including religious, political, literary, artistic, educational, scientific, medical, and many others. So Confucianism is/was a religion in some manifestations, a political science in others, a literary practice or medical tradition in others. Most often it was a constellation of several of those and more. The nature of that constellation differed depending on the particular historic moment and society within which Confucianism manifested.

Importantly, for both Confucius himself (as represented as a "person" in texts like *Confucius Analects*) and for most people who engaged what we now call Confucianism up until around the Song dynasty (960–1279 CE), Confucius, although regarded as a very important teacher and editor, was not considered the originator of the sacred, nor the provider of an idealized, heavenly ordained political order. Confucius was no Jesus or Buddha embodying other-worldly perfection, nor was he like Muhammad (and many Jewish and Christian kings before and after him) seen as an ideal ruler bringing an ordained political order to the earth. After all, Confucius was famously ineffective as a political advisor and, unlike Muhammad, never himself ruled. The Confucian tradition, however, did include reference to a golden age when Heaven's mandate had ruled on earth. This age, however, was seen as predating Confucius by several centuries and was associated rather with "Ancient Sage Kings" like Yao and Shun, who were purported to have ruled "a long time ago" – in the *Star Wars* mytho-historical sense of that phrase.

This vision of Confucianism focusing on the claimed historical sages of antiquity became less influential after the rise of so-called Neo-Confucianism. Neo-Confucianism is the name given in English to more religiously inclined forms of Confucianism which began to emerge in the Tang dynasty (618–907) and were systematized in the Song dynasty (960–1279) by a number of major figures, notably Zhu Xi (1130–1200). For this reason, in Japanese and Chinese one dominant stream of Neo-Confucianism is called "Song Learning" or "Zhu Xi Learning." Neo-Confucianism emerged both in reaction to and under the influence of Chan (Zen) Buddhism. Under Buddhist influence, new understandings of classic Confucian and Daoist texts and ideas generated a systematized cosmology linking individual practice with a metaphysical conception of the cosmos and ethical and political understandings of the importance of social structures like the family, country, and empire. This integrated system, Neo-Confucianism, became the basis of most forms of Confucianism which emerged thereafter, and indeed most understandings of Confucianism advanced today. It emerged out of a religious milieu and functioned for centuries as what was undeniably a form of individually centered (albeit socially engaged) religious practice (Yang 1967: 255–93). This tradition, both through its parallels with Buddhism (and the myth of the person Buddha) and through its emphasis on individual transformation, also further facilitated an ongoing elevation of Confucius (the alleged person) as an object of devotion and emulation.

Historical research into premodern Asia reveals a pluralist constellation of parameters constituting Confucianism in each different historical period and place. Confucianism is therefore best analyzed over the longue durée utilizing the plurality that its history possesses. This is an approach to the study of tradition that borrows much from contemporary trends in writing on religious history, which have been heavily affected by cultural and religious anthropology over the past decades, and which are broadly accepted in history, religious studies, and Asian studies disciplinary settings. Historians of Christianity, for instance, usually refer to their field these days as the History of World Christiani*ties*. They seek to help us understand the multiplicities and complexities in the history of the inter-action between Christianity and different parts of the world (Gilley and Stanley 2006). Contemporary historians of Christianity, Islam, and other religions often integrate the social and cultural history of affected areas with the histories of religious practice, and in postcolonial settings often also link these with the political histories of empire and modern colonial-ism to better understand how a religious tradition operated in a particular, concrete historical setting. This approach allows the diversity of history to show, and it also provides a model for studying links between belief and practice, text and action.

This basic outlook informs this book's method of defining what can or cannot be considered a Confucian action, statement, or person. Employing a very basic methodology long favored by many in the fields of history, anthropology, and religious studies, this book calls phenomena Confucian simply if they were regarded as such by people in their own historical contexts. People are regarded as "Confucians" if they were identified by themselves and/or others around them in terms which match the way Confucianism is used as a conceptual category today.[2] Texts or actions are considered Confucian if they were presented in their own time and space so as to be widely regarded as primarily Confucian. For Japan, this way of defining Confucianism is particularly handy because the beginnings of the history of Confucianism in Japan fell during the Chinese Tang dynasty, in a period of sectarian conflict where "Three schools" – Confucianism, Buddhism, and Daoism – critiqued each other, thereby providing an (at the time) innovatively clear set of indigenous self-delineations between these three traditions. As will be discussed in Chapter 1, in Japan the "Three schools" soon became Confucianism, Buddhism, and Shinto. So unlike Chinese history, in Japanese history we have an indigenously delineated scheme of self-identification of traditions right from the very beginnings of Japanese Confucianism.

Of course, in line with this methodology, actions and statements can be considered Confucian even when not made by a Confucian, as long as the statement or action was clearly meant to be identified in Confucian terms in the historical context of articulation or was commonly associated with Confucian practices in that time and place. So when Emperor Hirohito made a Neo-Confucian reference in announcing Japan's surrender in 1945, this does not make him a Neo-Confucian, but it certainly indicated that in this particular case he was deliberately employing Confucianism in the sense that he clearly wanted educated Asians (including Japanese) to read his comments through an inter-textual allusion which could be understood by them as part of the trans-Asian Confucian tradition. This manner of "defining" Confucianism is simple and historical. Ultimately the historical agents themselves judge what is Confucian (or not) in relation to the norms of their own times and societies, and that is what then also facilitates (and enforces) the presentation of a diversity of plural Confucianisms in this book.

Regarding Confucianism in religious terms is particularly useful when attempting comparative analysis of Confucianism with the other traditions which shared its geographic and cultural spaces in East Asia. Through most of the history of Confucianism, and through its entire history in Japan, East Asian historical actors on the ground have perceived Confucianism in comparison with and in relation to Buddhism. In later (post-sixteenth-century) history, such actors also often compared Confucianism with Christianity. Modern scholars routinely study Buddhism and Christianity as religions. For instance, Buddhism in the history of Tang China or Christianity in the history of Ming China are both studied as "religions." Both Tang Buddhism and Ming Christianity critically impacted the history of Confucianism in Japan (as will be discussed in Chapters 1 and 2). Local historical actors on the ground clearly identified Confucianism in parallel with the concepts "Buddhism" and "Christianity" (Xu 1855; NKBT 71; NST 28; NST 35; Ōkuwa 2006; Paramore 2009). This means that if we, on the one hand, accept the characterizations of these traditions as "religion," but refuse to accept the characterization of Confucianism as a religion, then we are buying into an inherently ahistorical set of comparative concepts. Since nearly everyone regards Buddhism and Christianity as religions, we have little choice but to regard Confucianism as a religion, at the very least when considering it in comparison.

This way of defining Confucianism stands in contrast to other methods. The most common competing ways to define Confucianism today are either to equate it with Chinese culture or to define it exclusively as political philosophy. These two ways of framing Confucianism are both related to the modernist construction of Confucianism as representative of a timeless Chinese culture. The practice of equating Confucianism with Chinese culture has a long history. Under the influence of Jesuit and other Western writings from China through the seventeenth century, a very specific image of China emerged in seventeenth- and eighteenth-century Europe describing Chinese political society in relation to a manufactured vision of Confucianism. At first, this image was regarded very positively. "Confucianism," as the reification of an essentialized Chinese culture, became the basis of Voltaire and other enlightenment figures' idolization of China (Jensen 1997; Marchand 2009: 21–2).

After a century or two of the European intelligentsia fawning over and idealizing this "Confucian culture," however, there came a counter-reaction in the late eighteenth century. That counter-reaction coincided with the Industrial Revolution and the rise of the second great wave of European maritime imperialism. Now from Kant to Hegel, everything Confucian was backward and that was the explanation for everything wrong about China (Schwab 1984; Marchand 2009: 22). Together with attitudes like anti-Semitism, this anti-Siniticism, with Confucianism as its primary content and referent, became a major part of the construction of the intellectual self-conception of modern Western Europe during its nineteenth-century period of global high imperialism (Marchand 2009: 21–8; Nirenberg 2013). The prevalence of anti-Siniticism in late nineteenth-century European thinking both informed and was bolstered by Western states' utilization of anti-Chinese cultural arguments in the construction of the unequal treaties through which they subjugated semi-colonial China. The lynchpin in this Western disparagement of Chinese culture was a vision of Confucianism which portrayed it as underpinning an inherently backward society.

This was the context within which the Westernizing, modernizing Japanese Meiji state post-1868 chose to airbrush Confucian influence out of the first official modern histories of Japan it commissioned. This was done partly for local political reasons: because, as will be discussed in Chapters 4 and 5, the Tokugawa state overthrown by the Meiji Restoration had been so closely associated with Confucianism toward the end (Makabe 2007). Mainly, however, it was to make sure the new Japan was as clearly differentiated as possible from free-fall China and the negative imagery of Confucianism through which the West justified its semi-colonization. This was particularly the case through the late 1800s as Japan's attempts to revise the unequal treaties were argued in relation to the nineteenth-century Western concept of "Civilization," of which China and Confucian values were held up by the Western powers and Western thought as the Asian antithesis (Kuo 2013). Meiji Japanese leaders correctly judged it in Japan's best interests not to be perceived by the Western powers in relation to a Confucianism that had become the West's marker of Chinese culture's backwardness. This was the Confucian image from which the Meiji state did everything it could to distance Japan.[3]

Looking at Confucianism outside of China thus opens up issues of global history and politics far beyond the scope of general religious history, linking into larger narratives of culture upon which the creation of the modern world order relied. This book looks to engage those larger issues through presenting a history of Confucianism in Japan with three main methodological aims: firstly, broaden our vision of Confucianism and make it historical by defining Confucianism in the pluralist terms favored by the voices of history; secondly, counter doctrine-centered approaches to Confucianism (notably those claiming it as "philosophy") by broadening the fields of action investigated to religion and culture in general; thirdly, counter nationalist (both Sinocentric and anti-Sinitic) renderings of Confucianism by demonstrating the cultural plurality of its various manifestations. Delivering this latter prong involves questioning at every turn Japanese nationalist readings of Confucianism, readings often wrapped up in a long history of Sinophobia related to both nineteenth-century European biases and Japan's own nativist history of anti-Chinese nationalism. However, it also requires awareness of how deeply the study of Confucianism in general is colored by often unconscious Sinocentric outlooks.

Confucianism today

Such a problematization of the history of the study of Confucianism also looks to speak to scholarship on new manifestations of Confucianism currently rising in East Asia. Although usually considered part of East Asia's "traditions," and therefore the past, Confucianism is on the rise in China today. Sociologists and political scientists are charting dynamic increases in the numbers of Chinese carrying out Confucian religious practice, identifying with Confucian doctrines and teachers, and seeing Confucianism as a solution to problems in society and politics. Researchers have also described the important role of the contemporary Chinese state and the Chinese Communist Party (CCP) in encouraging this rise in Confucianism, by using Confucianism in political ideology and state ritual, and identifying Confucianism overtly and symbolically with the Chinese nation and its culture (Callahan 2012, 2015; Sun 2013).

Most agree, however, that the resurgence of Confucianism in China is not simply a function of this state interest, but rather also has elements resembling a social movement. Kang Xiaoguang has recently argued that the resurgence of Confucianism in early twenty-first-century China should be seen as a "cultural nationalist movement" related to China's current stage of socio-economic development. Kang employs the theories of Samuel Huntington to argue that traditional culture, relatively strong at the beginning of a nation's trajectory of economic modernization and Westernization, will wane as that nation begins to become more economically independent and assertive in its "successful" emergence from the modernization process. In other words, according to Kang, "the rise of China as a great power" is a determining factor in feeding a rise in cultural nationalism that is manifested through social activism advocating a return to Chinese tradition as Confucianism. For Kang, himself an advocate of Confucian revival and a participant in state-supported public intellectual activity in China, this rise in Confucianism as a form of cultural nationalism should be welcomed (Kang in Yang and Tamney 2012: 71–2).[4]

Kang's argument relating power politics and the resurgence of traditional Confucian culture is convincing, not because of the theories lying behind it, but because, as will be discussed in the later chapters of this book, a similar process can be seen to have already occurred in mid-twentieth-century Japan. At that time, Japan was going through a period of industrial and economic growth, increase in global political influence, and rising nationalism similar to China today. Japanese history provides comparative evidence for Kang's claims. As I will discuss in the penultimate chapter of this book, Confucianism experienced a resurgence in Japan and its occupied Asian territories during the height of Japanese militarism, partly through state support, but also partly through a national hubris for Japan's steadily expanding position as a "great power." It sprang from a similar "cultural nationalist movement" as that glowingly described by Kang in contemporary China. This historical interaction between "cultural nationalism," Confucianism and fascism might lead some to a more problematic view than Kang as to whether the resurgence of Confucianism in China should be welcomed.

The political significance of the rise of China, and the role of Confucianism therein, is a subject that is attracting increasing attention, particularly among international relations theorists. David Kang, probably the most influential voice in this new discussion, has argued that Confucianism could play an immensely positive role in the future of international relations. Rather than associating Confucianism with cultural nationalism like Kang Xiaoguang, David Kang (they are unrelated) instead sees Confucianism as providing the basis of an international relations order which could be inherently more peaceful than the Westphalian and post-Westphalian orders of recent times. David Kang privileges the use of history to argue his point that in post-risen China, Confucian influence will be basically good, facilitating more peace and less conflict in the world (Kang 2007, 2010). This position has been opposed by Yuan-Kang Wang, who also uses history, but to counter David Kang's assessment of the pacifism of Confucianism. Wang instead argues that Confucianism also has inherently violent, war-like and aggressive aspects, and thereby might well encourage coercive behavior by a Confucian state. His main historic argument is that decisions made by Chinese empires to go to war were usually based on power political rather than philosophical reasons, with Confucianism being deployed in the ideological service of practical political decisions rather than vice versa (Wang 2011). In this way, Kang and Wang both use history to argue for the pros and cons of Confucianism's effect on international peace – Kang viewing it positively, and Wang seeing it as often irrelevant, but also at times ideologically dangerous. Historical study has thus become a prime weapon in a controversy raging over what Confucianism's place should be in the contemporary world. This, in effect, is an argument about the future nature of global society – an argument that, intriguingly, is being framed in relation to the history of Confucianism in East Asia.

The focus on Japanese history presented in this book might be useful for thinking more about these wider issues for a number of reasons. Firstly, simply because Japan is not China. If anyone will contend that Confucianism can be a universalist force for international good, then they must study Confucianism outside only a Chinese cultural setting. Looking at the long-term history of Confucianism in a non-Chinese cultural setting is particularly meaningful and necessary for considering what capacities that tradition might have in an international setting. Secondly, as David Kang has rightly pointed out, Japan is the most peripheral and most un-Sinicized of the East Asian countries where Confucianism flourished (Kang 2010). This makes it a particularly good example for comparison with China and for assessing the claimed universalist possibilities of Confucianism. Thirdly, Japan, through early modern and modern history until quite recently, was the most politically, militarily, and economically powerful state in East Asia, and indeed until the late 1980s the only Asian state considered to have been successful in the task of modernizing development. This is important, not because it denotes some normative achievement of Japan, but because it gives us a chance to historically observe the resurgence of Confucianism in a society (Japan) which has already passed through the processes of rapid industrialization, socio-economic development, and post-industrialization. This allows us to put into a longer historical perspective the kind of claims made above about Confucianism in the world today, as well as relativizing a range of other views on Confucianism's position in the world that have been advanced over the past decades.

Outline

This book proceeds chronologically, using a periodization of Japanese history in combination with thematic labels to navigate through the longue durée covered. Often the periods discussed in each chapter overlap, sometimes by hundreds of years. The thematic titles of each chapter also usually indicate only one of several manifestations of Confucianism in any given period.

Chapter 1, *Confucianism as cultural capital*, deals with Confucianism from the beginnings of an organized state in Japan in the middle of the first millennium CE, until the sixteenth century. It presents the early Japanese state as having come into being as part of the same processes of cultural transmission which established Confucianism for the first time in mid-first-millennium Japan. It argues that although Confucian ideas and ways of writing were centrally employed in the creation of the first organized Japanese imperial state through the seventh century, Confucianism was otherwise underrepresented in the institutions developed by the state, particularly in comparison with the continental examples upon which those institutions were modeled. The nature of Confucianism's manifestation in early Japan was also severely limited by the fact that it never seems to have moved beyond state institutions, and never seems to have been able to compete with Buddhism or any of the other religious traditions either within or outside the state. From the beginnings of Japan's medieval period in the twelfth century, however, Confucianism began to penetrate realms of life and culture beyond the state. Intriguingly, this occurred primarily through the mediation of Zen Buddhism. The second half of this chapter looks at how this Zen Buddhist-delivered Confucianism began to influence social life and culture in Japan, and how this lay the basis for the emergence of Confucianism as an influential independent tradition in Japan in the early modern period.

Chapters 2 to 4 deal with the period of Japanese history usually characterized as the early modern, from the late sixteenth through into the mid-nineteenth century. During this period, Confucianism came to penetrate nearly every facet of Japanese cultural and political life. It was undoubtedly the high point of Confucianism in Japan. Chapter 2, *Confucianism as religion*, attempts to explain the meteoric rise of Confucianism in the seventeenth century, discussing the period from the late 1500s up into the mid-1700s. It argues that the rise of Confucianism was facilitated primarily by the power of Neo-Confucian religious practice, which during the seventeenth century permeated Japanese society for the first time on a large scale. This spread of Neo-Confucian practice in independent forms throughout the country is explained in relation to two major socio-political changes which occurred in Japan at this time: firstly, the large-scale suppression of religion at the end of the Warring States period, a suppression which created the demand for the kind of religiosity which Neo-Confucianism offered; and secondly, the rapid increase in disposable income, leisure time, travel, and literacy which the Tokugawa settlement (the *pax* Tokugawa) offered to large segments of the population, notably among the samurai.

Chapter 3, *Confucianism as public sphere*, argues that this Confucian activity came to play the role of something like a public sphere in Tokugawa society, particularly from the 1700s onward. The chapter discusses examples coming from throughout the Tokugawa period, from 1600 to 1868. It first analyzes the nature of Confucianism's integration in the leisure learning networks which characterized early modern Japanese urban life from the seventeenth century. It argues that Confucian practice, notably including pedagogical practice, occupied a privileged position within this vibrant realm of social action. The chapter then moves on to demonstrate how, through the eighteenth century, particular Confucian pedagogical, self-cultivation, and discursive practices which had originated in that private leisure learning sphere were then integrated into state-led systems of training and socialization for the shogunal retainer samurai administrative class, with the aim of this system being rolled out into the domainal states. The chapter argues that both in this new state manifestation and in the continuing private networks and schools, key Japanese Confucian pedagogical and discursive practices, notably so-called social reading (*kaidoku*), facilitated political discussion which was both reasonable in nature (in the Rawls and Habermas sense) and at times affective on state decision-making processes. This led to Confucianism facilitating a public sphere which linked private and state commentators in an ongoing political discourse through the later Tokugawa period.

Chapter 4, *Confucianism as knowledge*, discusses the role of Confucianism in the development of useful knowledge in Japan, analyzing interactions between Confucianism and knowledge from as far back as the fifteenth century, forward into the early Meiji period of the 1870s. Focusing particularly on the field of medicine, the chapter demonstrates both the nature of traditional links between Confucianism and practical knowledge innovation in Japan, and the role of Confucianism in the late Tokugawa state's institutionalization of knowledge in the late 1700s and into the 1800s. It argues that these Confucian-led reforms resulted in a larger state engagement with knowledge in general, and in particular with Western knowledge. The chapter thus also touches upon the links between late Tokugawa Confucian-led state knowledge reform and the Western-style modernization projects of the Meiji state post-1868.

Chapters 5 and 6 deal with Confucianism in the modern period, beginning in 1868 and ending with the end of World War II in 1945. Chapter 5, *Confucianism as liberalism*, picks up the links made in Chapter 4 between Confucianism in the late Tokugawa period and the early stages of full-scale Western-style modernization. Focusing on the political field, it examines the way Japanese intellectuals and political leaders, particularly in the mid- to late nineteenth century, perceived liberal democracy as a Confucian form of ideal rule. Confucianism continued to be the dominant lens through which the developing ideals and systems of political liberalism, at the time on the rise globally, were understood in Japan right up until the end of the century. The chapter also touches on the links between Confucianism and early understandings of both capitalism and socialism.

Chapter 6, *Confucianism as fascism*, considers the broader history of Confucianism between 1868 and 1945. It argues that state repression of Confucianism by the new Meiji government, part of its broader anti-religious policy of the 1870s, severely weakened Confucianism, to a degree where it was later easily manipulated and exploited in the political confusion of the early twentieth century. The chapter argues that Japanese reconstructions of Confucianism as philosophy at the turn of the nineteenth into the twentieth century were instrumental in transforming Confucianism into a form ripe for later employment by ultra-nationalists and fascists. I thus see this "philosophical turn" as having played a key role in mediating between the early Meiji state suppression of Confucianism, and the later modern Japanese fascist state's valorization and utilization of the tradition. The chapter spends some time considering this most harrowing of Confucian transformations, analyzing the relationship between mid-twentieth-century political conservatism and Confucianism in comparative terms. It then moves on to analyze the nature of Confucianism's integration into the ideologies and practices of fascism in Japan, and its utilization in the propaganda of occupation and colonization in Japan's early and mid-twentieth-century colonial empire.

Chapter 7, *Confucianism as taboo*, presents some thoughts on the position of Confucianism in Japan since then – between 1945 and the present. Confucianism is usually considered extinct in Japan after 1945. This chapter considers the nature of Confucianism's disappearance from almost all aspects of Japanese life after World War II, linking that to contemporary Japanese ways of dealing with war memory and the country's general postwar ambivalence to its own longue durée Asian history. A short *Epilogue* muses on parallels in the modern histories of China and Japan and on what possible future there may or may not be for Confucianism in contemporary China in light of patterns revealed in Japanese history.

1   Confucianism as cultural capital

> On the sixth day of the eighth month in the autumn of the fifteenth year [284CE] a Prince from [the Korean state of] Paekche called Araki came before the court and presented two fine horses to the [Japanese] emperor... This Araki was very good at reading the [Confucian] classics... Hearing this, the emperor asked Araki, "Do you possess a fine Confucian professor [in Paekche]?" Araki replied, "There is one called Wani, he is excellent." Arata Wake and Kamunaki Wake were dispatched to Paekche to get Wani. In spring in the second month of the sixteenth year Wani arrived. Prince Uji no Waki Iratsuko took him as his teacher. He learnt various classics from Wani. There were none of them he could not master. Wani became the first keeper of the imperial books.
>
> (*Nihon Shoki* in NKBT 67: 370–3)[1]

So began the history of Confucianism in Japan. Confucian professors were fine gifts for princes who could use them as symbols of status and connection. As a prince would show his prowess and exhibit his own status by skillfully riding an especially fine stallion, so too a prince "able to master" all the Confucian classics taught by a fine teacher exhibited not only the status of "having" that teacher but also his own accomplishments in being able to "master" the material. This passage seems to be the first Japanese historical source narrating Confucianism's arrival in Japan. Whether this occurred in 284, as the source could be literally interpreted, or 402, as Peter Kornicki has suggested, or whether this story is just a work of complete fiction from the early eighth-century period in which *Nihon Shoki* was compiled, we will never really know.[2] What is clear is that Confucianism, its personnel, and texts were initially primarily perceived as part of the status symbolism of East Asian interstate relations.

The beginnings of Confucianism in Japan were thus closely intertwined with the beginnings of a Japanese state. The formation of a single dominant state in central Japan occurred from the fifth to the seventh centuries, concurrently with a new wave of importation and institutionalization of political and religious culture from mainland Asia – notably Korea. The impact of, most importantly, Buddhism, but also Confucianism, and other religious ideas associated with Daoism, accelerated dramatically during the seventh century. These religious, cultural, educational, and administrative paradigms provided many of the sociological tools necessary for the construction of a more complex centralized state capable of projecting and holding power over a large area (Como 2008; Ooms 2009).[3] The formulation of Confucianism in Japan and the formation of the Japanese state were thereby concurrent and symbiotic processes. Confucianism was not a prepackaged formula that arrived in a pre-prepared and already formed Japan. Confucianism in Japan was rather part of the processes that formed the early Japanese state itself, and conversely, these processes of state formation also helped to shape the particular early Japanese manifestation of Confucianism.

This chapter looks at the beginnings of Japanese Confucianism, from the beginnings of Japan itself in the middle of the first millennium CE, through to the end of the sixteenth century. The first half of the chapter examines the particular formulations of Confucianism that arose in early Japan (7CE–11CE). The second half looks at Japanese Confucianism in medieval Japan (12CE–16CE). Confucianism is identifiable as a major cultural influence from the very beginnings of early Japan, but the social integration of Confucianism was very limited. That was because its influence, in comparison to Confucian influence in China, Korea, and later Japan, was limited to the spheres of bureaucratic education. Concentrated among lower-ranking aristocrat officials of the imperial state, and practiced only in state institutions, the fortunes of Confucianism were inextricably linked to the fortunes of the imperial bureaucratic state structures. As will be discussed later, those structures were from the beginning comparatively vulnerable. When imperial institutions declined in the ninth–eleventh centuries Confucianism's place in Japanese society, already overly compartmentalized and isolated, became exceedingly marginalized. Questions to consider in relation to early Japanese Confucianism thus include the following: what was the nature of its role in state formation; how did it affect ideas on human interrelations within state structures and interstate relations within Japan and East Asia; and why was the scope of Confucian influence and activity restricted to the state sphere?

The second half of this chapter examines how Confucianism bounced back in the medieval period. From the twelfth into the sixteenth centuries Confucianism reemerged in new, more socially and culturally embedded formulations. Intriguingly, this initially occurred owing to, and under the patronage of, a new flourishing literary culture associated with the rise of Zen Buddhism. Confucianism's more theoretically complex, culturally diverse, and socially embedded character in this later period was in large part a function of its positioning within the Five Mountains Zen Buddhist cultural movement. Although more politically and socially embedded, popular, and intellectually developed than Confucianism in early Japan, medieval Japanese Confucianism was still predominantly limited to social circles which were literate or could afford to employ the literate: the Zen Buddhist clergy, the imperial aristocracy, and important elements in the new, emerging samurai nobility. Nonetheless, medieval Confucianism achieved enough social integration to influence some key aspects of Japanese life and developed a base of scholarship which influenced the emergence of the socially, politically, and culturally central Confucianism of the early modern period discussed in later chapters of this book. The second half of the chapter therefore looks to use this medieval history to consider how different social positionings and cultural packagings of Confucianism might affect not only the nature of its interaction with society, but also its inherent creative cultural, philosophical, and religious potentials. As will be touched upon in this chapter, and expanded upon in the coming chapters, the rise of *Neo*-Confucianism in China would play a large part in enabling these potentialities later in Japanese history.

Early Japan

State and civilization: Confucian universalism and the beginnings of Japan

There is no doubt Confucianism significantly affected not only the way the early Japanese state was conceptualized but also how that conceptualization was expressed in the first political texts. The *Kojiki*, for instance, one of the two core early texts legitimizing the Japanese state, and actually the most linguistically un-Chinese of the two, nevertheless opens with an introductory section which is modeled exactly on the style of the introduction to the *Wujing zhengyi*, a collection of the Confucian classics from the Tang period (618–907) (NST1: 10–17, 650). In other words, the introduction of the *Kojiki* mimics the form of the most famous Chinese Confucian commentary of the Tang period. The structure of the *Nihon Shoki*, the other core legitimizing text of the early Japanese state, is clearly based on Chinese dynastic histories which were part of the Confucian canon. In this sense, quite apart from the content of the earliest Japanese historical texts, the very form they are written in was highly derivative of Confucian textual tradition.

Conceptual paradigms sitting at the heart of Confucianism affected Japanese state formation much more deeply. The conceptualization of a state, notably the logic behind delineations of outer and inner, and the interaction of this logic with larger questions relating to the place of humans in the natural world, was crucially affected by Confucian paradigms. Confucian universalism in particular had a big influence on the early codification of principles of governance in early Japan. The formation of the early Japanese state occurred through a process of interaction with Korean kingdoms in the mid-first millennium CE. These interactions were military, political, cultural, and religious in nature. They were related to the emergence of enduring state identities, state violence (war), and early codification of principles of governance which, while certainly not being law in the modern sense, had enduring effects on the later development of state institutions including law. Positive Confucian influence on this codification of systems of governance needs to be resolved with the violence inherent in the consolidation of the early state. Thinking about the history of the early Japanese state thereby invites reflection upon the contradictions inherent in the utility of Confucian universalism to statecraft at a broader level – not just in early Japan, but also in later periods, and in other parts of the world.

Confucian influence in early Japanese statecraft manifested itself in two opposing directions. On the one hand, Confucian ideas were used to provide frameworks for mediation and consensus building in Japanese society, and between Japanese and foreign peoples. On the other hand, Confucian ideas were used to assist in recognizing a hierarchy between different societies which justified Japanese state violence against so-called barbarians.

Scholars of Chinese, Korean, and Japanese intellectual history often emphasize Confucianism's message of shared human values and respect for the other. Scholars in Japan have repeatedly cited *Shōtoku's Seventeen Article Constitution* (also called the *Seventeen Injunctions*) as a strong example of this.[4] *Shōtoku's Seventeen Article Constitution* is a list of principles of governance which tradition claims was written in 604 by the imperial regent, Prince Shōtoku.[5] In the centuries thereafter, Prince Shōtoku was discursively transformed into a kind of saint (Como 2008). Various Buddhist traditions claimed him as a bodhisattva, and he has been revered by those of all political colors since. His *Constitution* has been one of the most heavily referenced treatises in Japanese political history, right into the twenty-first century.[6] This is partly because of its flexible nature: hortatory rather than regulatory, consensus driven, and religiously pluralist. *Shōtoku's Seventeen Article Constitution* is correctly cited both as representative of the Buddhist nature of the early Japanese state and also as one of the most clearly Confucian-influenced texts in early Japanese history. This is indicative of the intellectually and religiously pluralist nature of this text, but also more generally of Japanese political culture at this time – an issue I will return to.

The main claim made by modern commentators about *Shōtoku's Seventeen Article Constitution*, however, has been that it represents a

"Japanese" idea of "harmony." How exclusivist the "Japaneseness" of this harmony is imagined to be has usually depended on the political color of the scholar and the moment in modern Japanese history they have worked within. Imperialist and nationalist scholarship in the mid-twentieth century valorized this as an exclusionary "Japanese value." Post-World War II Japanese scholarship challenged these readings by emphasizing the comparatively universalist perspective and clear Confucian influence on *Shōtoku's Seventeen Article Constitution* (Kurozumi 2006). Intriguingly, this later, more politically correct scholarship thereby did not actually challenge the valorization of early Japanese state codes inherent in the earlier nationalist readings but simply relocated the valorized ideas to a transnational Asian rather than exclusionary national Japanese discourse. "Asianizing" a previously "nationalist" narrative of early state formation or codification allowed that process to be discussed with the same positive value judgment as before. What is undeniable is that the references to harmony come from clearly Confucian sources.

The very first sentence of the first of the seventeen injunctions of this text is a line from the Confucian classic *The Book of Rites*, which also appears in *Confucius Analects*, "Harmony is to be valued, and contentiousness avoided" (NST 2: 12–13). The injunction continues, "When those above are harmonious and those below are conciliatory and there is concord in the discussion of all matters, the disposition of affairs comes about naturally" (NST 2: 12–13; De Bary 2005: 51). This injunction is quintessentially Confucian in the sense that it advises for a form of rule in which the use of force is unnecessary. Traditional understandings of Confucianism, both in Shōtoku's time, and in ours, are primarily based on conceptions of Confucian values that came into being in Han-dynasty China (206 BCE–220CE). Han-dynasty China classically defined Confucian values as humanitarian and conciliatory in opposition to the rule- and force-based political values of the Chinese Legalist tradition of thinkers like Han Fei (280–233BCE). The former was associated with the long-running Han dynasty, the latter with the brutal and short Qin dynasty (221–207BCE) that it replaced. This classical interpretation of the Confucian tradition sees it as recommending governance through ritual which conciliates as opposed to the Legalist tradition which sought to govern through rules backed up with coercive violence. This injunction, therefore, begins *Shōtoku's Seventeen Article Constitution* by clearly identifying it with the Confucian (conciliatory) rather than the Legalist (coercive) tradition and style of governance in East Asia. In other words, *Shōtoku's Seventeen Article Constitution* not only adopts Confucian terminology and quotes Confucian texts but also uses these following standard

Confucian political discourse patterns dating from the Han dynasty that claim for themselves a relatively conciliatory, harmonizing character.

This preference for rites as a preferred method of rule is also emphasized in the fourth injunction which, after quoting from another Confucian work, the *Classic of Filial Piety*, "rites must be the basis of rule," goes on to conclude that, "if the common people have rites, then the state will govern itself" (NST 2: 15). The emphasis on the centrality of the cultivation of mediating relationships is again represented in Injunction Nine, which after opening with a quote from *Confucius Analects*, "Trust is the basis of justice," goes on to conclude, "if there is trust between sovereign and vassal then nothing cannot be achieved, if there is no trust then all will be destroyed" (NST 2: 17–18). A similar emphasis on conciliatory human relations, this time between rulers and commoners, is presented in Injunction Sixteen, which opens with the quote from *Confucius Analects*, "the common people should be employed according to the season." This reference to the seasons is a warning to rulers not to demand corvée labor from the peasants in times of agricultural labor intensity such as harvest, because this would interfere with the peasant's livelihood (NST 2: 21–2).

All these injunctions share a characteristic of warning members of the ruling elite to emphasize conciliation and harmony in their relationships with others, including being aware of others' needs – even the needs of peasants. For the rulers this implied that they should moderate their use of coercion and force in their exercise of power. All of these injunctions clearly take Confucian textual sources as their bases, and make points which could indeed be characterized as representing basic Confucian approaches to social governance.[7] Confucian influence, thereby, emphasized conciliation and cooperation and militated against the use of force and violence in governance. This conciliatory character had a relatively egalitarian nature in that even the interests of the peasantry were considered worth taking into account.

This Confucian universalism, however, had another side. The rather moderating and civilizing aspect of Confucian influence just narrated went hand in hand with a Confucian world view which demarcated between different human societies in a clear hierarchy. By establishing a single universalist cultural idea of "civilization" upon which human societies could be comparatively judged, Confucianism recognized the possibility to grade human societies in a hierarchy with a central civilized state at the top, and barbaric peripheries at the bottom. This allowed the Confucian idea of "civilization" to be deployed in justifying the conquest of peripheral "barbarian" peoples and states. Such justifications of conquest can be found all through the classic Confucian texts. In the context of the Japanese archipelago, the Yamato state of Prince Shōtoku saw itself as the civilizing center. Its wars of conquest against other peoples in the archipelago, and indeed the taking and trading of these peoples as slaves, were justified using the same paradigms and language as in the Confucian classics. Non-Japanese, at this time meaning any peoples on the archipelago not willing to submit to the authority of the Yamato sovereign, were referred to in *Nihon Shoki* as "barbarians" using the same phrasing employed in the Chinese Confucian classic *The Book of Rites*.[8] Early Japanese state documents also mimic Confucian tradition in narrating the world in terms of a unipolar imperial order of civilization. They narrate the conduct of state ceremonies involving subjugated "barbarian" peoples and surrounding states along the lines of this logic (Naoki 1988: 27; Ooms 2009: 168). In this sense, Confucian universalism was used in Japan to justify ideas of cultural superiority and military domination.

Interestingly from the perspective of postcolonial history writing, the rewriting of Japanese history since World War II, including its highly critical approach to Japanese nationalism and militarism, has not led to much soul searching in regard to this role of the Confucian tradition. That is because most of the critique of early Japanese nationalist and imperialist historiography has been done from the perspective of the postcolonial nation states – notably Korea. Post-World War II perspectives on early Japanese history thereby emphasize the role of Korean states, the interaction of Japan with Korea, and Korean influence on Japan, and this is seen as sufficient revision of the old nationalist historical outlook. But these new historical perspectives do not pay much attention to the people who fall between the boundaries of the modern nation states and their premodern forerunners – "barbarians," not belonging to premodern Korean, Japanese, or any other states. Postcolonial history has not required too much criticism of the Confucian world order in relation to premodern Korea and Japan, because premodern Japanese texts recognized and acknowledged Korean kingdoms by name. "Barbarian," or *emishi* as they were most commonly referred to in Japanese sources of this period, was a signifier which identified only someone not part of a recognized kingly state, not Japan *or* Korea.

Most historians agree that the words used to identify Japanese and non-Japanese in the early history of the archipelago, rather than relating to racial or ethnic identity, were primarily politically formed categories. *Emishi* or "barbarian" in its premodern usage cannot be identified as a signifier of non-Japaneseness, because many non-Japanese, notably subjects of Korean kingdoms, were not called "barbarian." Conversely, "barbarian" did not signify non-Japanese in a modern ethnic sense either, because there are many examples in the historical sources where Japanese, through a change in political affiliation, quickly "became" *emishi*, or vice versa. *Emishi* barbarian and Japanese identity could be exchanged. Or to state this more precisely: the signifiers "barbarian" or "Japanese" could be swapped around fairly much on the whim of the post hoc political writer. *Emishi* could quickly become Japanese, and vice versa. The "civilized" and "barbarian" tags were quickly interchangeable, and thereby clearly not related to characteristics parallel to modern ideas of ethnos or race. Those submitting to the authority of a kingly court, be it Yamato, Silla, Paekche, or other, were civilized. Those not subjugated by one of these courts were barbarian. In the context of the Japanese archipelago, this meant that anyone not submitting to the Yamato court was characterized as what would later be interpreted to mean non-Japanese. Culture and civilization in the Confucian sense, therefore, and indeed the idea of harmony, were thereby rooted in a brutal politics of submission that, on the one hand, transcended (or did not imagine) ethnicity, but, on the other, institutionalized and legitimized as never before set relations of clan, class, and state power and the violence inherent therein.[9]

The postcolonial sensibilities that have dominated the rewriting of Korean and Japanese history, from both perspectives, have encouraged scholars to acknowledge the interaction between Korean and Japanese kingdoms in the processes of early Japanese state formation. Confucianism's role in encouraging "respect for the other" has been recognized, because that functioned in terms of state interactions – including with Korea. But its employment to justify the enslavement, integration, and even annihilation of the other has attracted less attention – because those "barbarian" others are not identified with the modern nation states whose ideologies, budgets, and underlying cultural power continue to ineluctably influence the direction of academic research today.

Postwar social history in Japan has made it clear that the premodern societies in Japan were made up of many people who fell between state boundaries, or simply sat outside of them. The classic example given by Amino Yoshihiko is of "people of the sea," who lived off sea-based trade and/or production processes like fishing, were sometimes nomadic, and almost always comparatively mobile. Historians like Amino have provided plenty of data and narrative about the people of Japan who did not fit with premodern state identities.[10] But intellectual historians and particularly those studying Confucianism have been slow to think about how the history of these peoples can be resolved with the rise of Confucian-inspired state structures and political discourses through Japanese history.

One important issue to consider in trying to better understand the history of Confucianism in relation to broader Japanese society is why

Confucianism had such an exclusionary and statist nature in early Japan. Rather than being an inherent element of some essential Confucian or Japanese identity, I would rather suggest that this state-centric logos was related to the particular way that Confucianism was *positioned* in early Japanese society. Confucianism was institutionalized in a particularly passive position within the early Japanese state. This passive and statist positioning was, ironically enough, deeply related to the high level of pluralism of Japanese society and its state institutions at this time. To better understand the nature of Confucianism in early Japan, and the role of Confucian universalism in the formation of the Japanese state, it is helpful to look at how it was positioned within the state, and how that affected the nature of its engagement with general society.

Positioning and pluralism: the institutionalization of Confucianism

Japanese state institutionalization of Confucianism was effected under direct influence from Korea, mainly by using institutional and legal examples from the Sui and Tang dynasties of China. The Sui dynasty (589–616), and particularly the very successful Tang dynasty (618–907) which followed it, were both particularly pluralist Chinese states. Although nearly all periods in Chinese history knew massive religious pluralism, in most periods from the beginning of the Common Era onward Confucianism held a preeminent position in the systems of state ritual practice which constituted the primary ideological apparatus of the empire. In the Han period (206BCE–220CE), when many Chinese institutions were formed, Confucianism was elevated to a position of orthodoxy above other religious traditions in the state (Yu 2005: 21–2). This superior position of Confucianism in the state, although relinquished to some extent during the Sui and Tang dynasties, was further developed in the Song (960–1276), Yuan (1271–1368), Ming (1368–1644), and Qing (1644–1911) dynasties. In other words, through most of Chinese history Confucianism held a dominant ritualistic position in the state. Whereas earlier and later Chinese dynastic states usually positioned Confucianism in a privileged position in the state above the other religious traditions, the Sui favored Buddhism, and the Tang were unusually favoring toward a range of other religious traditions including Daoism, Buddhism, and many others. This resulted in a comparatively diminished status for Confucianism.

The fact that the Tang, despite being considered one of the golden ages of Chinese history, is an exception to the rule of Confucian supremacy has been related by some scholars to other exceptional qualities of this state. Tang society's approach to gender is seen as different to earlier and particularly later periods of Chinese imperial history. Representations of noble women in Tang literature and art often portray a much more robust and active vision of femininity (Rothschild 2003: 54–6). The Tang is also generally regarded as having been a particularly culturally open and diverse Chinese state. The Tang dynasty's ruling house "had roots in the Turkic peoples" (Kohn 2000: 339). The state looked West and was more economically, socially, and culturally integrated with Central Asia than other Chinese states had been. This particular cultural characteristic of the Tang has been related by experts on Daoism to the particularly high level of Daoist influence in the Tang state, an influence which to some extent came at Confucian expense (Kohn 2000: 339).

The Tang is important in Japanese history not only because of the influences on Japan that emanated directly from Tang China but also because of the level of Tang influence on the Korean peninsula, particularly in the Korean state of Silla, which was the dominant power in southern Korea during the seventh century (McBride 2010: 3). From the sixth century, the Silla state identified itself with Buddhism, as did its northern Korean neighbor Koguryo. This meant that all the major continental states in touch with Japan in the seventh and eighth centuries, Sui and Tang China, Silla, Koguryo, and Bohai all identified with a non-Confucian tradition – usually Buddhism.[11] Herman Ooms has argued that continental Daoist influence was equally if not even more influential than Buddhism in eighth-century Japan. Direct references to Daoism in the Japanese historical texts are, as Ooms has put it, "elusive." But he argues nonetheless that many elements in Japanese society often attributed to Shinto or Confucian influence are actually Daoist "deposits," which can be shown to have a deep Daoist history (Ooms 2009: xviii; Barrett in Breen and Teeuwen 2000: 13–31). He thereby links the strong position of Daoism in Tang dynasty China to the particular religious plurality of early Japan.

Early Japanese state structures just happened to form at a moment in Chinese history when Confucianism was in many ways at its institutionally weakest. It is a singularly important fact then that it was this in many ways unusual and comparatively un-Confucian Chinese state – the Tang – which most directly influenced early Japanese state structures – including the place of Confucianism therein. For much of the eighth and ninth centuries, Tang China, Silla Korea, and early Japan all shared a political situation where despite formally having an imperial bureaucratic system of governance, aristocratic cliques and clans were in strong political positions and structurally undermined the imperial bureaucratic institutions. In Japan, however, the emperor and imperial institutions were much weaker than in the Tang. Because these institutions, particularly in Japan, were the locus of Confucian activity, this limited the capacity of Confucianism to be developed or utilized critically in society. This was particularly the case in Japan, where the imperial institutions were more often than not subjugated by the political power of aristocratic oligarch cliques. As Marian Ury has written, "a bureaucratic system carefully modelled after that of the Tang reached its apogee in the eighth century... by the beginning of the... tenth century, although the conception and rhetoric of Confucian government remained, as did its forms and usages, many of its functions were being carried out by other means" (Hall et al. 1999: 342).

Comparing Japanese and Tang state regulations, we can find solid evidence to suggest that Japanese political structures limited the power of the imperial bureaucracy and the reach of Confucian teachings within the imperial apparatus much more than in China. The most influential legal and administrative codes of early Japan, the *Yōrō Ritsuryō* (757), were closely based on the Tang *Kaiyuan Luling* (737) and earlier Chinese dynastic codes. Examination of the *Yōrō Ritsuryō* in comparison with the Sui and Tang codes reveals subtle differences that suggest the position of Confucianism in early Japan was even more constrained than in the Tang Chinese or Silla Korean model.

The Tang and earlier Chinese codes deal with Confucianism primarily as part of a chapter entitled "Regulations on Worship" (*Ciling*), or in some alternate versions "Regulations of the *Shenqi*." The *Shenqi* (literally meaning "Gods of Heaven and Earth") was a government department which regulated the important state rituals through which imperial power – the power of the emperor and thereby the empire – was legitimated. These "regulations" outline guidelines for the officials working in that department. These officials presided over important rituals in the cosmological system whereby the emperor's authority was legitimated through his mediation between the temporal world and the world of the Gods. In the Chinese codes, all of the rites are Confucian, and notably even include the *shidian* rite honoring Confucius (called *sekiten* or *shakuten* in Japanese) (Kornicki and McMullen 1996).

In the Japanese code, there is a parallel section in the same part of the code, also titled "Regulations on the *Jingi*" (the Japanese pronunciation of *Shenqi*), and also giving rules for the officials who serve in this department. The Japanese code, the *Yōrō ritsuryō*, even opens with a sentence lifted from the Chinese codes, identifying the *Shenqi* as referring to the "Gods of Heaven and Earth" (NST 3: 211–24).[12] Yet it seems clear the Gods imagined were different to those discussed in the Chinese codes. Notably, none of the rituals outlined in this section were Confucian. Although most of the text is very similar to the Chinese codes, the key

Confucian rite of *shidian* has been removed. The rites described are rather clearly limited to particular Shinto shrine rituals. In other words, in the Japanese codes the all-important rites to the Gods which justified imperial power had been cleansed of Confucian content. The most central positioning of Confucian content in the Chinese codes was done away with in the *Yōrō ritsuryō*.

In the Japanese codes Confucianism was instead limited to a separate chapter on the state Confucian academy (Ch: *Daxue*, Jp: *Daigaku*). This section also exists in the Chinese codes as a separate chapter. In the Japanese code, however, it is only in this section on the academy that Confucian religious practices are mentioned.

At the imperial academy and each of the provincial state academies every year on two occasions, in Spring and Autumn, the *shidian* ritual will be performed for Confucius and the ancient sages (NST 3: 262).

The same section also defines the Confucian canon of the state academy at that time, showing a preference for works of Zhou dynasty divination and rites.

The *Zhouyi* (Zhou Book of Changes), *The Book of Documents*, the *Rites of Zhou*, the *Yili*, the *Book of Rites*, the *Book of Songs*, and the *Zuochuan commentary of the Spring and Autumn Annals* should each be considered a "classic" [text in the canon]. *The Classic of Filial Piety* and *Confucius Analects* should also be learnt by scholars (NST 3: 263).[13]

Discussion of Confucian rites is therefore restricted in the Japanese codes to the academy only, showing us that it was only the academy staff who led these rituals.[14] In this sense the positioning of Confucianism in Japan was even more peripheral and constrained than its position in Tang China. Confucianism was removed from the imperial center and the central religious rites which justified imperial authority. Unlike in China, Confucian rites were not the prime vehicle for worship of the imperial ancestor gods. Confucian rites did not permeate the space of the imperial palace inner sanctum. Confucianism in early Japan did not occupy a structurally preeminent position in the state cosmology.

This led to Confucianism in early Japan having a particularly sequestered and bureaucratic character qua its social context. Confucianism clearly influenced the form of the earliest and most important Japanese historical documents such as the state histories discussed earlier. On a much larger level, the entire legal and administrative structure of the imperial state was based on Chinese models which were heavily influenced by Confucian thought. But Confucian practice was limited institutionally to spheres of government education which trained lower aristocrats who served in lower to mid levels of the imperial bureaucracy. It was less central to the religious practices which functioned to authenticate imperial rule.

Another indicator of the limited influence of early Japanese Confucianism is the lack of indigenous Japanese Confucian writing. Despite there being Japanese Buddhist treatises and Japanese works of both Japanese- and Chinese-language poetry extant from this period, there is little to nothing of the kind of memorial and commentary writing associated with Confucianism. This indicates Confucianism in early Japan was not only limited by social context but also limited in terms of intellectual content and capacity. Early Japanese Confucianism's problems of social context and intellectual content seem to have been related. On the one hand, the comparatively limited intellectual dynamism and creativity of Confucianism in Japan contributed to the lack of diffusion beyond the compartmentalized sphere of aristocrat bureaucrat training. On the other, Confucianism's prime social locus of operation in Japan being the state academy and the aristocrat–bureaucrat elite reinforced a particular focus on language learning and repetition rather than analysis and interpretation.

A good example of a viewpoint from early Japan which saw Confucianism as limited is that of the famous Buddhist monk Kūkai (774–835). Ironically enough Kūkai became the most well-known graduate of the early Japanese state's official Confucian academy, the *daigaku*, primarily through founding a new Buddhist sect, the Shingon school, which became one of the major streams of Japanese Buddhism. His main association with Confucianism other than his time at the academy was his authorship around 797 of the text *Sangō shīki*, in which he systematically argued against Confucianism and Daoism to assert the superiority of Buddhist teachings. The logic through which he did this sheds light on how Confucianism was seen by Japanese elites familiar with it at that time. Kūkai frames his argument in relation to filial piety. He first shows how Daoism is superior to Confucianism by arguing that Confucianism's teaching about other (metaphysical) worlds is constrained, thereby giving no understanding of where the souls of one's parents go after death. He then argues that Buddhism is superior to Daoism because it shows us more levels of the metaphysical universe, thus enlarging the realm within which we could communicate with our ancestors. His condemnation of Confucianism then is based on what we could primitively call the lack of religious and metaphysical aspects in Confucianism in the Japanese context, and the limitations on ancestor veneration this created (NKBT 71: 17–28; Kūkai 1972: 101–40).

This resonates with the late twentieth-century intellectual historian of Confucianism Wang Jiahua's argument that early Japanese Confucianism lacked creative power. He attributed this primarily to the particular nature of the Chinese Han and Tang dynasty Confucian traditions favored in the early Japanese state academy (Wang in Minamoto 1995: 78–9). These Chinese schools of Confucianism emphasized philological research which focused on the investigation of particular Chinese logograms and words instead of an understanding of the meaning and intention of the texts. This tendency to focus on the meaning of particular words rather than the meaning of content and ideas was probably strengthened in the Japanese context because the Confucian scholars' main tasks were related to language and translation. The centrality of the linguistic aspect in the Japanese context of Confucian education was reinforced by the fact that a major aim for aristocrat–bureaucrat students and teachers was to equip themselves with the linguistic and cultural knowledge necessary to conduct diplomacy and official commerce in the medium of elite Chinese language and ritual. The linguistic side of understanding Confucian texts was therefore particularly important to them from a practical perspective. Or to put it another way, Confucianism was valued more as the source of an applied practical knowledge (in this case linguistic and diplomatic ritual knowledge) than as a religious or philosophical system relevant to any deeper part of human existence.

The Confucianism of early Japan, in comparison with Confucianism in most other periods in Japan or China, was particularly instrumentalist and elitist, while at the same time being comparatively unreligious and unintellectual. Its exclusivist ties to the state and its confined practical role within the state structures limited its ability to diffuse through general culture and made its very existence vulnerable to political change. That change began to occur during the tenth century when particular noble clans and cliques, notably the Fujiwara, began to gain such dominance at the early Japanese court that they were able to permanently subvert most of the state structures of the imperial system (Breen and Teeuwen 2010: 140). Many state institutions ceased to function as instruments of bureaucratic rule. Notably the Confucian state academy, which was supposed to supply personnel for the imperial bureaucracy, became increasingly irrelevant as most government appointments were decided through patronage, in time becoming hereditary.

In fact, the ideal Confucian state academy system, comprising a central academy in the capital, and regional academies throughout the provinces, had never been realized in early Japan. The college in Dazaifu, the imperial outpost in Kyushu in charge of continental relations, was the only regional academy established, and by 1097 it had ceased to function (Smits 1995: 103). The Confucian academy in the capital, lacking sufficient funds to sustain itself, also sold positions. Eventually, even the leadership of the Confucian academy became hereditary, thereby diminishing the real-world value of Confucian scholarship in matters of appointment even within the academy itself. The central academy became increasingly irrelevant. Its decline can be discerned in the lack of numbers of teachers and funding. Interestingly, vegetables replaced meat as the sacrificial offering from 1163 onwards, although it is unclear if this was because of lack of funds, the rise of Buddhist sensibilities, or a combination of the two. The lack of state support and general malaise of Confucianism was demonstrated by the fact that after a fire in 1177 destroyed the Confucian academy buildings no one bothered to reconstruct them.[15] By the twelfth century the Confucianism of the imperial institutions was in a dire state.

Scholars of Japanese history interested in Confucianism often dismiss the weakness of Confucianism in the early Japanese state as simply one symptom of the overall weakness of the *ritsuryō* imperial government system in Japan (Kornicki and McMullen 1996: 70). However, we could rather turn this around to argue that the removal of Confucian ritual from the imperial structures, right from the very beginning of the organized Japanese imperial state, may have been one of the root causes of the weaknesses of that state over the long term. Furthermore, the fact that the field of action of Confucianism in early Japan was so limited, reaching only to state institutions, engaging only a limited number of the lower to mid-level ranks of the state functionaries, and with a constrained statist focus, was what made Confucianism so vulnerable to begin with. Confucianism faded with the imperial state structures because it had virtually no presence outside them.

So what consequences did this positioning and configuration of Confucianism in early Japan have for the role of Confucian universalism in that society, and what can this tell us about the nature of Confucian universalism more generally? Because Confucianism was limited to an instrumentalist role in the early Japanese state, and limited to its state institutions, it did not manifest itself as a broad social force, discourse, or set of practices through which creative approaches to governance or other individual or social practice could emerge. Someone like Kūkai experienced Confucianism as a set of socially and spiritually disengaged doctrines related to statist systems which regulated international relations and low-level state administration. He rejected Confucianism as limited. This was not the Confucianism of individual redemption and social reform seen in other periods of Chinese, Korean, and later Japanese history. It was not a broad social vision which could compete with, for instance, the integrated social, religious, and political vision of Buddhism. The social context, positioning, and practice of Confucianism seem to have been a major contingent factor in facilitating different possible developments of Confucian universalism. For Confucian universalism to be engaged creatively by those on the ground, in a way that allowed them to play a role in shaping the nature of the tradition, through their own commentaries, through spreading the tradition to other sections of society, or through changing the nature of its interaction with society, it needed to be socially positioned in relation to culture and society in a more creative way. This then gives us a lens for understanding the limitations and possibilities for the application of Confucianism in other geographic and temporal contexts – including, as I will come back to in this book's Epilogue, East Asia today.

Medieval Confucianism

Confucianism as Buddhism

Whereas Confucianism in early Japan manifested itself primarily through bureaucratic educational activities of the state academy, Confucianism in medieval Japan (twelfth to sixteenth centuries) manifested itself in a vibrant literary culture associated with Zen monasticism. Five Mountains Zen Culture, or *Gozan* Zen culture, is the name given to a wide-ranging movement associated with the rise of Zen Buddhist monasticism and practice in medieval Japan. Much important traditional Japanese art, literature, and poetry are associated with this movement, which was based in, but not limited to, the new Zen monasteries which were established and patronized by the new Japanese samurai-led shogunal states between the thirteenth and fifteenth centuries (Collcutt 1981: 57, 101, 125).

The Chan (Jp. *Zen*) Buddhist arrival in Japan that led to the Japanese Five Mountains Zen culture was significant not only in terms of its establishment of Zen in Japan but also as an importer of a newly integrated form of Chinese culture which emphasized artistic, literary, and religious practice and integrated non-Buddhist religious traditions, notably including Confucianism. Zen Buddhism's ability to penetrate Japanese society, however, was aided by the political schisms of the early medieval period, which brought new people to power who had vested interests in looking to the rise of a new Buddhist order to challenge the old Buddhist order that had been so closely associated with the corrupt imperial aristocracy.

As noted earlier, imperial Japan was already in decline by the tenth century. It was completely overthrown in 1185 when samurai warlords took power into their own hands. For centuries the aristocrats had ruled in the name of a usually impotent emperor, first through the imperial structures, then through Fujiwara family hegemony and inter-estate and inter-clan rivalry. The samurai rose as a new caste of people employed as muscle by the Fujiwara and other powerful families in the late Heian period. In a sense, then, the twelfth-century samurai usurpation of power was simply a new group of people pretending to protect the same old impotent imperial line, a power coup like the many before it. Culturally, however, it had huge impact. This is because the whole complex of aristocratic imperial culture and its institutions was challenged by the new samurai rulers, who did not derive their power directly from any imperial aristocratic lineage. The new samurai government, by moving the center of power to Kamakura (a new city many days travel to the east of the traditional imperial power base around Kyoto), to an extent indicated their rejection of the Kyoto-based cultural institutions of imperial power.

The imperial aristocracy had always kept strong links with the Buddhist monasteries, many of which were situated in the hills around Kyoto. These links were solidified through the practice of retired aristocrat officials, notably including the leaders of the Fujiwara clan, "retiring" from office into Buddhist monastaries as monks. This meant that many of the senior Buddhist monks were actually former aristocrats. Senior Buddhist clerics and the aristocracy became intimately interrelated elites. The removal of aristocrats from power and the rise of the samurai of the Kamakura shogunate thereby precipitated a "de-aristocratization" of the clergy. This was done partly through shogunal support for new monasteries, often from new traditions (Wang in Minamoto 1995: 86; Collcutt 1981: 57–62). Another technique was to encourage, through patronage, the establishment and importation from China of new sects of Buddhism – notably Chan/Zen.

Medieval Japanese Confucianism's positioning in the new vibrant cultural milieu of Five Mountains Zen culture gave it a comparatively more socially integrated, creative and transnational character. The Five Mountains Zen culture it was associated with represented a new force of continental cultural influence and individual Buddhist practice in Japan. This was partly related to the nature of Zen (Chan) Buddhism, partly related to the particular Chinese cultural influences it brought with it, and partly due to the particular social circumstances through which it came to enjoy significant patronage in Japan.

The Zen bridge to China, and the seeds of Neo-Confucianism

A particularity of Zen in comparison with other forms of Buddhism is its advocacy that adherents individually reach enlightenment in this current life. This leads to an emphasis on individual practice which some scholars have related to the individual creativity of art and literature associated with this movement (Pollack 1985: 4–5). In Song dynasty China – from where Zen was imported into Japan – art, literature, religion, and culture in general were particularly prized not only in the state sphere but also in the growing commercial world. Religiously, the Song was a particularly creative and competitive society. In Song China, Zen Buddhists had to compete with, among others, a rising new movement of popular Confucianism, now often called Neo-Confucianism, which harshly criticized Zen while also integrating Zen elements into its own world view. Zen Buddhists often reacted by similarly integrating elements of this Confucian culture into their own schematics. Zen Buddhists during this period thereby often responded to attacks by other sects or religions by emphasizing the doctrine of "The Combination of the Three Religions," suggesting that Zen represented a perfected synthesis of Buddhist, Daoist, and Confucian teachings. This Zen reaction sought to appropriate and integrate other religious teachings (Bodiford in Anderl 2012: 287; Collcutt 1981: 33).

Zen in medieval Japan, thereby, inherited Song-Yuan Buddhism's characteristic integration of cultural practice and tradition from other religions, and this critically affected its transmission of Confucianism. Medieval Japanese Confucianism, particularly under the stewardship of Gozan Zen culture, developed a number of characteristics that set it apart from earlier manifestations of Confucianism in Japan. Firstly, it was more transnational in the sense that it was more up to date with recent Confucian interpretive traditions from China and tried to keep abreast of these. Secondly, it was more creative: in the medieval period, Confucian treatises were written in Japan and Confucianism influenced secular and Buddhist literature. Even the imperial aristocracy, influenced by Zen approaches to Confucianism, wrote treatises which were deeply Confucian in outlook: former Emperor Hanazano's Admonitions to the Prince being a famous example (Goble 1995:66–68). Thirdly, through this secular literary influence and the Buddhist monastic networks, Confucianism was more broadly culturally integrated than it had been in early Japan. While tied closely to literature based in Zen monasteries, it was not limited to one school nor tied to only one political caste or group. Fourthly, although Confucianism was utilized by politicians, poets and monks in a variety of ways, the utility that Confucianism represented to the Japanese who engaged it in the medieval period was not as instrumentalist as it appears to have been in early Japan. It was not seen exclusively as a way to communicate with the Chinese state, nor as only a way to train bureaucrats. It was clearly valued in a more multidimensional way, and that is why it was integrated into the literary and philosophical outlooks of different Japanese in this period. This led to medieval Japanese Confucianism having long-lasting effects on elements of social practice – an issue I will come back to.

As discussed earlier, early Japanese Confucian theory seems to have been limited. It stuck with paradigms originated in the Han dynasty, and focused on interpretation of single words over attempts to understand, analyze, or develop the content of Confucian thought. Conversely, the Confucianism of Zen priests in the medieval period was directly influenced by the newest Confucian theories originated in the Song dynasty. This form of Confucianism, called "Song Confucianism," "Zhu Xi Learning," or most commonly in English "Neo-Confucianism," is still the dominant interpretation of Confucianism today. Developed by a number of thinkers before and during the early Song, and systematized by Zhu Xi (1120–1200) in the twelfth century, this form of Confucianism developed a metaphysics that systematically linked Confucian ethics and political thought to an explanation of the natural world influenced by Chan Buddhist and Daoist Yin Yang theory. By being based in this very modern (by thirteenth-century standards) Confucian discourse, Japanese medieval Confucianism already had a hugely more complex and theoretical base to develop upon than its earlier predecessor (Yao 2000: 97).

The fact that there was a regular flow of Zen monks moving between Japan and China through the thirteenth and fourteenth centuries, and that Japan under the Kamakura shogunate (1185–1333), and particularly under the Muromachi shogunate (1336–1573), carried out an active trade with China, meant continuous Chinese contact and influence. Recent Confucian commentaries and treatises kept arriving in Japan from China through the medieval period, representing a continuing influence on Japanese Confucianism. The increasing institutionalization of Neo-Confucianism as the basis of state examinations in China from the Yuan dynasty (1271–1368) and thereafter meant that the development of Chinese Confucian discourse continued along a path that could be paralleled in Japan. Neo-Confucianism represented a stable interpretative base, institutionalized on the continent and peninsula through the examinations system (Elman 2000). This created the capacity for Japanese Confucianism to have a more transnational character, in the sense that it could stay linked to the development of Confucian discourse in China and Korea, a development which was occurring within the same systematized discourse pattern of Neo-Confucian theory across all three countries. The medieval period did not see Neo-Confucianism popularized in

Japan, nor even clearly systematized, but it was the period in which Neo-Confucian conceptions began to make their way into Japanese thinking.

Japanese reacted to the systematized and theoretical discourse of Neo-Confucianism even in the medieval period by participating in it through actively printing the commentaries of Zhu Xi and others and, crucially, through writing their own commentaries on classic Confucian texts. The fact that Confucian study occurred primarily in a context of literary study, literary production, and religious practice in the Zen monasteries contributed to its more creative character and the willingness of practitioners to write their own interpretations. The fact that Confucian study occurred in this kind of creative environment – integrated into Buddhist monastic life, which in turn was itself often integrated into other social structures, like village life, or samurai household life – meant that Confucianism was also more socially integrated (Bodiford 1993: 108–21).

This meant that Confucianism was approached and regarded in much less instrumentalist terms than in early Japan. Confucianism was still often studied to equip scholar monks to carry out the diplomatic roles that were charged to them by various shogunal rulers dealing with China and Korea. But Confucianism was not institutionally positioned or perceived exclusively in those terms. In fact it is fairly clear that, at least from a Zen Buddhist perspective, Confucian teachings were truly related to the quest for enlightenment. Gidō Shūshin (1325–1388), for instance, one of the most important Zen monastic leaders, explained Confucianism as a kind of social manifestation of Buddhism's individual message.

If at first, through the transmission of Confucian action, you are made to know the benevolent way of humanity, then later, through the teaching of Buddhist religion, you will be awakened to the existence of Heavenly truth in your own nature. What could be better than this (Minamoto 1995: 99)?

Confucianism in medieval Japan then was integrated into a larger religious and literary movement enabling it to be perceived in a wide array of ways interacting with an array of human experience. Not being restricted to the compulsory schooling for government officers as it had been in early Japan liberated Confucianism to function on a broader social level where, under the umbrella of Five Mountain Zen culture, it spoke to a range of human experience and elicited a range of human response.

Practice, politics, and Shinto

The most enduring Confucian influence on general Japanese cultural practice through all history is undoubtedly its influence on funeral rites.

Standardization of funeral rites in the forms that led to the contemporary form of Japanese Buddhist funerals, which represent the mainstream funerary rites even today, began in the fourteenth century under Zen influence. William Bodiford has argued that key to this standardization was the importation of Chinese Chan [Zen] Buddhist practices which had internalized Confucian traditions of funerary rites (Bodiford 1993: 1, 185–7; Gerhart 2009: 165). The most socially embedded influence of Confucianism in Japanese history thus occurred through Zen mediation in the medieval period, centuries before Confucianism's golden age in Tokugawa Japan, and in spheres of social activity which were (and often still are) intensely religious. Zen mediation of that influence, and the fact that Confucianism was already integrated into the Zen practices before importation from China to Japan, means few were aware of its Confucian roots.

Medieval Confucianism, however, although thus reaching well beyond politics, also had a political side. The Five Mountain Zen Monastic order itself was actually a politically created social phenomenon. The Five Mountains represented a number of monasteries given government license – in China by the Song and later dynasties, in Medieval Japan by the Kamakura and Muromachi shogunates. There were other monasteries which did not receive this favored state position. So Five Mountain monasteries were particularly integrated with the shogunal states, and indeed did provide many of their interpreters and diplomats. Most shoguns were also patrons of the Five Mountains, and some of them even practiced Zen.[16] Under this Zen umbrella, however, Confucianism's relation to the state was definitely more removed. Shoguns of the Kamakura and Muromachi shogunates did not regularly patronize any independently Confucian institutions or institutionalize Confucian rites or practice.

The *Shidian* rite (Figure 1.1), however, was revived by the Southern dynasty during the so-called War of the Northern and Southern Dynasties in Japan. This was a fourteenth-century civil war between Emperor Godaigo (the Southern Court), who was attempting to revive direct imperial rule, and the Muromachi shogunate (who supported the so-called Northern Court with their own opposition candidate for emperor who accepted shogun rule) (Kuroda 1975: 294–7). Much has been made of the Southern Court's short-lived revival of the entire trappings of state Confucian ritualism during this period, something which had disappeared from the Heian state centuries before its fall. Wajima Yoshio has claimed that "the Southern Court's conduct of the *shidian* ritual, even in a time of war when there was little safety, demonstrated the importance of the ritual as a symbol of imperial court authority" (Wajima

Figure 1.1 Sekitenzu: a picture of the Shidian Rite (Shibunkai collection)

1965: 164–5). Whether this demonstrated any particular love for the Confucian tradition, however, or even a perception of its importance, is questionable. The Southern Court actually attempted to revive a whole host of religious traditions in the hope of increasing the cultural capital and legitimacy of their increasingly militarily ineffective claims to the throne. Emperor Godaigo also increased patronage for Zen, Shingon, and Tendai Buddhism, as well as various Shinto sects at the same time. Confucianism does not seem to have been anything particularly special. It seems this kind of patronage and revival of religious rites was primarily about attempting to emulate Song dynasty examples of imperial trappings (Collcutt 1981: 94).

In any case, the Southern Court was ultimately the loser in the conflict. Often not performed at all, at other times not able to proceed because the ritualistic implements had been stolen, by the late 1300s the imperial state *shidian* ritual had become a joke. In 1405, a few years after the end of effective Southern Court resistance to the Muromachi shogunate, a rare successfully prepared rendition of the ritual was turned into a farce when twenty-three drunken nobles, having physically forced their way into the reception hall, proceeded to drink and yell obscenities through the entire proceedings (Wajima 1965: 165). It was clear to anyone that the center of Confucian learning was not any longer the imperial state. It was instead the literary and Buddhist culture of Five Mountains Zen. In fact, even the holders of the titular Confucian positions in what was left of the imperial bureaucracy themselves acknowledged this through steadily adopting more of the teachings and practices of Song Confucianism from the Zen side (Wajima 1965: 92–199; Wang 1988: 128).

Zen-mediated medieval Confucianism influenced not only the Confucian scholars of the imperial house but even the substructure of Shinto thought and practice. Mark Teeuwen has argued that the concept of Shinto came into being during the thirteenth and fourteenth centuries under the influence of metaphysical readings of Yinyang thought imported from China at this time. Teeuwen attributes this influence to a number of Daoist texts (Teeuwen 2002: 252–4). In China at this time, however, Yinyang thought and the *Book of Changes* (*Yijing*) had been most powerfully harnessed in the metaphysical system of Zhu Xi – that is, Neo-Confucianism, the system that underpinned Gozan Zen Confucianism. Wajima Yoshio has shown how Shinto thinkers appropriated the "Buddhist, Confucian, Daoist, Three Teachings doctrine," which we saw earlier was so closely associated with the Five Mountains Zen tradition, to manufacture their own "Buddhist, Confucian, Shinto,

Three teachings doctrine" – a doctrine which was central to late fifteenth-century Shinto self-conceptualization (Wajima 1965: 159–162).

In other words, the birth of what Teeuwen calls "the concept of Shinto" (as an articulated religious tradition) appears to have occurred under the influence of the metaphysical Song Confucianism favored and spread by the Gozan priests, and indeed through their particular conceptualization of that Confucianism within the "three teachings doctrine." Or, as William Bodiford has concisely argued, "there is little doubt that the new Song interpretation of the *Yijing* as cosmology (instead of as a book of divination) helped Japanese conceptualize *shintō* in cosmological terms" (Bodiford in Anderl 2012: 287). In other words, the birth of Shinto as a concept (in Teeuwen's sense) occurred as a direct result of the influence of Song Confucianism, mediated through Japanese Gozan Zen. Confucianism enabled the creation of Shinto as we know it.

Ultimately, the story of medieval Japanese Confucianism is the story of the superiority of cultural forms over state ones. Even though operating under the umbrella of Buddhist culture and practiced predominantly by monks in Buddhist monasteries, the links of medieval Confucianism with cultural production and other cultural forms – Buddhism itself, but also very importantly literature – began to suggest that it had the capacity for a much wider impact than as only the exclusive learning of mid-level bureaucrats. Of course, in a society of incredibly limited literacy, it goes without saying that Confucianism in medieval Japan was still the preserve of a tiny elite. But it was an elite that valued Confucianism across a wider spectrum, that reproduced, developed, and propagated it, and that through its own relatively integrated social engagement allowed Confucianism to embed in several aspects of Japanese culture.

Importantly this embedding ultimately led to forms of Confucianism which integrated the remnants of the imperial Confucian institutions, eventually breathing life back into them and leading to a political reengagement with Confucianism. Already in the early fifteenth century, what may have been the first Japanese-language commentary on a Neo-Confucian text was authored by the court noble Ichijō Kanera (1402–1481) when he commentated the *Greater Learning* (*daxue*). The Kiyohara clan, notably under the leadership of Kiyohara Nobutaka (1475–1550), served as Confucian teachers around the court and also began to embrace Neo-Confucian interpretations. W. J. Boot argues that this was partly instigated by the need of nobles like the Kiyohara to sell their services on an emerging intellectual market where the primary consumers where members of the samurai elite (Boot, forthcoming). The emergence of this market went hand in hand with the increase in

samurai literacy which began through the sixteenth century and accelerated exponentially in the seventeenth.

The Confucianism of the medieval period thus began the process of a
much larger-scale engagement with Confucianism by large sections of
Japanese society. Led increasingly by the warlord leaders of the rising new
settlement of early modern Japan instead of the imperial aristocracy, this
new engagement would usher in the golden age of Confucianism under
Japan's Tokugawa shogunate (1603–1868), the regime that laid the
foundations of modern Japan.[17]

2   Confucianism as religion

> The Way of the Sages, what is recorded in the Six Classics, there is none
> of it which does not return to reverence for Heaven.
>
> Ogyū Sorai, *Benmei*, 1717 (NST 36: 120)

This is the first of three chapters which deal with Confucianism in early
modern Japan, in the period of the Tokugawa shogunate (1603–1868).
Confucianism in early modern Japan was vernacularized and popularized
and emerged as a powerful independent tradition of ideas, practice, and
politics. Eventually, it came to exercise an omnipresent influence over nearly
every field of Japanese cultural production, and to provide the intellectual
and linguistic frameworks through which even the sociologies and technologies of Western modernity would be recreated in Japan. The next three
chapters seek to reshape the contours through which we understand
Confucianism's role in early modern Japan by considering a Confucianism
not only of ideas, but of religious, political, cultural, and scientific practice.

This chapter, Chapter 2, will concentrate on how Confucianism
became grounded in Japanese society during the early modern period,
particularly in the seventeenth century. It will argue that it was the
religious aspects of *Neo-Confucianism*, notably its forms of practice, and
perceptions of the meanings of those practices, which crucially facilitated
Confucianism's social popularization and impact during this period.
Chapter 3 will examine the role of this newly socially embedded
Confucianism in the early modern Japanese public sphere, considering
how Confucian ideas and practices influenced general culture and politics. Chapter 4 will concentrate on Confucianism's role in the knowledge
order of early modern Japan, including in fields of Western learning.

Confucianism as independent tradition

Through the first half of the seventeenth century, Neo-Confucianism
emerged and was popularized in Japan as a separate religious tradition
led by teachers who identified themselves primarily as Confucians.

Although Confucian ideas were present in Japan pre-1600, people interested in these ideas remained primarily attached to other traditions like Buddhism.[1] But by the early 1600s, there were a significant number of Confucian specialists in Japan identifying themselves primarily as Confucians, and usually also as Neo-Confucians. Below I consider how Confucianism emerged as an active independent tradition, firstly by charting the emergence of *The Way of Heaven*, a syncretist tradition, the popularization of which can be seen as marking the transition of Confucianism into an independent popular religious tradition in Japan at the turn of the sixteenth into the seventeenth century. I will then briefly examine the ideas, social positioning, and practices of several overtly Confucian scholars of the early to mid-Tokugawa period.

Over the last three decades, some Japanese historians have come to describe the rise of Neo-Confucianism in the seventeenth century in relation to a more general milieu of religious activity, which, rather than being state-oriented, actually emphasized "the individual's way of living in real society," "the nature of the subject's individual morals, rather than aspects of social system, organization or structure" (Bitō 1993: 32–5). In other words, Confucianism's sociality in the very early Tokugawa period when it first emerged into popular culture is currently seen as the product of a tension between Neo-Confucianism's regimes of individualized practice on the one hand, and the reality of Tokugawa political society on the other.

Ōkuwa Hitoshi, one of the most important contemporary writers on medieval and early modern Japanese religion, recently argued that the rise of Confucianism in seventeenth-century Japan should be explained in terms of a popular demand for a kind of religiosity that Neo-Confucianism was able to provide. Rather than being an imposition by the state, the forms of Confucianism and Confucian-indigenous syncretism which emerged in seventeenth-century Japan responded to the norms of the general population, whose "daily lives relied on religion" (Ōkuwa 2012: 114). This chapter follows this approach in arguing that the Japanese embrace of Neo-Confucian religious sensibilities was key to the rise of Confucianism in early Tokugawa Japan. Neo-Confucianism afforded a new kind of individual-centric moral religious practice in Japan which often possessed an inherently political (although usually not governing) character.

This chapter will look at this rise in Japanese Confucian practice partly through focus on a number of well-known early and mid-Tokugawa Confucians, notably Kumazawa Banzan (1619–1694), Yamaga Sokō (1622–1685), Hayashi Razan (1583–1653), Yamazaki Ansai (1619–1682), and Ogyū Sorai (1666–1728). I will focus particularly on their approach to the *practice* of Confucianism and how that conception of practice interacted with trans-Asian models of Neo-Confucianism. The traditional way to historicize these figures has been to focus on their ideas, to contrast those ideas, and thereby demonstrate their roles in establishing separate factions of Confucianism in Japan. Indeed many of these Confucians did claim legitimacy for themselves or their schools through identifying their own ideas with particular factional traditions within trans-Asian Neo-Confucianism. Major early Tokugawa period scholars like Hayashi Razan, Yamazaki Ansai, and Kaibara Ekken (1630–1714) claimed to be defenders of the "orthodox" School of Principle trend in Neo-Confucianism. They thus came to be seen as followers of the Chinese Song dynasty scholar Zhu Xi and were labeled by others "Scholars of Zhu Xi Learning" (*Shushigakusha*). Other early figures, notably Nakae Tōju (1608–1648) and Kumazawa Banzan, would become associated with the "School of Mind" trend in Neo-Confucianism associated in China and Korea with the early Ming figure Wang Yangming (1472–1529). They thus came to be labeled "Scholars of Yangming Learning" (*Yōmeigakusha*). Indigenous Japanese trends which emerged at the turn of the seventeenth into the eighteenth century would later see figures like Itō Jinsai (1627–1705) and Ogyū Sorai labeled "Scholars of Ancient Learning" (*Kogakusha*). This created a rough classification of three factional trends in Japanese Neo-Confucianism: (1) Zhu Xi Learning, (2) Yangming Learning, (3) Ancient Learning.[2]

These identifications of different intellectual trends are significant because they show the development by early modern Japanese Confucians of forms of self-identification which relied upon Chinese-originated, trans-Asian models of Confucian school affiliation. So there is some utility to this approach as a means of linking different trends in Japanese Confucianism to continental trends. Analyzing the relationship between different Tokugawa interpretations of Confucianism only through these kinds of intellectual "school" categorizations, however, would occlude (and in earlier research has occluded) many of the most socially and culturally significant aspects of Confucianism's legacy in Japan. Rather than focusing on these kinds of *differences of thought*, this chapter instead looks to identify *similarities of practice* between different streams of Confucianism in early modern Japan. It argues that, despite coming from a range of different intellectual schools of Confucianism, and disagreeing with each other on many theoretical issues, in terms of practice, context, and sociality, the Way of Heaven teachings, and the Confucianism of all these figures shared most or all of the following similarities:

1. A clear focus on Neo-Confucian *practice* as outlined in key texts edited by Zhu Xi in the Song, and developed through practice in Ming dynasty China: notably the "Method of the Heart" (*xinfa*).
2. A syncretist tendency to present Neo-Confucian practice in relation to, or even *as*, Shintoism, Military Thought, or other indigenous-Japanese non-Buddhist traditions.
3. A vision of post-Han contemporary imperial Chinese society as a completely separate and ruptured society from the ideal historic Confucian age of Yao and Shun.
4. A related capacity to create a space for Japanese nationalist sensibilities and to criticize contemporary imperial China from a Confucian perspective.[3]
5. Use of Neo-Confucianism to give meaning to the life of samurai in the new peaceful Tokugawa order.
6. Criticized by others as potentially or actually politically subversive.

Before directly engaging Japanese Confucianism in its early modern manifestation, however, it is first necessary to think about the nature of Neo-Confucianism itself. In particular, it might be helpful to consider what marked *Neo*-Confucianism as so different from earlier forms of Confucianism and how that difference was related to broader historic changes of socio-economic context, in both China and Japan.

Unleashing the power of Neo-Confucianism

This chapter contends that Confucianism's new place in Japanese society was facilitated primarily by the capacities inherent in Neo-Confucian practice. Through the eleventh and twelfth centuries, both the primary system of Neo-Confucian practice (self-cultivation) and Neo-Confucian metaphysics were originated in China. This occurred partly as a reaction to the rise of Buddhism in China. Neo-Confucianism represented a new form of Confucianism in China, the origin of which was bound up with an attempt to adapt Confucianism so that it could compete with Buddhism's comprehensive cosmology and its relationship to a concrete regime of religious practice. It is no surprise then that in Japan, where Buddhism was deeply embedded in society, Confucianism first gained broad traction in this new, comparatively religious, and deeply Buddhist-inspired Neo-Confucian manifestation.

In China, Neo-Confucianism superseded earlier forms of Confucianism theoretically in its systematization of an approach to individual practice set in relation to a comprehensive metaphysical vision of the universe. The classical canon of Confucianism, based around the Five Classics (*Book of Rites, Book of Songs/Poetry, Book of Documents, Book of Changes, Spring and*

Autumn Annals), was augmented with the Neo-Confucian Canon of The Four Books (*The Greater Learning, The Doctrine of the Mean, Confucius Analects, Mencius*). *The Greater Learning* and *The Doctrine of the Mean* were two relatively short, relatively metaphysical sections of the *Book of Rites*, now reclassified as "books" in their own right. *Confucius Analects* and *Mencius* were two ancient semi-canonical writings of Confucian teachers which had not clearly belonged to the "Classics" before the Song, but were now identified as elements of the new core canon. The combination of these four emphasized the moralist and pedagogical inclination of Neo-Confucianism and provided the requisite doctrinal material to support Zhu Xi, and his Song predecessors Cheng Yi (1033–1107) and Cheng Hao's (1032–1085) integration of real-life moral and social practice into a holistic cosmological order. In particular, the practice of "self-cultivation," seen as the primary method for *becoming* a "gentleman," emerged as a key element in Neo-Confucian religiosity.

The curricula of early temple schools and samurai schools in medieval Japan demonstrate that important elements in the Four Book canon associated with Neo-Confucianism, notably the *Greater Learning* and *Doctrine of the Mean*, were being taken up as elements in some forms of Japanese education as early as the thirteenth century.[4] The canonical changes associated with Neo-Confucianism were thus present in Japan at least three centuries before 1600. So why did it catch on as a separate tradition, embraced in its systematic entirety, only hundreds of years later in the seventeenth century? In short, the answer lies to a large extent in major socio-economic changes which occurred in Japanese society through the sixteenth and seventeenth centuries. The implications of some of these changes, for instance, increased literacy, crucially facilitated the social penetration of Neo-Confucian ideas and practices.

Song China (960–1279), where Neo-Confucianism arose, possessed an unprecedentedly active and integrated trading economy, had a population with unusually high levels of leisure time and literacy, and began to adopt political structures and practices which limited the power of local land-owning elites in favor of central imperial power and nominally meritocratic processes of government appointment. These changes, together with the rise of a relatively unfettered trading economy, initially served to support the status of literate trans-imperial elites, often at the expense of the traditional power of the landed gentry. This process of social change in the Song has been described by some twentieth-century historians as an alternative East Asian form of "modernity," or "early modernity" (Naitō 1972: 305–10). This socio-economic situation created the increased literacy and trans-local elite networks through which Neo-Confucian ideas and practice rapidly spread across China. And this new social order was in turn supported by Neo-Confucian ideas and networks. Neo-Confucianism facilitated an alternate form of imperial ideology focused on individual aspirational, rather than conservative aristocratic, action. It also provided justifications of power which were universal and moral in nature, rather than particularist and purely lineage based.

Tokugawa Japan was at its core a feudal order governed by warriors, and thereby inherently different to this post-Song imperial Chinese settlement. However, through the shogunate's practice of regular fief transfers, its concentration of the samurai elite in castle towns off the land, and most notably through the massive increase in agricultural production, wealth, trade, and consequently leisure time and literacy which occurred through the seventeenth century, Tokugawa Japan in many socio-economic respects did come to resemble the kind of "early-modernity" historians have associated with post-Song imperial China. The gentry (samurai) were removed from permanent land holding, a mobile trading economy came into existence, and literary and commercial publishing flourished. This provided the basic social and technological elements which facilitated the kind of society some scholars have called "public" (as will be discussed further in the next chapter). It was also, and often for the same reasons, very conducive to the popularization of Neo-Confucianism. Notably, a nationally mobile and networked elite, high literacy among them, and a commercial publishing and distribution industry to service that literacy, seem to have been instrumental in facilitating the popularization of Neo-Confucianism in both China and Japan. In other words, Tokugawa Japan from 1600, although a totally different political and cultural order to Song China in the twelfth century, nevertheless took Japanese society into new realms of literacy, leisure, and human mobility somewhat reminiscent of the post-Song imperial Chinese settlement.

These socio-economic changes, and notably the manifestation of a highly literate population and national commercial literary industry, were the *means* through which Neo-Confucianism *could* become popularized, *if* people were interested in it. But the core reason there was interest, why Neo-Confucianism did then become popular, is related to the new social circumstances in which Japanese found themselves during the construction of the new socio-political order established through the late sixteenth- and early seventeenth-century reunification of Japan.

Religion and politics

Neo-Confucianism emerged as an independent and influential tradition of practice and thought in a larger context of religious reformation, destruction, and renewal which swept through sixteenth- and early seventeenth-century Japan. The wars of the sixteenth century laid waste to large parts of Japan, including the cultural capital Kyoto (Berry 1994). The last phases of the wars, particularly from the 1570s, also brought significant destruction to non-traditional Buddhist institutions and Buddhist-aligned peasant communities (Souryri 2001: 181–95). Some Buddhist sects' and Buddhist-aligned peasant states' attempts to resist the reunifying samurai armies of Oda Nobunaga (1534–1582) and Toyotomi Hideyoshi (1536? –1598) led to the systematic eradication of some of the more active, spiritual, and popular Buddhist sects at the hands of these same warlords, and the destruction of the Buddhist institutions associated with them. Catholicism – a major religion in late sixteenth- and early seventeenth-century Japan – was also attacked by Toyotomi Hideyoshi, and from 1614 the Tokugawa shogunate began to carry out a more systematic repression, eventually achieving near eradication of the religion by the 1640s (Gonoi 2002).

In short, the late 1500s and early 1600s saw the warlord states, and later the Tokugawa shogunate, systematically eradicate several of the most active religions in Japan – particularly those which had dynamic regimes of individual practice. Some of the most popular religious groupings and faiths, notably Jōdo Shinshū (Shin-sect) Buddhism and Roman Catholic Christianity, were ruthlessly crushed during this period. At the same time, and perhaps not coincidentally, new religious movements not associated with Buddhism began to spring up and gain rapidly in popularity. Chief among these was the practice of the so-called Way of Heaven (*Tentō*) tradition, more religiously inclined movements around Military Learning, and independent streams of Shinto.

The religious sociality of Neo-Confucianism's positioning in early seventeenth-century society as a separate tradition was related to this context. This is most clearly flagged by the level of state suppression it attracted early on. The early seventeenth-century Japanese image of Confucianism as politically subversive is often overlooked in mainstream historical writing, dazzled as it is by Confucianism's relationship with state ideology in China, and its much warmer later relationship with the late Tokugawa state. Yet there are plenty of references to the earlier subversive image of early Tokugawa Confucianism. Beatrice Bodart-Bailey has demonstrated how even European writers in the early modern period, relying on seventeenth-century accounts from Japan, perceived Confucianism in Japan as a "suppressed" religious tradition (Bodart-Bailey 1993: 293–314). One of the most famous Japanese Confucians of the mid-Tokugawa period, Arai Hakuseki (1657–1725), writing in the early 1700s when Confucianism was enjoying unprecedented state patronage and influence, also reflected back upon the early and mid-seventeenth century as a period during which many Confucians in Japan were subject to state suppression.

Under the previous [first four] shoguns even superior persons mistook those who spoke about Confucianism for followers of Christianity. This was the situation until I first began to study. Such explanations were perhaps part of a trick by the Buddhists, who, having gained the upper hand, wanted to get rid of us Confucians as well. But one of my greatest doubts for a long time was that a teaching such as our Confucianism could resemble Christianity (Arai 1907: 550; Bodart-Bailey 1993: 300–1).

Confucianism in early Tokugawa Japan thus had a contradictory nature. On the one hand, it was a tradition which clearly looked to serve the state. On the other hand, by trying to influence politics from out of religious or moral conviction, and through their religiosity, Confucians were seen by the state as a potential threat to the emergent feudal political order.

The Way of Heaven

The interaction between Neo-Confucianism and the tradition of subversive popular religions is best illustrated by a syncretist religion highly popular in late sixteenth- and early seventeenth-century Japan called "The Way of Heaven" (Ch. *Tiandao*, Jp. *Tentō*). The Way of Heaven explained creation and the universe through a set of metaphysics employing yin and yang and reminiscent of Daoist teaching, *onmyōdō* practice, and most obviously Neo-Confucianism. For many years, modern scholarship misidentified sixteenth- and seventeenth-century Japanese Way of Heaven texts as either Christian or Neo-Confucian (Yamamoto 1985). The Way of Heaven certainly bears similarities to both. It sets Heaven as a primary deistic-like object of worship. The most popular "Way of Heaven" text in Japan, *Shingaku Gorinsho* (*The Five Ethics of the Learning of the Heart*), opens with a reference to this devotional object.

The Way of Heaven is Lord of all in Heaven and Earth. Because it has no form, it cannot be seen. However, the ordered progression of the seasons, the times of harvest, the birth of humanity, the flowering fruit, the creation of the five grains, all of these are works of The Way of Heaven (NST 28: 257).

In East Asia, the Christian God was often translated as "Lord of Heaven" or sometimes just "Heaven." This, combined with the fact that the tradition had a central deity at all, is probably what led scholars to misinterpret it as a form of Catholicism. Otherwise, the tradition was remarkably similar to Neo-Confucianism, especially as it began to be developed in early Tokugawa Japan. For instance, the "Way of Heaven" emphasis on

Confucian ethics, not unusual in itself even in medieval Japanese thinking, was couched in a new vocabulary, overtly employing Neo-Confucian terms.

Benevolence, Justice, Ritual, Wisdom and Trust, these are the creations through which people at all times enact virtue. Benevolence is compassion and love for people, it is what realizes charity. Justice is what allows the reasonable realization of Principle in all things. Rites is respect for those in high places, reconciliation with those below and between them, it should not be treated lightly or scorned. Wisdom means discernment of core wisdom. ... When one realizes Principle correctly, this is called discerning true wisdom. Trust means not deceiving. The action of benevolence, justice, ritual and wisdom cannot occur without trust. Heaven is one with the truth, and humanity is one with trust. In this way, Heaven and humanity are joined as one body (NST 28: 258).

Benevolence, Justice, Ritual, Wisdom, and Trust are the Five Ethics related to the Five Relations of Confucianism found in the fourth Neo-Confucian text, the *Mencius*. The "principle" referred to here is also a quintessential Neo-Confucian idea, synonymous in Neo-Confucian metaphysics with an inherently good "human nature" (Ch. *xing*, Jp. *sei*). The Way of Heaven emphasized not only Neo-Confucian vocabulary but notably also Neo-Confucian forms of religious practice, notably the "Method of the Heart-Mind" (*xinfa*), the quintessential form of Neo-Confucian practice, especially as popularized through the Ming dynasty (de Bary 1981).

One must make sure not to lose sight of the truth of one's heart/mind, and serve with one's heart/mind set, and one's face holding the correct expression, in the perfect state of attention. Respecting the illustrious virtue referred to earlier, and the three truths, this brings purification of the heart (NST 28: 257–8).

The reference to "illustrious virtue" in the above quote is again Neo-Confucian, referring to the opening line of the *Greater Learning*: "What the Greater Learning teaches is to illustrate illustrious virtue" (Legge 1983: 356). The Way of Heaven also emphasized "seriousness" as a key element of the Method of the Heart, as the main way to "rectify the heart." In the Way of Heaven, "seriousness," a key Neo-Confucian virtue, meant not simply respecting superiors, but a certain psychological state – "doing things not haphazardly, but regarding them as matters of the greatest import, this is seriousness" (NST 28: 257). This matches the interpretation which many Japanese Neo-Confucian thinkers attach to "seriousness," a key concept for Zhu Xi (Pak 2002: 72).

The "Method of the Heart-Mind" is one of the defining elements of Zhu Xi and post-Zhu Xi approaches to Confucianism. It is thus a core practice element of Neo-Confucianism. Zhu Xi himself linked this method to a section in *Confucius Analects* which reads:

Yan Yuan asked about benevolence. The Master said, "To return to the observance of the rites through overcoming the self constitutes benevolence. If for a
single day a man could return to the observance of the rites through overcoming
himself, then the whole Empire would consider benevolence to be his. However,
the practice of benevolence depends on oneself alone, and not on others". Yan
Yuan said, "I should like you to list the steps of that process". The Master said,
"Do not look unless it is in accordance with the rites; do not listen unless it is in
accordance with the rites; do not speak unless it is in accordance with the rites; do
not move unless it is in accordance with the rites" (Zhu 1983: 131–2; Legge 1983:
250; Lau 1979: 112).

Zhu Xi completed his commentary on this passage by stating:

In my humble opinion, the questions and answers of this paragraph transmit the
essential meaning of the method of the mind/heart (Zhu 1983: 132).

This emphasis on a religious method of self-cultivation which, although
an individual responsibility and practice, had social consequences, was
also a core element in seventeenth-century Japanese Neo-Confucianism,
as is the emphasis on "seriousness" and conformity to rites or ritual
propriety seen in the quotes above (de Bary 1989: 33).

Another link with the particular seventeenth-century Japanese manifestation of Neo-Confucianism can be seen in the way the Shinto, Buddhist, and
Confucian traditions are referred to in Way of Heaven texts. Way of Heaven
texts in Japan emphasize Japanese tradition and are positive about Shinto.
They are negative about Buddhist practice. While positive about
Confucianism in its "original" state, they can also be quite negative about
aspects of later Chinese history (anything from 200BC or so onwards),
contrasting this with a more positive image of Japan. Shinto in Japan is
likened to the "original" good Confucianism of Yao and Shun (pre-700BC),
thereby creating a Shinto-Confucian synthetic position lined up against
Buddhism, and possessing a Japanese national character which while
acknowledging debts to ancient Chinese culture distances itself from the
China of "recent times" (*kinsei*) – meaning the last 2000 years or so.

Japanese Shinto enacts true essence by rectifying our hearts, succoring the masses
and practicing charity. The Way of Yao and Shun also activates this true essence.
In China this is called Confucianism, in Japan it is called Shinto. The name is
different but the heart is the same. After the time of Emperor Jinmu in the reign of
Emperor Kinmei, The Buddhism of India came to Japan. It taught of inexplicable
transformations of gods, and by fooling people caused them to take this teaching
to heart and for Shinto to decline (NST 28: 261).

Importantly, this Shinto-Confucian synthesis is achieved primarily by
reading the Shinto tradition through Neo-Confucian frameworks. The
sentence "Japanese Shinto rectifies our hearts" resonates with the key

idea of Neo-Confucian Heart practice as articulated in the Greater Learning – "rectifying the heart" (*zhengxin*) (Legge 1983: 357).

Confucianism, Confucians, and the Tokugawa state

This kind of reproduction of Neo-Confucian ideas and practices within Japanese cultural religious forms observed in the "Way of Heaven" can also be seen in the way many of the first overtly Confucian independent scholars both represented themselves and were represented by others. Japanese Confucians in the early seventeenth century tended to have a tense relationship with political authority, even when they were in government service.

Kumazawa Banzan

The Confucian scholar who most directly participated in early seventeenth-century domestic Japanese politics, and yet ultimately best represents the image of Confucianism as subversive, is Kumazawa Banzan. Kumazawa was a samurai in the service of domain lord Ikeda Mitsumasa (1609–1682) of Bizen Okayama domain who governed one of the larger domains in western Japan. At the height of his influence in Mitsumasa's administration, Kumazawa held a position similar to prime minister of the provincial government, and received 5,000 *koku* (Paramore 2009: 99).[5] He led a major program of reform in Okayama which was designed to increase agricultural production, improve administration, and give samurai a central role in society by putting samurai administrators back into the agricultural villages of the domain, having them use their learning and power to effect agricultural innovation and reform (McMullen 1999: 116–119). This brought him into conflict with the central shogunal government because the shogunate instead favored moving all samurai into castle towns, and having villages and agriculture administered by local peasant leaders, responsible to the domainal administration in the castle towns.

At the root of this difference in perspective was the role of the samurai in government. The shogunate policy was designed to contain and control samurai power. Centralizing them in groups in large towns meant they could be under constant peer surveillance and isolated from any potential support from or influence on or by the peasant classes. Kumazawa's idea was by contrast to have the samurai embedded within the agricultural production units (the peasant villages), using book knowledge to teach peasants in production. He saw samurai leading peasants, not simply massed as a potential threat against them. The reason that he saw no conflict inherent in this situation was that he imagined samurai being disciplined not by social forces (the Tokugawa method of peer pressure and hierarchical control in the cities) but rather by individual discipline gained through religious practice: Neo-Confucian cultivation of the self, rectification of the mind/heart.

His political outlook was thus directly linked to his particular religious world view which privileged individual morality gained through self-cultivating practice. This was inherently Neo-Confucian, and in Kumazawa's case was related to the Yangming School of Mind Confucianism which paid particular attention to the section of the *Greater Learning*, the first book of the Neo-Confucian canon, which calls upon the gentleman to "rectify the mind/heart." The "technique/method of the mind/heart" (*xinfa*) calls for Confucian practice through various means, including reading, quiet sitting, and others, to reach an individual enlightenment of truth. Once in this "state of goodness," the subject would then be morally upright and would administer their office in a way which would bring the greater good to the family, state and empire – that is, the community. Central to this ideal was individual practice focused on developing seriousness as a form of rectification of the mind. Banzan explained it as follows.

"Seriousness" is the virtue of the heart/mind. You should never be distanced from it. Depending on the focus of a person's heart, they are called a "gentleman" or a "small man." Paying attention only to external appearances, and not feeling shame in one's internal heart is called being distanced from this. This is the state of the ordinary fellow. The gentleman makes his internal self his focus ... If one reveres a sober heart and self-knowledge, then how could one ever do what is bad or unjust. When you have no desire for immoral enjoyments and follow justice, then you are one with the Principle of Heaven. There is nothing more important than this seriousness. And there is only one seriousness, and it is the difference between focusing on the internal or the external. This is what separates the gentleman from the small man (NST 30: 182).

This explanation in large part follows examples from the Song originators of standard Neo-Confucianism, Zhu Xi and the Cheng brothers. Kumazawa even included diagrams illustrating the outcomes of practice adapted from Song interpretations of the *Book of Changes* (de Bary 1989: 30–5, 79–87; Sawada 1993; NST 30: 106–7).

Kumazawa, likely because of the inherent conflict between his own administrative approach to the role of the samurai and that of the shogunate, gave up his position of political influence in his domain under strong shogunate pressure (McMullen 1999: 117–119). Senior shogunal ministers (*rōjū*), as part of their pressure on the domainal lord Ikeda over Banzan's reforms, insinuated that his ideas were secretly Christian. The shogunate's own pet Neo-Confucian scholar Hayashi Razan, by the

1650s deeply entrenched in shogunate service, also authored and had distributed a literary tract alleging that Banzan's ideas had inspired an attempted ronin rebellion against the shogunate in Shizuoka and that his teachings were no more than a "mutation of Christianity." Kumazawa was also accused of links with "heretical" military thought traditions (Paramore 2009: 80–101). Kumazawa stood down from his positions of influence around 1657 in Okayama, withdrew to Kyoto around 1662, and was later banished to a state of "semi-exile" in Kii from 1667 (McMullen 1999: 113–30). In Kyoto, he was uninvolved in issues of politics or administration, and instead devoted himself to literary criticism and writing. Much of this interacted notably both with Japanese indigenous tradition and also with the religious side of Neo-Confucian teachings (McMullen 1999: 256–8).

Yamaga Sokō

Yamaga Sokō, a contemporary of Kumazawa, is another example of a major early Tokugawa Confucian who emphasized Neo-Confucian practice, integrated Confucianism with indigenous Japanese traditions, and was persecuted by elements within the shogunate. The nature of the attacks on Yamaga were very similar to those against Kumazawa. His ideas were also alleged to be "heretical" and were associated with instances of civil disorder. Like Kumazawa, Yamaga was particularly charged with inspiring ronin activity and linked to forms of "military thought" which were popular among ronin and regarded as subversive or dangerous (Paramore 2009: 91–2).

Yamaga was indeed very seriously interested in both Zhu Xi-style Neo-Confucianism and Japanese traditions of Military Learning. Maeda Tsutomu, one of the most influential contemporary historians of Tokugawa Confucianism, reads Yamaga's ideas predominantly as a synthesis of Military and Neo-Confucian outlooks. He sees that synthesis as being related to a broader change in the nature of Military Learning in Japan, where, in the early seventeenth century, it was transformed from a mere collection of military knowledge and techniques to a life philosophy, a tradition in many ways reminiscent of a religion (Maeda 1996: 135–42).

Until the late 1500s "Military Learning," as the name suggests, had constituted a range of scholarship and practical learning techniques on everything from the use of weapons to more complex ideas on strategy. Because this latter element included works like those of the Chinese strategist Sunzi, it had an intellectual character and was related to Chinese traditional religion. But it was not anything like a world view in itself. It was primarily a set of practical techniques and tactics to be used in the civil war.

In the 1600s, however, writers like Hōjō Ujinaga (1609–1670) transformed "Military Learning" into a tradition with a world view in some ways resembling a religious outlook (Maeda 1996: 140). This was done partly with the help of Confucianism, notably Neo-Confucian theory, as can be seen in the following quote from one of his most widely distributed works.

If one wants to safely defend the state and stop bandits from entering from outside, then one should begin with good domestic governance. The basis of good domestic governance lies in building castles. But "building castles" does not simply mean digging a moat, constructing a rampart and holding fast. The empire should be seen as a castle, the state as a castle, each family of subjects should be seen as a castle, when alone, your body should be the castle. "If the body (individual person) is cultivated, then the family will be regulated, if the family is regulated, then the state will be rightly governed, if the state is rightly governed, then the whole realm will be tranquil and happy." This method is applicable from the great to the small (people) without discrimination (Hōjō Ujinaga, *Shikan Yōhō*, in Ishioka 1967: 185).

The quote contained within the citation above is from a key section in the first of the Four Books of Neo-Confucianism, *The Greater Learning*. The overall message also matches.

The ancients who wished to illustrate illustrious virtue throughout the empire first ordered well their own states. Wishing to order well their states, they first regulated their families. Wishing to regulate their families, they first cultivated their persons. Wishing to cultivate their persons, they first rectified their hearts. Wishing to rectify their hearts, they first sought to be sincere in their thoughts. Wishing to be sincere in their thoughts, they first extended to the utmost their knowledge. Such extension of knowledge lay in the investigation of things. Things being investigated, knowledge became complete. Their knowledge being complete, their thoughts were sincere. Their thoughts being sincere, their hearts were then rectified. Their hearts being rectified, their persons were cultivated. Their persons being cultivated, their families were regulated. Their families being regulated, their States were rightly governed. Their states being rightly governed, the whole realm was made tranquil and happy. From the Emperor down to the masses, all rests on the cultivation of the person (Legge 1983: 357–359).

So sixteenth-century Military Learning can be seen to some extent as a new intellectual and religious tradition which came into being in Japan partly by employing overarching Neo-Confucian structures. Military thought was making this transformation around the time Yamaga was active. This in itself is an interesting interaction. Teachers regarded primarily as Military Learning figures like Hōjō utilized

Neo-Confucianism. Confucians like Yamaga relied heavily on Military Learning.

The development of Yamaga's own Confucianism had some similarities with Kumazawa. He advocated Confucianism be used centrally in governance. He saw this happening primarily through Neo-Confucianism providing a framework for the cultivation of the individual samurai as an administrative official. For Yamaga, retention of the samurai warrior identity of this administrator was also essential (NST 32: 31–2). Yet the key to the overall function of the system he imagined was still the individual (samurai) and his/her cultivation. The Neo-Confucian idea of self-cultivation was thus a core element in Yamaga's famous invention of the "Way of the Samurai" (Benesch 2014).

But Yamaga's conceptualization of Neo-Confucian practice was innovative and socially embedded. Yamaga, disturbed by the passivity he associated with the prevalence of Zen-associated practices of quietude, emphasized the underlying Neo-Confucian idea of changing the nature of *qi* (ether) in a person (Ch. *huaqi* Jp. *ki wo kasuru*). This process he saw as potentially involving physical action, including military training. For Yamaga, these forms of activity were also more fitting to a warrior than quiet sitting.

Because the Heart is made up of *qi*, then when the *qi* is in a state of quietude, then the heart will also be in quietude. When the *qi* moves, then the heart also moves. In this way Heart and *qi* are not two different ways, they cannot be separated. Seeing the heart is internal and *qi* is something that moves externally, the basis of "cultivating the person and being in your heart" must initially be achieved through cultivating *qi* (NST 32: 36–7).

For Yamaga, training *qi* was the key element in Neo-Confucian practice of "cultivating the person and being in your heart." This could be done not only through the Heart but also through the "Self" (Jp. *mi*, Ch. *shen*), a word in Japanese which also meant the physical "body." Yamaga's emphasis on rites and the body is thus an emphasis on physical forms of practice: rites, but also martial practice. For Yamaga, physical action, not just quiet contemplation, could be part of the Neo-Confucian Way.

In seeking to transform and utilize *qi*, rather than simply suppress it, Yamaga's approach could be conceived as running against elements of the Neo-Confucian "Method of the Heart-Mind." Indeed, much has been made of Yamaga's willingness to break with Neo-Confucian moralism by creating his own critical interpretations of Confucian metaphysics (Maruyama 1974: 39–50). In this sense, Yamaga can indeed be seen as one of the earliest radical critics of Neo-Confucian interpretations in Japan. Yet even he privileged the Neo-Confucian practice of self-cultivation (if through a rather unusually physically dynamic means) as the core of a Confucian life. And although his theorization was innovative, it still worked in basic Neo-Confucian terms: principle, ether, practice. Thus even in this case of the early seventeenth-century Japanese Confucian most critical of Neo-Confucian theory, Neo-Confucian religious practice (self-cultivation) still occupied center stage. Peace relied on good employment of the samurai, and the most important requirement for good employment of the samurai was their own self-cultivation – to be achieved through the practice of self-cultivation and rites.

Whereas Kumazawa was considered suspicious because of his emphasis on Method of Mind practice, which seemed to some too similar to Christianity, Yamaga's reference to the military arts was used by his enemies to associate him with suspicious military arts practices, and the generally poorly regarded ronin rabble of the times. For both Kumazawa and Yamaga, their focus on religious practice, while, on the one hand, providing a basis for them to engage Confucianism with the society around them, also left them open to suspicion of state subversion.

Hayashi Razan

Intriguingly, however, early and mid-seventeenth-century Confucians closely associated with the shogunal state also embraced the religious possibilities offered by Neo-Confucianism and used these to try to engage Confucianism with other movements in Japanese society. Hayashi Razan, for instance, spent much of his later career trying to resolve Neo-Confucianism with aspects of Shinto (Nosco 1984: 166–87). Hayashi Razan is an interesting example of an early Confucian who both spent a lot of time trying to repackage Confucianism in Japanese cultural terms, notably through integration with Shinto, and also served the shogunal state. Hayashi Razan is considered one of the most "state friendly" or "state serving" manifestations of a Confucian in Japanese history. A servant and scribe of the first Tokugawa Shogun, Ieyasu, he was portrayed by later histories, incorrectly as it turned out, as a Neo-Confucian Tokugawa state ideologue (Maruyama 1974: 15).[6] He was, however, doubtless an active propagandist for the Tokugawa shogunate, both domestically and in diplomatic writing, publicly holding up Tokugawa rule of Japan as a moral blueprint on many occasions. Yet even this most famous of early seventeenth-century Confucian shogunal servants had his doubts about the nature of his relationship with the feudal samurai order of the Tokugawas. In 1611, Hayashi Razan wrote from the seat of Tokugawa Ieyasu's court in Sunpu to a Confucian he considered his teacher, Fujiwara Seika (1561–1619), expressing the tension he saw between his privileged position as scribe to the shogun and his calling as a Confucian.[7] In this letter, Hayashi basically condemns his own participation in what he regards as the morally questionable government of the Tokugawas, which he reveals through quoting Mencius, "I 'agree with the current customs and consent with an impure age' and pretend that I do this for the sage of harmony" (Hayashi, translation by Boot, in de Bary et al. 2005: 53).

Even for Hayashi, then, there was a tension between Neo-Confucianism and his social position. Certainly many other rising Neo-Confucians saw Hayashi's loyalties as divided. The general condemnation of Hayashi among his contemporary Confucians is even more telling than his own doubts, because they reveal a more general and public critical tenor in seventeenth-century Confucian writing. Yamazaki Ansai, for instance, wrote:

Who is this Hayashi? He is someone known for degrading filial piety . . . He does not discuss [the examples of the ancient Chinese sage kings] Yao and Shun before our prince [the Tokugawa Shogun]. This shows disrespect for the prince (Yamazaki 1978: 510).

For Nakae Tōju, it was also clear.

Hayashi Razan has an excellent memory and wide erudition. He proclaims the Way of the Confucians, but this is just pretty words. He learns the law of the Buddhists and has outrageously shaved his head [like a Buddhist monk] . . . yet he calls himself a true Confucian. In Japan there are no sages, heterodoxies are renewed by the day and multiply each month. The theories of heretics and witches compete with each other for dominance, filling the ears and eyes of the common people, and plunging the realm into filth and squalor (NST 29: 19).

Yamazaki Ansai (1619–1682) and Nakae Tōju (1608–1648) are regarded as sitting at opposite ends of the Tokugawa Confucian spectrum. Yamazaki Ansai was an adamant follower of the Song teachings of Zhu Xi, Nakae Tōju was associated with the Ming teachings of Wang Yangming. But they agreed about Hayashi Razan. By presenting himself as a Buddhist monk, he broke the cardinal Confucian virtue of filial piety. And by not daring to hold up Confucian ideals in remonstrance to the prince, he plunged the country into filth and squalor. This of course shows a belief on Nakae's part that one's own convictions should be put above state norms.

Nakae was one of a rising wave of active Confucian scholars in the early 1600s who profiled themselves very differently to Hayashi. Many of these scholars were influenced by the Ming thinker Wang Yangming and other currents of Neo-Confucian thinking which, while clearly being descendants of the tradition of Neo-Confucianism established in the Song, did not conform to Ming Chinese or Choson Korean state orthodoxies. Fujiwara Seika, Nakae Tōju, and Kumazawa Banzan, three of the most famous early seventeenth-century Japanese Confucians, were all happy to identify themselves with Wang Yangming's interpretations in Neo-Confucianism (NST 28: 47, 451). For them, Confucianism certainly did not need to conform to the intellectual orthodoxy of continental states.

Yamazaki Ansai

But even Japanese Confucians attracted to ideas of orthodoxy tended to embrace these elements of Ming Confucian practice and to look to embed Confucianism in Japanese religious tradition. The most interesting and influential attempt to synthesize Shinto and Confucianism, and also possibly the most religious manifestation of Neo-Confucianism in seventeenth-century Japan, was advanced by Yamazaki Ansai. Although never enjoying the extent of shogunate patronage attained by the Hayashi clan, nor as much direct political power as the likes of Kumazawa Banzan, Yamazaki is nevertheless remembered as one of the key Confucian thinkers of the seventeenth century.

He was employed toward the end of his career by Hoshina Masayuki (1611–1673), a son of the second Shogun Tokugawa Hidetada, brother of the third Shogun Tokugawa Iemitsu, and one of the most powerful lords and shogunal cabinet members under the fourth Shogun Tokugawa Ietsuna (1641–1680; in office 1651–1680). Modern scholars emphasize Yamazaki's importance because they consider his particular synthesis of Shinto and Neo-Confucianism laid the basis for the development of nationalist ideological paradigms later in the Tokugawa period. These paradigms are seen as having influenced the Meiji Restoration and the formation of the modern Japanese state in the late nineteenth century. Herman Ooms, for instance, considers Yamazaki's ideas to have laid the basis for what he labels "Tokugawa ideology," a world view which Ooms once implied continued on even into the contemporary 1980s he was writing in (Ooms 1985).[8]

Yamazaki's ideas, and particularly the forms of practice he led in his well-attended Confucian schools, closely followed Neo-Confucian methods of self-cultivation and practice. Yamazaki regarded his school as a bastion of "orthodox" Zhu Xi Neo-Confucianism. Yet Yamazaki's interpretation and practice of the Method of the Heart-Mind, like that of most other Japanese Confucians at this time, was also influenced by post-Song developments in Neo-Confucianism. Yamazaki followed the systems and ideas on practice of Zhu Xi, but as interpreted and developed by later

Ming Neo-Confucians. Yamazaki followed the Ming scholars associated with orthodox Zhu Xi thought and particularly the Korean scholar Yi Toegye. But Yamazaki, like Yi Toegye, although being proud of his Zhu Xi orthodoxy, was actually very much influenced by the significant religious turn discernible in Ming dynasty Neo-Confucianism. One of his most famous texts, *Keisaishin*, opens by emphasizing the state of seriousness that rectification of the heart, according to Zhu Xi, relied upon in Neo-Confucian practice.

"Seriousness" this one word embodies the practice which is the beginning and end of Confucian learning. It is eternal. Ever since the beginning of Heaven and Earth generation through generation the true line of the sages' transmission of the Method of the Heart has not gone beyond this one word "seriousness" (NST 31: 80).

Unlike Yamaga, Yamazaki stayed true to the core message of Neo-Confucianism, following Mencius to see human nature as originally good, and each individual's mission as recovery of that original inherent goodness.

The "human nature" given by heavenly command resides in the human heart. Therefore "residing in the heart" (Ch. *sunxin*, Jp. *zonshin*) and cultivating human nature is how one serves Heaven. The core of "residing in cultivation" is nothing other than this. It is "seriousness" alone (Yamazaki in Pak 2002: 73).

When you read the Greater Learning you find the two words "rectify [the] heart" ... The heart is what directs the self/body and is the basis of all action. Therefore, when you rectify the heart, then you cultivate the self and govern all action (Yamazaki in Pak 2002: 71).

Like Yamaga, however, Yamazaki sought to integrate Confucianism with an indigenous Japanese tradition. In Yamaga's case, the local tradition of choice was Military Learning, in Yamazaki's case, Shinto. Both of them used Neo-Confucian spiritual practices to breathe new life into indigenous Japanese traditions, thereby systematizing but also sacralizing those traditions. Neo-Confucianism was used to introduce systematic methods of religious practice into the Japanese traditions as core features.[9]

Yamazaki also shared with Yamaga an historical outlook on the Confucian tradition which facilitated a kind of cultural and temporal relativism. Yamazaki argued that rituals conforming to Confucian ideals could be originated in any appropriate time and space. Hoshina Masayuki, while employing Yamazaki as a teacher, and in a document that Yamazaki appears to have edited, wrote the following.

Cheng Yi says, the basis of rites spring from the passion of the people, which was then simply guided by the sages. The instrumentality of rites springs from the daily customs of the masses, the sages simply ritualized these. If the sages appeared again before us they would definitely ritualize the clothing and instruments of today (Hoshina in Pak 2002: 78).

This claim by Cheng Yi, one of the founding fathers of Neo-Confucianism in the Song, that rites spring from daily customs is exploited by Hoshina/ Yamazaki to argue that the culture of the here and now could also, theoretically, become the basis for rites. Given that the culture of the here and now was the culture of military Japan (not civil China), this was a significant claim. It could be interpreted as a step toward indigenization. Certainly within a couple of decades, scholars like Ogyū Sorai were mounting very sophisticated defenses of the equality of contemporary Japanese forms with Chinese culture, as we shall explore further below.

This quote also shows that Yamazaki's famous focus on seriousness as the basis of Heart Practice was linked to a prizing of ritual. In this case, the utility of ritual was emphasized in relation to the masses. Ritual should be the means by which the ideals of Neo-Confucianism interact with the real world. This also contextualizes the present-ist outlook on the form of ritual seen earlier. In this way, even Yamazaki, the most rabid Zhu Xi-inclined and anti-Wang Yangming Confucian in Japan, nevertheless emphasized the Method of the Heart-Mind, and the culturally and temporally relativist aspects hidden within Ming interpretations of Song Neo-Confucian thought.

Similarly Kaibara Ekken, another of the most famous early Japanese Neo-Confucians, even when railing against Wang Yangming, still emphasized that: "All the teachings established by the sages of old, without exception, were the learning of the mind[/heart]" (Sawada 1993: 2). Kaibara Ekken was a path-breaking Confucian both in his embrace of new scientific research and in his use of Confucianism to articulate and spread scientific developments. He was also a leading figure in the vernacularization and popularization of Confucian learning in Japan. In relation to the popularization of Neo-Confucian practice, Janine Sawada has commented that the vernacular writings of Kaibara Ekken in particular "led to significant popularization of the notion that mind-discipline leads to social well-being" (Sawada 1998: 108). This religious outlook was related to his popularization of scientific principles, as will be discussed further in Chapter 4.

We can thereby discern a similarity in approach of most Confucian practitioners in seventeenth-century Japan. All of these Confucians were deeply affected by Neo-Confucian religious sensibility, which came to occupy a central part of their own ideas and practices. Many of them deployed Neo-Confucian forms of religious practice centrally. Many of them tried to combine Neo-Confucianism, particularly its methodology, but also its metaphysics and ethical outlook, with other non-Buddhist traditions present in Japan: The Way of Heaven, Military Learning, Shinto. In all these combinations, the element of Neo-Confucianism most emphasized was its approach to religious practice, notably the Method of the Heart practice *xinfa*.

Their attempts to combine Neo-Confucianism with other traditions, their approach to and deployment of Neo-Confucian religious practice, and particularly their attempts to argue for the position of Confucianism within the new Tokugawa state all indicate an underlying tension between Neo-Confucianism and its socio-political environment. Of course, Neo-Confucianism, as a separate tradition with its own separate practices was a new phenomenon in Japan, and therefore one could assume it would face some tension in its relationship with society at large. But a more immediate underlying problem for Neo-Confucianism in Tokugawa Japan was the disparity between the individual, moral, and sometimes by association meritocratic outlook of Neo-Confucianism, and the reality of hereditary feudal warrior rule under the Tokugawa shogunate.

I believe that most of the major early and mid-seventeenth-century Confucians, and indeed many of those who came later, can be understood through this prism of tension between the imperatives of Neo-Confucianism and those of the hereditary feudal order (Paramore 2012b). In the case of someone like Kumazawa, the tension between the way the state operated and his Neo-Confucian ideals was obvious. Yamaga Sokō's entire ideological system was set up almost to prove the necessity of Neo-Confucian forms of practice in a warrior society. But even elements of seventeenth-century Japanese Confucianism which most served state ideological purposes can be viewed as attempts to resolve the tension between Confucianism and the nature of feudal warrior rule in Japan. For instance, Yamazaki Ansai made a point of rejecting the Confucian doctrine which allowed for (indeed, justified) the replacement of an unvirtuous ruler. Neo-Confucian readings of the doctrine of Heaven's Mandate (Ch. *Tianming*, Jp. *Tenmei*) linked the ruler's morality to the legitimacy of their dynastic rule. Yamazaki's rejection of this element of Neo-Confucian discourse, while simultaneously claiming to be a defender of Neo-Confucian orthodoxy, can be viewed as an attempt to adapt Neo-Confucianism to the political situation in Japan – to mitigate against the inherent tensions between this moralistic and potentially meritocratic ideology and the reality of the Tokugawa state. Even the most pro-state thinkers like Yamazaki and Hayashi therefore seem to have had at the base of their ideas an understanding of the inherent tension between Neo-Confucianism and the feudal state.

Ogyū Sorai: Rejecting Neo-Confucianism and its consequences

The most theoretically creative attempt to resolve this and other tensions inherent in Neo-Confucianism's sociality in early modern Japan, and particularly its relationship with culture and politics, was initiated by Ogyū Sorai in the first decades of the eighteenth century. Ogyū is usually considered the greatest of Japanese Confucians. Unlike most other Japanese Confucians both before and after him, Ogyū categorically rejected Song Neo-Confucianism. His criticism of Song Neo-Confucianism cut to its core by rejecting the Four Books canon upon which it was based, a canon which had enjoyed wide-ranging acceptance across East Asia for the previous half millennium. The most significant implication of Ogyū's rejection of the Four Books was that by rejecting *Mencius*, a text which he saw as deeply flawed, he could reject one of the core ideas of Neo-Confucianism presented in the *Mencius*: the inherent goodness of human nature.[10] Without the idea of an inherently and originally good human nature, the basis of Neo-Confucian practice – *fuxing* – returning to the original human nature meant nothing. Why cultivate a return to your original nature if that original nature was not inherently good? According to Ogyū, individual cultivation was not the answer. The idea of ordinary individuals "cultivating" themselves into sages was ridiculous. People could not become sages through individual conduct. The sages were rather figures in history who were sages by virtue of their noble birth – a grace bestowed upon them by Heaven. The Way was their way, a way of politics, ordained by Heaven, and transmitted at a particular historical period in a historical act to "the ancient sage kings," the mythical (historical for Ogyū) kings of ancient Zhou China (pre-700BC). These were the only true sages as far as Ogyū was concerned.

The Way of the Ancient Kings was constructed by the Ancient Kings. It is not the way of Heaven and Earth, nor of Nature. Using their virtues of intelligence, clarity and wisdom, and receiving Heaven's mandate, they were sovereign over the realm. Their minds were focused entirely on their duty to bring peace to [govern] the realm. Committing their enormous spiritual and mental powers to the task, they created the Way, which people of the realms through the generations enacted. How is this Nature (NST 36: 14; Ogyū 1998: 6, 2006: 142)?

Ogyū's Confucian Way thus clearly emphasized human intervention, artifice not nature, in Maruyama's famous interpretation relating it to

Hobbes (Maruyama 1974: 227–8). This formulation also had the Confucian Way as something relative to space and time, period and culture. Invented at a particular moment in time in a particular cultural-historical context, and enacted in different places and cultures through different methods. Ogyū thereby emphasized the inherent diversity of the nature of the Way in historic practice: "The Way of the Ancient Kings is multi-faceted" (NST 36: 19). This meant it needed to be realized again by learning from that cultural-historical context – by recovering the language and culture, the rites and music, of that time. Copying the China of later imperial times (post-Tang, including the Song and Ming) was mistaken as they had already lost the Way of the ancient sage kings, notably through their abolition of the feudal order and its customs during the Han dynasty. Ogyū thus resolved the tension between Confucianism and feudalism by recasting Confucianism as historically feudal.

The "ancient sage kings" of the Five Classics did not have an imperial bureaucratic government, but rather a feudal regime, like Japan under the Tokugawas. Just like the Japanese of the Tokugawa period, the Chinese Sage Kings of Antiquity also based their rule on lord–vassal relations, as outlined in the ancient classic texts, mediated through rites and music. Ogyū's contemporary Japan of the Tokugawa period thus did not need to try to mimic China, not even that ancient China of the sages. Rather, those in the present needed to have rites and music that *functioned* in the same way the rites and music of the ancient sage kings had functioned in their time and place. Tokugawa Japan should originate cultural forms (rites and music) that worked following the model of the origination of rites and music in ancient China, which had occurred in a kind of divine revelation from Heaven. This then also introduced a very creative element into Ogyū's scheme. The *new* rites and music of today should *function* like those of the ancients, and therefore like the ritual forms of the ancients they should be *naturally integrated with local culture*.

How can latter generations know the original words of their ancestors? One thousand years pass. Customs change, and physical realities deteriorate. One cannot rely on the present readings of the old words. How can we possibly transport ourselves back into the time of Confucius and ... receive instruction at first hand? Space *and* time are after all different (Ogyū in NST 36: 190; Minear 1976: 17).

In this way, Ogyū completely politicized Confucianism not simply by saying that it was political, but also by demonstrating that it could be disengaged from a normative foreign cultural or metaphysical system and instead be interpreted as an act of creative politics particular to the time, place, and culture of its operation.

These ideas of Ogyū, innovative as they were, did not come from nowhere. One aspect shared with earlier and later writing in Japan was an attempt to create a system which put Japan on a par with contemporary China, which paid due respect to Japanese culture and histories of governance by integrating them into the story. Already in 1669 Yamaga Sokō had suggested that Japan, not China, should be seen as the "Central Kingdom" of Confucian theory (Kurozumi 2006: 25). Ogyū achieved this harmonization primarily not through some form of primitive Japanese nationalism but through a theoretically more complex formulation, by relativizing time and culture, to both disengage the last 1500 years of Chinese history from Confucian ideals and also to offer a way for Japan to engage this ancient tradition through a culturally integrated creative process.

Ogyū thus systematically removed many of the tensions that existed between Neo-Confucians and the order of the Tokugawa regime. His school became wildly popular in his own later years and through the period directly after his death in 1728. The brilliance of his scholarship meant that his ideas had a wide impact on all forms of Confucianism in Japan. Intriguingly, however, Sorai-school scholarship, the tendency in Japanese Confucianism which followed his wholesale rejection of Neo-Confucianism, declined rapidly during the late eighteenth century. It was replaced by a tenacious resurgence in the popularity of orthodox Neo-Confucianism following the teachings of Zhu Xi (Ishikawa 1960 256–9). Crucially, however, this second Japanese rise of Neo-Confucianism post-Sorai integrated many aspects of Sorai's thought into their own outlook.

Watanabe Hiroshi has related the declining fortunes of Sorai Confucianism as a school to its lack of emphasis on individual practice. The lack of practice meant that Sorai scholars often pinned all their hopes on immediate political impact, failure of which seems to have often led to withdrawal from responsible behavior in general. He quotes one of the major Japanese literary figures of the late eighteenth century, Ōta Nanpo (1749–1823), to illustrate this claim.

Since Sorai, scholars seem to think that unless they are going to become one of the shogunal elders [ministers] and rule the realm, scholarship itself is useless. So it is not surprising that they fall to delinquent and amoral behavior (Ōta Nanpo in Watanabe 2012: 185).

Sorai Confucianism's rise thus further illustrates the inherent tensions between Neo-Confucianism, on the one hand, and the Tokugawa political order and elements of Japanese martial culture, on the other. Sorai Confucianism's fall, however, also demonstrates what a creative force that tension had become in the intellectual, political, and religious life of mid-Tokugawa-period Japan. The tension almost sustained Confucianism. By the time of the rise of Ogyū Sorai's school in the early decades of the eighteenth century, Neo-Confucianism had already become a norm of individual religious and social pedagogical practice across Japan. The tensions inherent in it were tensions through which the Japanese polity operated. As the next chapter will argue, this tension was part of a wide-ranging sociality which supported something like a public sphere in Japan. Within that public sphere, new practices originated by Ogyū, notably practices of pedagogy and debate, also played a major role. So although Ogyū's rejection of Neo-Confucian practice brought limitations to the endurance of Sorai Confucianism itself, on the other hand, new practices originated by Ogyū would inform the continued development of a prime social role for Neo-Confucianism in the later Tokugawa period, as will be explored in the next chapter.

3   Confucianism as public sphere

The Way is the Principle of Heaven, Earth and Public. People receive it through human nature. The sages made learning to cultivate it. ... Without the impartial mind the Way cannot be elucidated. Without a balanced mood, it cannot be related to substantial issues. You cannot construct the Way with [just] impartiality and balance. But in order to advance the Way one must most definitely begin with impartiality and balance.

Bitō Jishū, Professor in the Confucian Academy of the Tokugawa
Shogunate (NST 47: 261–7)

The constructive tension between Confucian principles and the feudal structure of Tokugawa society discussed in the previous chapter was enabled and sustained in large part by the location of Confucian practice in early modern Japan primarily *outside* the institutions and structures of the state. This was a major difference between early modern Japan and contemporaneous China and Korea. In Ming and Qing China and Choson Korea, state examinations were a track to attaining state employment and social status. Confucian activity therefore revolved around the state. Academies, whether public or private, trained students mainly to pass the examinations the state set. The state therefore had a powerful means of influencing the Confucian academic agenda. The fact that the most prestigious academies in China and Korea were directly run by the state and presided over the examinations further institutionally integrated the worlds of academy, practice, and state.

In Tokugawa Japan, however, Confucian practice, teaching, study, and writing occurred in small private schools and reading groups. The vast majority of professional Confucian scholars made their livelihood principally from monies extracted in student fees. The students did not come to these schools to pass state examinations, because for most of the Tokugawa period there were no state examinations. Even when the state did run a few examinations in the early 1800s, only the highest hereditary status samurai (*hatamoto* and *goke'nin*) in the Tokugawa houses could participate (Hashimoto 1994; Paramore 2012c). There was no sustained link between Confucian study and government appointment.

Yet, despite the study and practice of Confucianism in Japan generally having no direct effects on career prospects, earning potential or government status, tens of thousands of Japanese of all status studied in Confucian schools at any given moment during most of the mid- and late Tokugawa periods, supporting at any given time many hundreds of professional Confucian scholars who ran these schools (Ishikawa 1960). The Confucian private schools were enthusiastically populated – primarily by low-status samurai who had no hereditary claims to significant office, but also by townspeople, and even by peasants and Buddhist priests. This mass Confucian activity, based in the private sphere, reached a peak in the late 1700s and early 1800s and continued to be massively popular right through the Meiji Restoration until finally displaced by the new modern school system at the end of the 1870s. This chapter will argue that this activity, and its deep influence on other forms of cultural activity in early modern Japan, led to the formation of something like a public sphere.

There has been considerable discussion among historians of Japan over the last twenty years about the applicability of the term "public sphere" to late Tokugawa and Meiji history (Mitani 2004). In most of these discussions, the term "public sphere" is understood generally in line with the ideas of the German political philosopher Jürgen Habermas. The core to Habermas's idea of the public sphere is that it links broad opinion with governance carried out through state "public institutions" (Habermas 1991). This is what differentiates the concept of the public sphere from more wishy-washy concepts like "civil society" (Kaviraj and Khilnani 2001). A public sphere is not just a talk fest. The term "public sphere" indicates an open discussion which interacts with politics and influences governance. According to Habermas and some others like Rawls, the nature of that interaction is positively colored by the rational and/or reasonable nature of discussion. In other words, defining aspects of a public sphere are forms of discourse which (1) influence the state and impact governance, (2) are reasonable and/or rational in nature (Finlayson 2011). This chapter will argue that Confucianism active in the private sphere of early modern Japan ultimately reached a position where it was able to exercise significant influence on governance. This occurred usually not in the revolutionary manner feared by the opponents of Yamaga Sokō and Kumazawa Banzan, but more commonly through stable cultural systems and continuing traditions which developed through the eighteenth century. As will be discussed in the next chapter, these cultural systems of communication and interaction came to be increasingly closely integrated into state institutions of education, research, bureaucracy, and diplomacy from the late eighteenth through the early nineteenth century. And as will be elucidated upon below, this discourse was indeed predominantly reasonable and rational in nature.

Most scholars who have written recently on public intellectual activity in Tokugawa Japan have tended to downplay the role of the state and Confucianism in early modern Japanese culture and society. Eiko Ikegami, in her opus on Tokugawa networks *Bonds of Civility*, did not talk directly about publicness or a public sphere. She instead began with the term "civil society," but rejecting it moved on to the term "civility." For her, "under the firm hand of the Tokugawa shoguns, Japan did not develop a civic associational domain that fit with the Western notion of civil society" (Ikegami 2005: 19). Ikegami takes this view because for her the dominant binding element in the associations of cultural activity in the Tokugawa period was "aesthetics," rather than politics. What I describe in this chapter as "leisure learning" or "social learning," she thus described as "aesthetic socializing" (Ikegami 2005: 4). Ikegami was right that an important motivation and activity which occurred in these circles was socializing, and that many of the circles revolved around aesthetic interests. Socializing, however, including cross-class and cross-status socializing, occurred in many different spaces in Tokugawa Japan. For example, people often socialized in the so-called "pleasure quarters" of the major cities– the early modern versions of bars, theaters, and night clubs. But circles for the study of poetry, art, Confucianism, weapons training, Dutch Learning, and so forth were just that: *study* circles. Learning was the prime activity, not aesthetics. As I will outline below, much of that learning revolved around issues which had a political edge and was conducted in a manner which facilitated reasonable debate.

My emphasis on the "learning" aspect of these circles is also informed by the fact that most schools identified themselves as a form of "learning" – *gaku* in Japanese. They dealt primarily in "learning" (*gaku*) and "teaching" (*oshie*). As in most other premodern societies, cultures and languages, the same word used to indicate "teaching" in Japanese *oshie* was also used to indicate elements we would today perhaps rather classify as "religion." Indeed the interaction between "learning" and "religion" in the Tokugawa period, in particular the way learning was perceived as an at least semi-religious experience, is key to understanding the significance of the "leisure learning" movements. The link between religious movements and civil society, particularly in non-Western societies, is an important element in contemporary theoretical discussion of what the terms "civil society" and "public sphere" might or could mean (Habermas and Cronin 2008; Habermas and Mendieta 2002). Below I will suggest that particular forms of Confucian practice generated in Tokugawa Japan, together with the particular social positioning of Confucianism in that society, led to its educational and religious aspects facilitating something like a public sphere.

Confucianism and culture

Before moving on to discuss the practices lying behind this Confucian public sphere, it is first necessary to explain the expansion of Confucian penetration into general Japanese society during the mid-Tokugawa period – the central social positioning of Confucianism which facilitated public sphere-related practice. This broad social and cultural penetration was intimately linked to the growth of private Confucian schools (*juku*) and study groups and to the increasing influence of Confucian ideas and practices outside Confucian circles – in art, literature, and other representations of general culture.

The rise in the popularity of Confucianism in general society during the course of the seventeenth and eighteenth centuries occurred in the context of a widespread expansion in private, informal learning conducted through private schools and study groups in a range of fields (not just Confucianism) which occurred across all the castle towns and cities of the Japanese archipelago during this period. This massive expansion of leisure learning was enabled by widespread changes in the nature of the Japanese economy, infrastructure, society, and politics which occurred during the seventeenth century. The major driver of these changes was increased disposable income among Japanese, which was to a significant extent linked to the nature of early Tokugawa rule. Firstly, Tokugawa rule brought peace. Peace alone created a significantly better environment for agricultural cultivation (the main source of production in the still overwhelmingly agricultural economy) and trade. Agricultural production was further assisted by the comparatively interventionist nature of the rule of the Tokugawas and many of the domain lords under them in the first century of the Edo period. Both the Tokugawa overlords and many local domain lords facilitated large-scale land reclamation projects in the seventeenth century, allowing more land to be cultivated. This in turn grew the population. Trade, by facilitating a more efficient exchange in goods, led to increases in disposable income, which in turn meant more time for leisure. But trade in itself also facilitated leisure directly by providing national byways and networks through which leisure activities, including learning, could be propagated and carried out on a national basis – through travel, book distribution, and so on.

Particular aspects and policies of Tokugawa rule in the seventeenth century directly facilitated the networks and markets of leisure learning. One of the primary policies through which the Tokugawas sought to ensure the loyalty of domain lords was the alternate attendance system (*sankinkōtai*) introduced in 1635.[1] This system required domain lords from all over the country, with their large families and samurai and servant retinues, to reside in Edo in alternate years. This instigated hundreds of regular journeys per year (from each of the more than 200 domains) of groups in each instance of hundreds, often thousands of the wealthier and higher-status members of Japanese society. This brought mass, well-funded travel across the country, and then long-term residence of tens or hundreds of thousands of those with the most leisure time and income, together in Edo. Edo thus grew to become the greatest city in the world with a population of over one million in the late seventeenth century. The concentration of so many people, and so much wealth and status, not only in Edo but also along the highways and byways and in the intervening cities and highway towns of Japan, the constant movement of these people back and forth between and through different urban centers created a newly networked and culturally vibrant society (Vaporis 2008).

The fact that many people of high status and wealth were living away from home also encouraged trade between the different regions of Japan. Before alternate attendance was introduced, the Tokugawa government had tried to keep domain lords busy by requiring them to improve the "military infrastructure" of their own and other regions of Japan. This predominantly entailed building and maintaining trunk roads which linked the regions of the country, as well as building castles and other security points along these roads to secure them, and garrisoning these secure points. This meant that by the third decade of the seventeenth century Japan had a strong network of good, well-secured, state-maintained roads linking the major centers of the country. Tokugawa policy of controlling external contact and sea journeys by Japanese also effected a pacification and securing of the domestic seaways which had always been the prime routes for the domestic trade of goods in Japan (Arano 1992). The aim in all these reforms for the Tokugawa overlords was a further militarist securitization of the country. But a side effect was to make movement and trade across Japan, and interconnection between its peoples, easier than ever before.

In the early to mid-Tokugawa period, the people most able to take advantage of the increase in leisure time, disposable income, and capacity for secure movement were members of the samurai caste (men, women and children). There were multiple reasons for this. Firstly, there was location. Samurai were required to reside in castle towns, so they were always in a relatively urban environment, concentrated with other samurai as well as the richer merchants in towns which, even in the provinces, often had populations of over 10,000. Moreover, many samurai were required to regularly travel with their lords to Edo, putting them for periods of a year or more in Edo, the urban center par excellence. So samurai were more urbanized and in general more mobile that the average Japanese.

Moreover, the governance system of the Tokugawas meant that most of the low-class samurai (the overwhelming majority of samurai) had leisure time. The structures of Tokugawa administration were in essence military. The senior samurai lords and their most senior families (the *hatamoto* and *goke'nin*) played the major management roles, and the core role of the lower samurai was envisaged as ground troops. But there was no war. Because management positions were allocated to *hatamoto* and *goke'nin* family members in a primarily hereditary process, there was usually no route for "ordinary" samurai to rise to a meaningful administrative function. Their duties were things like "guard duty." With the rise in population (also among the samurai), and overwhelming peace and good order, there were not many hours per week "guarding" required. So they had plenty of spare time. This led samurai to sometimes lead, and often take part in, a whole range of leisure learning activities in fields as diverse as the military arts, agricultural technology, poetry, medicine, and Confucianism. Many of them enjoyed a kind of permanent *otium*. Although this social change was qualitatively different to what Hayami Akira, in relation to the contemporaneous Japanese peasantry, has referred to as the "industrious revolution," the parallels are intriguing (Hayami 2009, 2003; de Vries 2008). Both cases involve the availability of extra time being ploughed into an increased application of knowledge – in the case of Hayami's generic peasant for increased production, in the case of the generic samurai for what an economist might call "no goal in particular," a European humanities academic might call "*bildung*," and what in Confucian terms is called "self-cultivation."

Indeed, the third reason why samurai were often involved in leisure learning, and particularly in Confucian and Military leisure learning, was the nature of their self-identity, especially as it related to society at large. As touched on in the previous chapter, the early Tokugawa period saw the Warring States-period self-conception of the samurai primarily in terms of combat and individual courage replaced by an ideal which saw samurai as guardians of the social order in a broader sense, bringing peace to the land as much through their individual exemplary moral conduct and social engagement as through their military service. This was the Way of the Samurai originated by Yamaga Sokō: *bunbu ryōdō* (the Dual Way of Scholar and Warrior). The advent of this "Way" saw scholarly cultivation (Jp. *bun*, Ch. *wen*) combined on equal (or higher) footing alongside military cultivation (Jp. *bu*, Ch. *wu*) as a core self-defining feature of a samurai. With the advent of *bunbu ryōdō*, the samurai needed to be learned. Being learned increasingly became a core defining feature of being a samurai, whose new role Yamaga likened to that of a "teacher" in the following terms.

The Scholarly Way constitutes his heart, but externally he keeps the tools of a Warrior to hand. The three classes of the common people automatically take him as their teacher and look up to him. By following his teachings they come to know the [inherently good] original nature. This is how the Way of the Samurai arises (NST 32: 32).

Samurai were thus transformed, at least in Yamaga's ideal, into Confucian teachers, leading the commoners to personal enlightenment through recovery of the original nature, the shared single "principle" of Neo-Confucianism. The samurai was to become a kind of Neo-Confucian missionary, exemplifying and teaching a salvational ideal to the common people.

Leisure learning, however, was not only a samurai affair. Depending on the activity, the place, and the particular school, a leisure study group might be dominated by traders, artisans, or peasants. Indeed there are famous examples of Confucian schools predominantly attended by commoners, for instance the merchant-dominated Confucian academy of the Kaitokudō in Osaka (Najita 1987). It was also not at all rare for Confucian scholars to be non-samurai. Some of the most famous Confucian scholars of the middle and later period such as Itō Jinsai, Nakai Chikusan, Bitō Jishū, and Shibano Ritsuzan were not born samurai. Their market of students was also mixed, but tended to have more samurai than not. Given that in most areas samurai represented less than five percent of the total population, this was significant. In cities like Edo which had larger samurai populations, the leisure learning had higher number of samurai, and in cities like Osaka where there were many wealthy non-samurai, these people also played leading roles.

The practice of leisure learning in early modern Japan was particularly interesting in the way it encouraged a diversification of interests, skills, and networks, and sometimes a bifurcation of the nature of status and skill based on a particular field. As Ikegami has explained, leisure learning "supplied individual citizens with occasions for exchanging their feudal identities ... for identities otherwise defined" (Ikegami 2005: 14). Network research has demonstrated that it was very common for urban dwellers with the means to simultaneously take part in a number of different study circles or schools practicing different arts. Diaries from urban dwellers in Tokugawa Japan give us examples of people who regularly attended circles for painting, Confucianism, poetry, and military arts, and who would have relatives and friends they mixed with in these circles who might then be doing Dutch Studies or National Learning. So there was a huge human network of overlap between the different interests (Beerens 2006: 199).[2]

There was thus overlap and interchange between the participants in different leisure learning activities, including Confucianism. Confucianism, however, held a particularly privileged place within the field of the different kinds of schools and learning groups. This privileged position was related to the nature of what was taught in Confucian schools, how these skills linked into other activities, and how Confucianism and Confucian schools were perceived within the broader context of leisure learning.

Confucian activity, including practice, was usually based on book learning. This meant that a core part of the activity that occurred in most Confucian schools and study groups involved reading – in the broadest sense, from the acquisition of advanced literacy, through to achieving sufficient knowledge of the canonical base of Neo-Confucianism so one could understand the range of references occurring in Chinese texts. Literacy in the broad sense of Confucian learning thereby also included understanding the textual roots of and thinking behind the cosmological system used by Neo-Confucianism – a cosmological system that also underlay the way Chinese medical and scientific texts had explained the human body and the physical environment ever since the Song dynasty. Confucianism's role in increasing literacy in Chinese in this broad sense was then vital for people who were in groups studying medicine, agricultural technique, or many other pursuits which relied on texts from China written in Chinese. The massive popularity and increase in literacy in Chinese literature dominated the fields of not just Chinese, but also Japanese-language literary studies and many other cultural fields in the leisure learning environment. This literary influence extended to the visual arts. The key role of Confucian schools in the overall function of the learning environment, and particularly the fields that used literary tools, explains the rapidly increasing permeation of Confucian ideas, values, and references into all aspects of cultural life in Japan through the late seventeenth century. Most people active in cultural production had received a good degree of Confucian schooling.

Leisure learning focusing on Western technique and science is ironically enough one of the best examples of the deep influence of

Confucianism throughout the leisure learning field. Western Learning in early modern Japan was crucially affected by Confucianism and internalized various Confucian pedagogical and literary forms. The study of Western science in Tokugawa Japan was usually called "Dutch Learning" (*rangaku*). This was because after the settlement of Tokugawa foreign and trade policy in the 1630s and 1640s, the Dutch were left as the only European trading partners of Japan. Long-term contact between Dutch in Nagasaki and the official Dutch interpreters employed by the shogunate at Nagasaki facilitated a flow of Western information and knowledge delivered through the Dutch language. Current understandings of the nature of how Western knowledge was transmitted into mainstream Tokugawa Japan through "Dutch Learning" are unduly influenced by sectarian writings of some Japanese "Dutch Learning" scholars of the late eighteenth and early nineteenth centuries. These figures, like Sugita Genpaku (1733–1817), were private scholars who had set up school businesses in Edo and other cities. They sought to delineate themselves from other traditions of learning, notably Chinese medicine and Confucianism, by arguing that their practice of Dutch Learning was completely different to other forms of leisure and medical learning in Japan (Horiuchi 2003: 166–70; NST 64).

In reality, however, "Dutch Learning" was much more closely integrated with practices of Confucianism than these figures, and later historical outlooks privileging them, would admit. Dutch medical knowledge and medical technique was transmitted in Japanese society predominantly through the networks of traditional Chinese medical practitioners (Hübner 2014; Nakamura 2005). The greatest overlap in all the knowledge professions in Tokugawa Japan was between doctors and Confucian scholars. Itō Jinsai, for instance, came from a medical family, as did the famous Confucian Kaibara Ekken, who actually studied Dutch Learning in Nagasaki. So what was later called Dutch Learning was initially begun among doctors of Chinese medicine, many of whom also worked as Confucian teachers. Sugita Genpaku himself, for instance, came from a family of traditional (read Chinese) medical practitioners. The entire Chinese medical theory they used, moreover, was heavily influenced by and integrated with Confucian theory, as we shall see in the next chapter (Fujikawa 1941).

As will be elaborated upon in the next chapter, Confucian state advisors, particularly after the 1790s, were also instrumental in having Dutch Learning – medical knowledge and technique, language study, geography, and study of Western society in general – integrated into the emerging knowledge institutions of the Tokugawa state. Scholars like Timon Screech have emphasized negative views of Dutch Studies by

some Confucians and Tokugawa officials, but as I have argued elsewhere, the involvement of major Confucians and state officials in promoting Dutch Studies through the late eighteenth and early nineteenth
centuries problematizes the old sectarian way of seeing this history
(Paramore 2012c; Screech 1996: 42–6). Network analysis also shows
that participants in the most influential Dutch Learning and Neo-
Confucian circles overlapped significantly. Confucianism underlay the
reception of Western knowledge in Tokugawa Japan – conceptually,
linguistically, and sociologically.

Similarly "National Learning" (*kokugaku*), or Japanese Nativism, is
often, following the sectarian rhetoric of its later practitioners, usually
depicted as standing starkly at odds with Confucianism in general, and
Neo-Confucianism in particular. National Learning, particularly under
its most famous practitioner Motoori Norinaga (1730–1801), framed its
own discourse as a radical "Japanese indigenous" attack upon the foreign
"Chinese Confucian" tradition. Yet, as Peter Flueckiger has pointed out,
the basic logic of National Learning worked along Confucian parameters
(Flueckiger 2008: 212). The theoretical basis of later National Learning
from at least the eighteenth century onwards, as already pointed out by
Maruyama Masao in the 1940s, was deeply based on the concepts and
world views of the greatest Tokugawa Confucian scholar of all, Ogyū
Sorai (Maruyama 1974). National Learning, like Western Learning,
while profiling itself against Confucianism, actually worked within the
conceptual, linguistic, and organizational order of Confucian pedagogy
and theory. Thus even the most popular and influential religious,
intellectual, and political tradition of all in the Tokugawa period other
than Confucianism, National Learning, was heavily reliant upon
Confucianism theoretically, often integrated with it in practice, and
often also overlapping in membership.

By the late seventeenth century, Confucianism was palpable in nearly
every genre of cultural production. One of the most prolific and commer-
cially successful playwrights of the Tokugawa period, Chikamatsu
Monzaemon (1653–1724), framed much of his work around the resolution of individual passion and ideas of social duty clearly framed in
relation to prevalent samurai conceptions of Confucian morals.
Ironically, it is in the comic love tragedies of Chikamatsu, set in urban
environments and depicting close social interactions between commoners
and samurai, where Confucian themes are most prevalent. These plays
are often considered particularly modern works, not only because they are
set in dense mercantile urban environments, in an environment inferring
class interaction and tension, and often love-themed, but also because of
the way the main narrative usually weaves around a conflict between

unavoidable social mores and rules, on the one hand, and individual emotional response on the other.

The magic of Chikamatsu's love-suicide literature, what makes it attractive and work so well in narrative, is that Chikamatsu, on the one hand, encourages us to sympathize with characters who have broken basic rules, making them the tragic emotional heroes of the story, but, on the other hand, is merciless in concluding that it is these characters' own responsibility to resolve their individual mistakes – usually through suicide. For instance, Chūbei, the main character in *Courier for Hell* (*Meido no hikyaku*), also known as *Chūbei and Umegawa*, commits fraud and steals money from a client in order to pay off a pleasure house so he can live with his girlfriend and former courtesan Umegawa. Chikamatsu has us sympathize completely with the hapless Chūbei, yet at no stage does the writer indicate that there could be any more just outcome than our hero and heroine's deaths – which ultimately occur as the climactic conclusion to the play (Chikamatsu 1961).

Kurozumi Makoto points out that Chikamatsu thereby puts forward an ethics of unlimited individual responsibility. Ultimately, only the individual who has transgressed can be held accountable – there is no broader social context.[3] But this unlimited individual responsibility also interacts with a mystical idea of fate. The final scene often includes Buddhist references to meeting in Heaven afterwards, and sometimes on stage in the puppet theater or in kabuki productions, design elements like falling flowers are added to stress this aspect. But even then, underlying the Buddhist references is a restatement of the prime Neo-Confucian theme, the emphasis on individual responsibility seen through the individual's inability to take responsibility for his father (and therefore the social order)'s suffering, and his comic hope that being blindfolded from seeing his father's suffering will somehow suspend the reality of his betrayal of filial piety.

Chūbei: I am guilty of the crime and I am ready for my punishment! I know that I cannot escape death. I humbly request you to pray for my repose. But the sight of my father's anguish will prove an obstacle to my salvation. Please, as a kindness, cover my face (Chikamatsu 1961: 194).

Despite the Buddhist dressing, the overriding thematic context of the story is deeply related to Neo-Confucian values. Moreover, as Minamoto Ryōen has indicated, the thematic context of the play is related to quite particular changes in Neo-Confucian theory which were occurring in Japan precisely at that time (Minamoto 1969: 73–5). Minamoto famously argued that during the mid-Tokugawa period, socio-political changes caused a change in Confucian thinking which was then reflected in popular culture. Early Tokugawa Confucianism focused on cultivation of an individual's morals as the basis of social order – for instance in Kumazawa and Yamaga. The increase in social mores and legal and institutional control through the course of the seventeenth century, however, meant that individual samurai ethics were increasingly no longer seen as key to social order. The political and social order had stabilized to an extent where individual morality seemed almost politically superfluous. A Confucian sphere of discourse then gradually emerged which no longer required the private and public values to match ethically. Individual attitudes could now be admitted as being at odds with the norms of society, because social order did not rely upon individual action. A plurality of ethical outlooks, and of ethical (and thereby potentially political) opinions, was perfectly acceptable. Minamoto particularly relates this new form of Confucianism to the ideas of Ogyū Sorai, whose separation of the political and moral realms Minamoto explained sociologically in these terms (Minamoto 1969: 73–5).

The creative tension of the main narrative in famous Chikamatsu works like *The Love Suicides at Sonezaki* or *The Messenger from Hell* have been seen by scholars like Minamoto as to some extent mirroring this change in ethical outlook in the development of Japanese Confucianism. There is no doubt Chikamatsu Monzaemon was closely related to Confucian circles. Itō Jinsai, one of the most famous Confucians in Kyoto during the rise of Chikamatsu's literary career, mentions "plays in the neighborhood theaters" influencing his work. The most famous account given by Chikamatsu himself on the art of writing survives in a work edited by one of Itō Jinsai's students, Hozumi Ikan (1692–1769), who, as Watanabe Hiroshi notes, "was a close friend of Chikamatsu's, and whose son won fame as a playwright using the pen name Chikamatsu Hanji" (Watanabe 2012: 127).

Like many major Confucian scholars of the time, Chikamatsu was the son of a divested low-level samurai. This was also the case for one of the most famous poets of the Tokugawa period, Matsuo Bashō (1644–1694). Despite working predominantly in Japanese-language poetry, as opposed to the Chinese poetry tradition which was also very popular at that time, Bashō liberally employed references to Chinese literature and philosophy which relied upon Confucian knowledge to be understood. The most famous artists of the Tokugawa period were also intimately integrated with book culture because they often learned their trades and earned a significant amount of their income cutting illustrations in the wood-block printing enterprises which provided the backbone of the flourishing Japanese publishing industry. This was the case for early artists like Hishikawa Moronobu (1618–1694), as for later stars like Katsushika Hokusai (1760–1849). They worked alongside Confucian scholars and the Confucian-educated literati who constituted the bulk of authors of the books they illustrated. As well as artists thus having a close integration with Confucian circles, Confucians themselves often practiced painting. One of the most actively Confucian rulers of Japan, the Tokugawa shogunal regent Matsudaira Sadanobu (1759–1829) (Figure 3.1) (shogunal regent and *rōjū* 1787–1793) was himself an accomplished painter who also used that medium and other artistic forms in governance (Screech 2000).

Practice, pedagogy, and public administration

For Matsudaira, painting was only one of a range of arts which he applied as a form of personal Neo-Confucian practice. Matsudaira Sadanobu's personal approach to Neo-Confucian practice is worth considering in detail, not only because he was one of the most powerful individuals in Tokugawa Japan, but more importantly because of his role in institutionalizing certain forms of Neo-Confucian practice in the apparatus of the late Tokugawa state. As will be discussed further in the next chapter, Matsudaira Sadanobu overhauled the knowledge institutions of the shogunal state through a major process of shogunal reform in the late 1780s and 1790s. The reforms changed and expanded the state roles of the Confucian Academy and other important medical and scientific institutions. Part of this process included appointing a range of new reformist Confucian scholars from outside Edo into key positions in the state apparatus. These appointees, in particular the so-called Three Kansei Professors, Shibano Ritsuzan (1736–1807), Bitō Jishū (1747–1813), and Koga Seiri (1750–1817), had developed in private academies in Osaka and Kyoto, and trialed in the regional states (*han*), a range of new ideas to reform the bureaucratic functions and mechanisms of government. All of these appointees were Neo-Confucians. Matsudaira himself, like many of these appointees, followed Neo-Confucian teachings of self-cultivation and moral improvement. Devoted to individual practice as a means of bettering himself and thereby the world, Matsudaira even authored a number of works about his own experience of self-cultivation. Below I will briefly use these writings to try to reconstruct what Matsudaira concretely meant by Neo-Confucian practice. I will then examine the more significant issue of how he institutionalized similar forms of Neo-Confucian practice among the shogunal samurai elite at the end of the 1700s through his reform drive, thereby using religious practice to attempt to engender a change in the machinery and nature of government, and the mentality of those directing it.

Matsudaira Sadanobu's *Record of Spiritual Exercises* (*Shugyōroku*) (1826) is a description of how his own individual Confucian practice

Figure 3.1 Matsudaira Sadanobu self-portrait (1788)

fitted into his broader life and thoughts. One commonly noted aspect of Neo-Confucian practice which was clearly also important to Matsudaira was control over "desire" (*yoku*). Many commentators link ideas over the control of desire in Neo-Confucianism to practices of abstention from the enjoyment of sex, food, and money – a form of asceticism. In Matsudaira's writings, there are links made between Neo-Confucianism and an ascetic outlook on life (Matsudaira 1942: 183–7). Matsudaira's account of Confucian practice also makes clear, however, that for him practice was more than just ascetics and that abstention was not supposed to mean a blanket restriction on passion or emotionality. This can be seen in the way Matsudaira delineated between the negative force of "desire" (*yoku*) and the often positive trait of "passion" (*jō*).

Carnal desire is an endless [insatiable] form of "the base passion (*bonjō*) of human physicality (*jinsei*)." In other words, it is all desire *yoku*. It is not "true [good] passion (*makoto no jō*)" (Matsudaira 1942: 184).

Thus for Matsudaira, although "desire" and "base passion" were bad, "true passion" was inherently good. Following from this, Matsudaira's vision of the Way of self-cultivation emphasized much more than just asceticism. As well as a negative narrative of what to avoid, Matsudaira also indicated a positive program of self-cultivation through active practice. Matsudaira's own practice exemplifies this positive approach.

Matsudaira identified his own practice as something called *jūdō*, which he claimed followed the teachings of a man called Suzuki Kiyobei (Suzuki Kunitaka) (Matsudaira 1942: 181). Judo is today the name of a modern Olympic sport based on jujitsu hand-to-hand combat traditions, but invented in the 1880s by the modernizing educator Kanō Jigorō (1860–1938). So what could have Matsudaira meant when he referred to judo a hundred years before Kanō invented it? Matsudaira tells his reader that this jūdō, which forms the basis of his own Confucian practice of self-cultivation, was popular at the time he took it up, particularly among quite a few of the domain lords. He narrates his own introduction to this "Way" by Kuki Takamura (1727–1820), Lord of Sanda, in what is now Hyōgo Prefecture (Matsudaira 1942: 182). Perhaps due to the popularity of this practice at the time, Matsudaira in his account saw no need to concretely explain how this practice was conducted. From other sources, however, this jūdō has been identified as indeed a form of jujitsu closely identified with Suzuki Kunitaka and currently referred to as *Kitōryū jūjitsu* (jujitsu of the Kitō school). This particular school of jujitsu training dates back to the mid-seventeenth century and is noted for emphasizing the benefits of jujitsu training for the purpose of Confucian self-cultivation.[4] Suzuki mixed in a bit of Shinto mysticism, but the art remained predominantly a form of martial arts practice adapted for Confucian self-cultivation purposes.

The nature of Kitōryū practice and its relationship to Confucianism is clearly articulated in the written doctrines of the school. According to these sources, jujitsu is practiced mainly in order to return one to the state of one's "original body" (*hontai*). In the literature of this school, this "original body" plays the same role as "original nature" (*honsei*) in more orthodox texts of Neo-Confucian practice. Return to the "origin" is achieved, just as in Neo-Confucianism, through controlling one's *ki* (*Ch. qi*). By getting *ki* under control, one reaches "illumination of virtue" (*kyorei*), a phrase taken from Zhu Xi's commentary of the *Greater Learning* (Imamura 1966: 364).[5] Kitōryū's system of self-cultivation is thus narrated through references to *The Greater Learning* using exactly the same textual explanatory background as Neo-Confucian self-cultivation. The only difference is that the "original nature" of standard Neo-Confucianism is replaced by the word "original *body*." The location of original virtue and inherent good in Kitōryū jujitsu is thus the physical body. The transplantation of the usual Neo-Confucian "human nature" from the abstract individual to the concreteness of the individual's body is significant. Given the nature of the practice, the physical element is more pronounced and clearly defined.

Our school begins by pointing out the practice of the original body (*hontai*). If we ask what is the original body, it is the illumination (*kyorei*) which lies behind the heart/mind, it is the shape of the godly *ki* of stillness, it is what is called the original body (Imamura 1966: 364).

This passage in all respects mirrors Neo-Confucian descriptions of practice, including the appropriation of the Zhu Xi term *kyorei* from Zhu's commentary on the *Greater Learning*.[6] The important difference with standard Neo-Confucianism is of course that they are doing jujitsu. There is an inherent emphasis on physicality both in the written description and in practice. Jujitsu, although practiced in this context to cultivate one's own self, is still conducted through the inherently relational, social, non-individual context of partnered throwing practice (*randori*). The above-quoted section thus immediately continues,

When you face your opponent, when your opponent is before you, at the moment when your awareness of this arises, agitation arises. If you become agitated then your body/self (*mi*) is ineffective. Looking at your opponent, but then with a still heart, with virtue illuminated / clean spirit, facing peacefully, in possession of the original body – this is called the wisdom of stillness (Imamura 1966: 364).

Thus the practice that Matsudaira followed and advocated was inherently positive about physicality, achieved through dynamic physical action, and requiring a social setting of relational engagement with another human being. Although Matsudaira's general discussion of self-cultivation in his account sometimes talks about avoiding sexual and gastronomic lust, the actual practice had nothing to do with abstinence or negation of passion. In fact, quite the opposite, it required energetic engagement. The outcome of the practice may have included lowering of desire, as part of an overall control of *ki*, but the practice itself was jujitsu.

The unique feature of this kind of practice, as opposed to other practices like quiet sitting, or indeed ascetic abstention, is that it is relational and socially embedded, both because the practice by its very nature involves physical relations with another person and because the practice confirms the samurai practitioner's social utility as a soldier. There is a social context, it is a lived tradition, practiced within a field of set social interactions, in space devoted to this (the *dōjō*), within communities who similarly identify the position of this religious practice with their own traditions and ways of life.

This adaptation of Confucian self-cultivation to samurai culture through this particular form of jujitsu, and its practice by Matsudaira, is significant because it facilitated, possibly for the first time, a systematic integration of Confucian practice into the emerging pedagogical structures of the state. Matsudaira Sadanobu was not content to practice self-cultivation himself. His reform of the educational and bureaucratic apparatus of the Tokugawa state allowed him to institutionalize this approach to individual practice in the emerging state pedagogical systems. He did this partly through the introduction of an examination system for the senior vassals of the Tokugawa house, the senior samurai who came to occupy many of the administrative posts in the Tokugawa bureaucracy. This examination system had two elements: military and literary. The examination curriculum was thus an articulation of the late Tokugawa state's vision of Yamaga Sokō's idea of *bunbu ryōdo* (Dual Way of Warrior and Literati). The two basic elements of the examination system were: (1) Confucian Practice (jujitsu, in its Neo-Confucian form), and (2) Confucian Learning (through texts).

The Confucian examination system in Japanese manifestation

Through the 1790s, Matsudaira's appointees in the shogunate began to attempt to roll out an examination system designed to influence appointment in the shogunal state over a sustained period. Half a century earlier, in the Kyōhō Reforms of the 1720s, Matsudaira's grandfather Shogun Tokugawa Yoshimune had attempted to introduce an examinations system. He was, however, ultimately unsuccessful. Matsudaira Sadanobu took the Kyōhō Reforms as an administrative model, but looked to improve them. One legacy of the earlier attempts to introduce examinations was that shogunal retainers, although not tested on Confucian or literary skills, were sometimes tested in the martial arts. They were required to occasionally demonstrate military skill through tests called *bugei kinmi* (assessments of martial arts). In the 1790s, Sadanobu began his introduction of an examination system by regularizing these military "assessments" as individual examinations, and adding to them "scholarly assessments" (*gakumon kinmi*): examinations in scholarly skills based around the Neo-Confucian Four Books and other classical texts. The idea was that these two "assessments," the "martial arts assessment" (*bugei kinmi*) and "scholarly assessment" (*gakumon kinmi*), would then become the dual core of an examinations system which could influence the order of appointment and promotion (Paramore 2012c).

The military skills tested in the examinations standardized under Matsudaira Sadanobu and later under his appointees included jujitsu. Therefore, this military aspect of the examination system can be seen to have been, for its initiator at least, a form of Confucian religious practice. Jujitsu was clearly seen by a large number of the samurai elite as a form of self-cultivation, an inherently Neo-Confucian practice. Confucian practice in this Tokugawa Japanese manifestation was obviously innovative, an adaptation of an element of samurai culture, and in this sense uniquely linked to the place and culture where it arose. Yet it was a practice which for many of the most influential people doing it was clearly a form of Neo-Confucianism.

Just like this physical military element, the practice of the "scholarly" element in the examinations was also more complex and more strangely "Japanized" than one may first realize. Chinese and Korean Confucian examinations were primarily written examinations. After studying, memorizing, and practicing writing for years or decades, the Chinese candidate would write essays: the famous eight-legged format of the Ming, for instance. The late Tokugawa shogunate's literary examinations, by contrast, were inherently interactive. The "scholarly assessment," depending on level, was conducted using one or both of two core pedagogical methods, Japanese in origin. These methods were *sodoku* (base reading) and *kaidoku* (social reading). These were originally pedagogical rather than testing practices which had arisen in the private sphere of the leisure learning schools and circles.

In many other Confucian cultures, a core pedagogical practice was lecturing. Lecturing had also been tried in Japan as a primary means of spreading Confucian learning among the governing classes, notably by Muro Kyūso (1658–1734) in the early 1700s. But the consensus on lecturing by the late 1700s was that it was a counter-productive practice which turned people off Confucianism rather than engaging them. Shibano Ritsuzan, one of the great Confucian reformers and initiators of the shogunal examination system under Matsudaira, described former attempts to introduce compulsory Confucian lectures for shogunal retainers at Edo Castle in the following terms.

They [shogunal retainers] all came to the lecture because it was required by their work, one person from each department, all sitting in lines. Whatever was said in the lecture, none of it entered their ears. They just sat in their rows day dreaming about the floating world [popular entertainments]. The lecture served no purpose whatsoever (Shibano in Takimoto 1914: 143).

Shibano Ritsuzan, the most influential figure in the Shogunal Confucian Academy in the 1790s, was thus clearly of the opinion that lecturing was not an effective way to engage samurai interest. After all, as he explained, each person was different and had different skills and interests, so this kind of broad brush pedagogy was unlikely to be effective (142–6). Instead, he recommended what from at least the mid-1700s had become the two core forms of reading practices in Japanese Confucian schools: "plain reading" (*sodoku*) and "social reading" (*kaidoku*).

Plain reading

"Plain reading" was a primarily didactic device whereby a student would orally read out a classic (usually Confucian) Chinese-language text (written in Chinese) in a form of (orally articulated) Japanese. For elementary students, the main aim was to be able to instantaneously reproduce the text verbally in Japanese, but "plain reading" also often involved a short explication of terms and quotes embedded within it. "Plain reading," therefore, while at its simplest entailing instantaneous translation of a classic Chinese text into Japanese, at its most complex was an exercise which demonstrated knowledge of the textual context and intersecting textual relations behind a classic work. The core of the skill was to read the Classical Chinese text out verbally in a form of Japanese. It was an oral rather than written practice. This was also an interpretative act because choices made in deciding exactly how to verbalize certain words and passages in Japanese also often showed knowledge of or allegiance to a particular interpretation or interpretative tradition. "Plain reading" was therefore taught from the most basic literacy level. It involved acquiring knowledge of classic Neo-Confucian texts, usually beginning with the *Greater Learning*, and then followed by the other Four Books of the Neo-Confucian canon: the *Doctrine of the Mean*, *Confucius Analects*, and *Mencius*. But at a higher level, it was also often an exercise in inter-textual interpretation, where the student, through her/his choice of Japanese reading, demonstrated an understanding of a particular interpretative tradition. It therefore also potentially taught students how to relate different classic Chinese texts and traditions to each other.

"Plain reading" is therefore an example of Confucian pedagogical practice which was of great utility to most other leisure learning activities. For people studying poetry, for instance, Confucian training gave them not only advanced literacy in general, but in particular the ability to interpret allusions to Chinese classical literature which pepper even Japanese language poetry; similarly for people who might be studying military arts texts. For people studying Western Learning, even though

Figure 3.2 A meeting of the Sorai School (Historiographical Institute of the University of Tokyo)

obviously allusions to Chinese literature would not appear in the original Dutch texts, the skill of inter-textual interpretation and translation inherent in "plain reading" was useful. More crucially, because Western Learning scholars often used Chinese-language translations of Western books and primers on Western knowledge, "plain reading" equipped them with skills necessary to fully utilize the main secondary literature and apparatus they had available to them to interpret Western culture – all written in Chinese.

It is instructive that it was this practice, not essays, which was used for primary examining in the new Shogunal examination system. It was completely based in reading of Confucian texts and explanation of Confucian ideas, but it was also a practical *skill*, and the act of testing rested on the candidate proving their capacity to use this skill. It was therefore inherently different to the eight-legged examination essays of the Chinese empires.

Social reading

Matsudaira Sadanobu's idea of jujitsu as Neo-Confucian self-cultivation was novel, but its primary aim of recovery of the individual's perfect original moral state was also quintessentially Neo-Confucianism. The practice of "social reading" (*kaidoku*), however, emerged from Japanese Confucian circles which opposed Neo-Confucianism and its focus on individual morality. As Maeda Tsutomu has noted, "social reading" was a pedagogically, socially, and politically central form of critical practice not only in Tokugawa Confucian circles but also in many other forms of Tokugawa leisure learning (Maeda 2009: 13–25). It seems to have originated, however, in the Confucian practice of Tokugawa Japan's most famous Confucian, Ogyū Sorai (1666–1728).

As discussed in the previous chapter, Ogyū Sorai's critical stance to Neo-Confucianism is what most scholars focus upon in narrating the importance of his impact on Tokugawa society. Aside from his Confucian theories and ideas, however, Ogyū was also an innovative educator and established new ways of communal studying, new forms of scholarly practice which it could be argued lent from religious tradition. Most importantly, the main new scholarly practice he is credited with, "social reading" (*kaidoku*), was for Ogyū a core method of reaching the truth of the Confucian Way.

Ogyū mentioned social reading in his instructions for students, *Master Sorai's Responsals* (*Sorai sensei tōmonsho*), a leaflet published in 1726 using the allegory of an exchange of letters between student and teacher to outline his ideas on education. Following his overall methodology of recovery of the ancient Way, Ogyū saw pedagogy as an attempt to recreate the scholarly practice of idealized ancient times.

In ancient times they used the word "friend-master [master *and* friend]". Through the cultivation of friendship they spread knowledge and advanced learning ... a school atmosphere permeated by friendly exchange was the most important element [in the ideal educational practices of the ancients] (Ogyū in NKBT 94: 171).

Social reading is mentioned fairly shortly after this in another passage discussing the method through which texts should be read.

When one meets with people from the same town and carries out Social Reading (*kaidoku*) amongst a group of friends, then sometimes East will be mentioned and East will be understood. In far-flung places, where one lacks the support of friends, scholarship cannot be undertaken very easily (Ogyū in Nakamura 1966 (NKBT 94): 173; Ogyū and Yamashita 1994: 93).

Here Sorai is talking about how to approach a text, but his key point is that the participant in "social reading" should not seek to use the group dynamic simply to push earlier views, but rather to cooperate to arrive at *new* understandings through discussion. His idea of social reading was thus centered around an idea of reasonable discussion which resonates with ideas from more recent political philosophy, notably by Habermas (figure 3.2). This approach underlay this technique's capacity to facilitate political discussion within scholarly communities in Japan through the eighteenth and nineteenth centuries.[7]

Later institutionalization of "social reading" practice gives more insight into the relationship between openness to interpretation inherent in this approach and the potential of public sphere discourse. Although probably first launched in Ogyū Sorai's school, "social reading" was most power-fully institutionalized by Neo-Confucian scholars who competed *against* the Sorai School during the late eighteenth century of state reforms led by Matsudaira Sadanobu. Bitō Jishū, a Confucian scholar originally based in the Kansai, and later one of Matsudaira's key professorial appointees at the Shogunate Academy in Edo, linked the Neo-Confucian Zhu Xi idea of the "impartial mind" (Jp. *kyoshin*, Ch. *xuxin*) to define the originally anti-Neo-Confucian Sorai's practice of "social reading" in new Neo-Confucian terms (Maeda 2009: 26–7).[8] This was picked up in the way domainal school ordinances described "social reading."

When one is carrying out social reading, one must maintain an impartial mind and a balanced mood so that this practice benefits you. You should not emphasize convincing others of a previously held position or adopt an argumentative tone of voice (NKSS 6: 110).

This example from the regulations of the Kobe-han school Kyōrindō shows "social reading" being redeployed by Neo-Confucians not only as an intellectual, pedagogical, and communicative form but also as a form of self-cultivation. Many other references of this kind indicate that, at least by the turn of the nineteenth century, "social reading" was the standard approach to education in the resurgently expanding network of Neo-Confucian schools in Japan. The adoption of this practice by Neo-Confucian schools is important, not only because the new state institutions and examinations were all run by Neo-Confucians but also because in the domainal and private school sectors Neo-Confucian schools experienced a resurgence of popularity at the expense of Sorai school institutions through the late eighteenth and nineteenth centuries (Ishikawa 1960: 256–8).

The later social interpretations of social reading thus also led to a combination of educative public practice with individual religious practice in mid- to late Tokugawa Neo-Confucianism – a combination which provided a robust basis for individual engagement with the public sphere in the Tokugawa order. Figures central in institutionalizing "social reading" practice into state schools cut down on practices like "lecturing" which were more hierarchical and only facilitated one-way communication. As Shibano Ritsuzan put it, "they (samurai) don't listen to lectures, no matter what you are saying" (Shibano in Takimoto 1914: 143). In this sense, Matsudaira can be seen as having played a role in further spreading and strengthening Confucian practices associated with the growth of a public sphere discourse around Confucianism, or what we might call a Confucian public sphere.

In the quote which opens this chapter, Bitō Jishū, defining the Way around the turn of the eighteenth into the nineteenth century, used the word that is now used in modern Japanese to refer to "publicness." It was clear that his idea of an "impartial mind" and its relationship to how controversial issues should be discussed were central to his conception of the political Way, which for him was intimately related to Confucian education (NST 47: 261–7).[9] The openness and reasonableness inherent in this approach resonate with contemporary theories of the public sphere by thinkers like Habermas or Rawls, which rely on "reasonableness" in public debate as one of the core preconditions necessary for a functional public sphere.[10]

An example of how robust political criticism had become by the late eighteenth century is provided by the quote below, from a widely distributed memorial to his feudal lord written by Koga Seiri, at the time head of his domainal state academy, and very soon after appointed one of the leaders of the Shogunal Academy in Edo.

As our country is under a regime of generals, the path of selection/election is closed. Particularly in domains such as ours [Saga], the damage of the hereditary system is not to be avoided. Those with hereditary status are negligent, and those without do not serve. This is why the spirit of the gentleman/samurai cannot be enacted, and why custom can so degenerate (Koga in Takimoto 1914: 160).

Orthodox state Neo-Confucians of the mid- and late Tokugawa period, like Koga, were a far cry from fawning lackeys like Hayashi Razan. There had been a clear change in the nature of discourse, where even closely state-aligned scholars were in a position to, in certain circumstances and media, trenchantly criticize the underlying structures of the polity. But they were also capable, usually, of tempering their opinions, of withdrawing to a reasonable, sustainable position of engagement within the reality of the polity. As Maeda Tsutomu and Watanabe Hiroshi have both recently pointed out, this allowed late Tokugawa Neo-Confucians to sustain their social critique over a long period. Mid- to late Tokugawa period Neo-Confucianism in particular, more so than other intellectual streams or forms of Confucianism in Japan, developed a robust capacity to sustain public debate over a range of issues, including on issues in tension with Tokugawa state policy, over the long term (Maeda 2009: 24–5; Watanabe 2012: 181–95).

Neo-Confucian figures in the late eighteenth- and early nineteenth-century Japanese Confucian world as diverse as Rai Shunsui, Rai Sanyō, Koga Seiri, Koga Tōan, Bitō Jishū, and Shibano Ritsuzan, all managed to combine Confucian activity and later often high office in the emerging state academic institutions with sometimes trenchant critique of the status quo. This was a combination of reasonableness, critique and practicality which Watanabe implies may have been related to their practice of self-cultivation, entailing as it did self-discipline, and also the hope of attaining a state of grace on an individual level, even if activity in the social world was not working out (Watanabe 2012: 185). I believe it was also likely related to the fact that their core professional activity as Japanese Confucian scholars, social reading, had them constantly debating each other. This was a form of rational, reasonable but also inherently disputational activity which these Confucian scholars and most educated members of the population understood as a functional discursive form, and a normal part of daily life.

The social and political relevance of this form was added to by the fact that it moved out well beyond strictly Confucian circles of study. Social reading was a core practice among many other kinds of politically relevant leisure learning circles, notably in the traditions of "Dutch Studies" (studies of Western science and medicine), "National Learning" (Nativism), and even Buddhism. All these traditions came to rely on meta-theories, larger concepts, and most importantly core methods of practice that originated in Confucian circles: notably including "social reading." Sugita Genpaku, the most famous "Dutch Learning" scholar of Tokugawa Japan, recommended "social reading." Important translation publications in Dutch Learning were the outcomes of "social reading" sessions. Motoori Norinaga, the most famous exponent of National Learning, even kept a "social reading" diary of group reading sessions he participated in (Maeda 2009: 19–21). Medical academy syllabi listed social reading as a primary method of instruction (Mori 1933: 210). It is this underlying Confucian pulse through the spectrum of Japanese leisure learning that frames my description of mid- and late Tokugawa Japan as having led to a Confucian public sphere.

As noted in the previous chapter, even very early Japanese Confucians were often seen in a political light, and sometimes suffered as a result. An underlying tension between certain Confucian ideals and the nature of the Tokugawa state propelled Confucian ideas, people, and practices into a central position in the articulation and sometimes resolution of those tensions. Sometimes, as in the case of Chikamatsu Monzaemon's writing, that tension led to a discourse not so critical of the state, nor overtly political – more a simple expression of tensions inherent in society. However, particularly from the late seventeenth century, and increasingly through the course of the eighteenth and early nineteenth centuries, the creative force of this tension became more active in mainstream political society and was increasingly formulated as political discourse – in forms both acceptable and unacceptable to the regime, from figures both aligned with and opposed to it.

Liberation Confucianism: Radical politics in the Confucian public sphere

This Confucian public sphere was not without an edge. As is normal with any historical enquiry, the most historical sources I use in this book were preserved by those whose descendants and followers lived on. The ones who survived, and whose reforms survived, like Matsudaira, become the agents of history. But there were also Neo-Confucians in Tokugawa Japan who ended up dead as a result of their public sphere activism. The best example is Ōshio Heihachirō (1793–1837).

Ōshio was a samurai who had served for nearly thirty years as an officer in the magistracy of the Eastern quarter of Osaka – the Tokugawa shogunate appointed governorate of the biggest commercial city in Japan. In March 1837, during a terrible urban famine, caused partly by merchant stock-piling of rice for market manipulation, Ōshio launched an armed uprising against the shogunate. He had resigned his position a couple of years earlier due to dissatisfaction with the way the magistrate of the time carried out his duties. In the intervening period, he earned a good living running his own private Confucian school. As the conditions of famine got worse through 1836, however, he devoted all his energy to petitioning figures in the shogunate to relieve suffering among the people of Osaka. He justified this intervention in politics in terms of the Neo-Confucian principle that teaching and action should be one. He called for both direct state support in rice and also for the state to intervene to free up the privately stock-piled rice already in Osaka so it could be consumed and the market manipulation ended. Nothing was done.

He then sold his book collection to raise funds and began to organize a peasant army. Ōshio was a relatively famous Confucian scholar. He had studied under Rai Sanyō who had famously nicknamed him "the little Wang Yangming." In preparing for the uprising, however, he was able to employ a non-Confucian skill he was also well known for – spear combat. The spear was one of the weapons that samurai were trained in, but was also the weapon traditionally used by peasants when employed in combat during the Warring States and earlier periods. Ōshio's idea was to launch a rebellion with about 300 men he had trained in the weeks before, first taking both the Eastern quarter and Western quarter magistrates' offices – the center of military rule in the city – and then set fire to as many of the rich merchant compounds as possible. The plan was then to use the chaos to raid these compounds for hoarded rice and also for money that could then be redistributed to the people to buy rice and ease suffering. This was the kind of Confucian-inspired samurai uprising the shogunate had feared 150 years earlier in the days of Yamaga Sokō and Kumazawa Banzan.

Ōshio's uprising, however, was undermined when two samurai who were also part of the plot revealed it to the magistrates. Ōshio brought forward the planning and assembled one hundred men after setting fire to his own house as a signal. With the earlier intelligence, the shoguante forces in Osaka had already assembled an army with heavy weaponry in Osaka Castle. By the time Ōshio's men came into confrontation with the shogunate forces they numbered around 300, many of them trained, but armed mainly with spears. The shogunate forces, however, deployed cannon and musket units against the rebels and soon overwhelmed them. Shogunate fire-power was more than enough to end the rebellion in one short confrontation near the ports. Ōshio managed to escape, but was found forty days later hiding at a residence in the city. He committed suicide in prison while awaiting what surely would have been a much more gruesome execution. Militarily, therefore, the rebellion was over: a disaster.

The fact that Ōshio was such a well-known Confucian scholar, and a former samurai officer of the city magistracy, however, meant that the rebellion continued to have major repercussions across Japan even after it was crushed. Most scholars agree that it significantly fed into anti-shogunate feeling in the long term. It has also been linked to a string of rebellions that broke out in the following months in other parts of Japan. The Bingo Mihara Rebellion, in the castle town of Mihara in present-day Hiroshima Prefecture in May of the same year, the so-called Ikuta Yorozu Rebellion in Kashiwazaki, Echigo, current Niigata Prefecture, in July of the same year, and the so-called Yamadaya Taisuke Riot in Nose, Setsu, current-day Osaka Prefecture, in August of the same year were all linked to Ōshio Heihachirō's rebellion, with the instigators labeling themselves or labeled by others as "followers of Ōshio" (Newmark 2014).

This in itself is interesting, because in fact the leaders of these other rebellions identified with other intellectual and religious movements which had no links to Ōshio's Confucianism. Ikuta Yorozu (1801–1837), for instance, was like Ōshio, a samurai who had given up service a couple of years before the rebellion he led. But Ikuta was no Confucian. He was instead a well-known scholar of National Learning, a nativist rabidly opposed to Confucianism. He had been one of the early students of Hirata Atsutane (1776–1843), one of the most famous and popularly influential nativist leaders. Hirata Atsutane is regarded as having popularized Nativism mainly through institutionalizing a range of practices which formed the basis of a network of schools throughout Japan based on Hirata's teachings – schools which later played a major role in advancing "Revere the emperor, expel the barbarians" *sōnō jōi* ideology, and in providing much of the organizational network for the rebellions of the 1860s which would bring down the Tokugawa shogunate and effect the Meiji Restoration (McNally 2005). So Ikuta Yorozu's rebellion, although militarily quite a farce, even less effective than Ōshio's attempt, was in many ways a taste of things to come for opposition to the Tokugawa shogunate: led by a nativist thinker who brought together samurai and wealthier peasant members in a religious movement which could be translated into radical political action against the state. It is interesting then that this first outbreak of such nativist anti-state violence was inspired by a much larger, more influential, but also clearly Confucian-inspired rebellion led by Ōshio Heihachirō.[11]

Ōshio Heihachirō is also interesting because of the close connections he had not only to most Confucian scholars in Osaka but also to some of the most influential and highly positioned Confucians serving the shogunate in Edo. These included Koga Tōan, with whom he was a regular correspondent (Aiso 2003). Koga Tōan was one of the most influential Confucian advisors to the Tokugawa shogunate, mainly in terms of his advice on foreign affairs informed by his deep learning in Dutch Studies. He was also the son of Koga Seiri, quoted above unfavorably characterizing the Tokugawa shogunate as a "regime of generals," and yet a central figure of state Confucianism, as we shall see in the next chapter.

Ōshio was part of the same Confucian public sphere networks as figures deeply embedded in the shogunal state, on the one hand, and was also the inspiration for rebellion by nativists, on the other. Here we can see the extent of the public sphere – networks of political debate stretching from the inner sanctums of the state to some of the most geographically and politically peripheral players in Japan. The traitor Ōshio's world was the same world and the same public sphere as that of Bitō Jishū and other close Tokugawa state officials. The Confucian public sphere was diverse and dynamic, it linked revolutionaries with the heads of the state academies in intimate study groups of "friendly interaction." It involved political activity from memorial writing to armed rebellion. Regardless of the position or the means of activity, however, it was a continuing dialogue which brought together many and had achieved a means and style through which political discussion could be held across a surprisingly wide (if not universal) breadth of Japan, its social classes, and outlooks.

4 Confucianism as knowledge

> Confucianism is the Way of Benevolence, Medicine is the Technique of Benevolence.
>
> Kagawa Shūan, Confucian and Medical Scholar (*Ippondō Yakusen* [*Pharmaceutical Selection of the Ippon School*], 1731 (manuscript in University of Tokyo Library))

Confucianism critically affected not only the religious, cultural, and political life of early modern Japan but also the fields of science, medicine, and technology. Confucianism in Tokugawa Japan was involved in the importation and development of "useful knowledge" in the form of agricultural and industrial technique from China, and medicine, industrial technology, and military intelligence from China, Korea, Manchuria, Holland, and beyond. In the later Tokugawa period, Confucianism was instrumental in facilitating engagement with a wide array of Western science and technology. Confucianism was also vital for importing and developing a form of useful knowledge often not emphasized in history of science scholarship, yet vital for economic development in the non-Western modern: knowledge of Western statecraft and systems of governance – the sociological technologies of Western imperialism.

"Useful knowledge" is a term in the fields of economic history and the history of science used to identify knowledge which has practical application. It has been defined as, "technology in its widest sense is [as] the manipulation of nature for human material gain" (Mokyr 2002: 3–4, 284). Since the 1970s, studies on the sociology of knowledge and the interdisciplinary study of STS (Science, Technology, Society) have emphasized the key role of socio-political factors in determining whether a society is supportive or obstructive of technological innovation and its application.[1] By contrast, writing on early modern Japan seldom engages the complex socio-political dynamics of knowledge development.[2] The history of knowledge transfer and development in early modern Japan has rather often been reduced to overly simplistic questions of how "open" Japanese society was to the "foreign" element represented by new technology. Narrations of early modern Japan touching on knowledge transfer thereby often conform to a very out-of-date vision of Tokugawa Japan as a "closed country," and still sometimes portray reception of Western knowledge as a victory over an imagined suppressing traditional state. This in turn plays into traditional flattening representations by the likes of G.W.F. Hegel which incorrectly portrayed premodern Asian societies as inherently static and caught in an ahistorical vacuum of religiously induced developmental stagnation.[3] This chapter instead tries to understand the development of knowledge in early modern Japan through the more socially embedded approaches ones sees in current STS scholarship. I argue that Confucianism in early modern Japan facilitated social practices, structures, and institutions which supported technological development, and encouraged ways of thinking and approaches to the position of knowledge in general society which were crucial in promoting technological innovation through the period.

This chapter traces Confucianism's role in knowledge development through four chronological phases. Firstly, we investigate Confucianism's role in the establishment and growth of private schools and knowledge networks through the course of the seventeenth century. To do this, I will begin by analyzing the role of Confucianism in the rise of the networks of private medical schools and clinics which disseminated medical knowledge throughout Japan before the Tokugawa settlement, during the course of the fifteenth and sixteenth centuries. I use medicine here as a case study illustrative of the knowledge field in general. Medical schools provided some of the earliest models of private knowledge institutions in Japan, making medicine a particularly illuminating case which I will come back to throughout the chapter. Secondly, the chapter will examine the Tokugawa regime's attempts to institutionalize knowledge through the state-led reforms of the eighteenth century. These reforms ultimately led the Tokugawa state into an ambitious program of construction and nationalization of academies, research centers, schools, and hospitals. I will show how these reforms were motivated by the ascendancy of a particular Confucian ideal of the utility of knowledge for the state. This ideal emphasized the state's role in providing welfare for the people in times of need – notably including famine. I will suggest that the advance of science and technology through the eighteenth and into the nineteenth century was not only closely related to this Confucian ideal of state paternalism and egalitarianism but also closely tied in with new Confucian practices of pedagogy described in the previous chapter. Thirdly, the chapter discusses how this Confucian-led state institutionalization of knowledge came to support Japanese engagement with Western science, technique, and method – particularly in the late eighteenth and early nineteenth centuries. Both the political leaders of state knowledge reform in this period, and the

Confucians they appointed into key positions, favored the use of Western knowledge and institutionalized the integration of the teaching of Western methods in state institutions. Fourthly, the chapter concludes by considering the significance of this institutionalization for the knowledge boom which occurred in Japan in the late nineteenth century, after the Meiji Restoration.

Confucianism and knowledge dissemination in the private sphere

One of the earliest forms of knowledge institutionalized in private schools and academies throughout Japan was medicine. Both the creation of networks of medical schools and the link between Confucianism and medical learning in Japan predate the early modern period. The rise of medical knowledge and its link to Confucianism in Japan both date from out of the Japanese Warring States period (fifteenth and sixteenth centuries), the violence of which encouraged a heightened interest in medicine.

Xiaozhu Furen Liangfang ("Effective Treatments for Women with Commentary") is a classic text of traditional Chinese medical gynecology. Reprinted on many occasions during the Ming and Qing dynasties, it is an expanded version of the late Southern Song early Mongol period, *Furen liangfang daquan* ("Complete Collected Effective Treatments for Women"), by the famous Chinese medical expert Chen Ziming (1190–1270), with important scholarly commentaries added by two later doctors of the Ming dynasty: Xiong Zongli (1415–1487) and Xue Ji (1487–1559) (Chen 1985; Xue 1976). Both these Ming commentaries played crucial roles in the development of medicine in Japan. Xiong Zongli was one of the most prolific medical writers, editors, and collectors of medical texts in the Ming dynasty. He is particularly well remembered for his role in the medical world of Fujian Province, the part of China which had the closest trade relations with Japan through much of the medieval and early modern periods.[4] In 1528, Xiong's *Mingfang lei zheng yishu daquan* (Encyclopedia of Medicine) became the first medical book printed in Japan (Xiong 1988).[5]

Asai no Sōzui (?–1531), the publisher of this text in Japan, was a gynecologist in Sakai with a deep interest in Confucianism. In addition to the *Encyclopedia of Medicine*, he also organized for one of the first printings in Japan of *Confucius Analects*, which occurred the year after he died. Sōzui's social status as a Zen monk was typical of both medical practitioners and those with an interest in Confucianism in the early sixteenth century. Like many other medical practitioners, he had probably been drawn out of his home monastery, Daitokuji, in order to service the great need for doctors that arose in the Warring States period. At the time his specialization in gynecology was closely related to the treatment of battle wounds, both forms of medicine focused on dealing with loss of blood and invasive situations (Sugimoto 1989: 214).[6]

Just as the foundations for a widespread and systematic approach to medicine had been laid in China in times of war (during the conflict between the Southern Song and the Mongols in the late thirteenth century), so too in Japan the foundations for the systemization of medical knowledge lay in the Warring States period of the fifteenth and sixteenth centuries. And just as this systematic approach to medicine was then institutionalized in China under the pax-Mongolia (the stable warrior rule of the Mongol Yuan dynasty), so too a systematized approach to medicine came to be institutionalized in Japan under the pax-Tokugawa (the stable warrior rule of the Edo shogunate).

While Asai and many others in his time remained monks, later in that century, doctors began to secularize, leaving the clergy and instead establishing lineage-based private schools which served both individual and samurai house patrons. The rise of Confucianism within a similar private school culture deepened the institutional links between Confucianism and medicine. Many of the Confucian private schools which emerged in the early seventeenth century began as side-ventures of medical families. Many of the most well-known Confucians of the Edo period were doctors, or from doctor families. Itō Jinsai and Ogyū Sorai are the most famous examples (Yoshikawa 1983).

Furthermore, through most of the Tokugawa period the development and categorization of medical knowledge and theory followed Confucian frameworks. This is clearly illustrated in some of the most famous popular Tokugawa medical texts, for instance those written by Kaibara Ekken. Kaibara's popular health manual *Yōjōkun*, published widely in 1713, was an instruction manual for how to lead a healthy life. The contents of the book covered general health advice, diet, hygiene, disease prevention, basic pharmacology and the use of drugs, geriatric medicine, pediatrics, acupuncture, and heat therapy. All of this, however, was couched in overtly Neo-Confucian terms, emphasizing the control of *qi* in a Neo-Confucian framework as the overall object of medical knowledge (Saigusa 1956: 27–33).

This is to be expected given that the Chinese Song dynasty Li Zhu approach to medicine underlay most systematic understandings of medicine in the early Tokugawa period and also provided the basis for standardizing and organizing the eclectic array of medical knowledge which the later Tokugawa state institutionalized in its state academies from the late eighteenth century. The importation of Li Zhu approaches to Japan is associated with the Confucian Ashikaga School graduate Tashiro Sanki's (1473–1544) study visit in Ming China between 1487 and 1489 (KISS 72: 28). The Li Zhu approach was a theorization of medicine based in the metaphysics of Song Confucianism, and theoretically integrated within it. Japanese reforms to the Li Zhu approach at the end of the seventeenth century also occurred in parallel with reforms in Confucian theory. Reform to the Li Zhu system in Japan was identified with Chinese models of an "Ancient Learning" school of medicine. Japanese doctors in turn associated this movement in medical theory with Neo-Classicist "Ancient Learning" schools of Confucianism rising at the same time in Japan. For example, Gotō Konzan (1659–1733), one of the notable leaders of this movement of medical reform, specifically located his criticism of Song-Yuan medicine and revival of late Han period medicine in relation to Itō Jinsai's attacks on Neo-Confucian Song learning and attempts to revive Han period Confucianism to replace it (Fujikawa 1941: 280–2, 342–3; Tsuji 2013: 41–52).

Gotō's most famous and influential student, Kagawa Shūan (1683–1755), also studied Confucianism under Itō Jinsai and portrayed his continuation of Gotō's reformist "Ancient Learning" approach to medicine as a wing of the Confucian Ancient Learning movement led by Itō (Machi 1999: 52). The introduction to his most famous medical treatise, *Kōyu igen*, opens with Kagawa discussing his study under Itō and Gotō and explaining the link between Confucianism and medicine in his own choice of study.

The thousands of words of the wise and sagely all ultimately revolve around the cultivation of the self (Jp. *shūshin*, Ch. *xiushen*). So why do some not cultivate themselves? The core of the matter is people need to be free of sickness in order to cultivate themselves. If their self/body is sick, then they cannot practice loyalty and filial piety. So how can they be healed (KISS 65: 21)?

He explains how this question led him from Itō Jinsai's Confucian school to go and study medicine with Gotō. The very practical outlook seen in early modern medical texts was thus sometimes intimately related to a wish to practically realize the Confucian Way.[7] Not only the rise of the Ancient Learning approach (*kohōgaku*) but also the rise of evidentialist learning (*kōshōgaku*) approaches were articulated in Confucian terms and paralleled Confucian developments. Importantly, however, despite often being represented as competing schools, all these tendencies cooperated with and influenced each other, and also interacted with scholars and doctors who identified themselves as experts in Western (Dutch) medicine (Kosato 2014: 178–206). The development of the trajectories of academic discourse in medicine thus followed Confucian trends and were argued in Confucian terms.

The theoretical context of medicine in early modern Japan, as in medieval and early modern China, was thus firmly Confucian. The main difference between the Chinese and Japanese cases was the role of the state. Confucianism saw the state as obliged to play a role in the welfare of the people, and medicine was one area particularly emphasized. Confucian medical theory in China assumed a state role. The orthodox, standardized medical practices which emerged in China from the thirteenth century were linked to the central position of Confucian learning in the state, and the consequent state institutionalization of knowledge. Chen Ziming, for instance, was professor of medicine at the state Confucian academy in Jiankang (Nanjing) County. He had grown up in a medical family business, but used his position in this famous Confucian academy to argue for an empire wide standardization of medicine. Xue Ji, the Ming figure whose medical commentaries would influence late Tokugawa state medical orthodoxy, was in his own time a doctor to the Chinese emperor and a professor at the imperial medical academy – a state institution established by the Ming state along the lines of classical Confucian models. In China, from the beginnings of the standardization of medicine in the late Song early Yuan, through into the Ming, there was a clear awareness of a Confucian idealized model of state stewardship of medicine, and occasional attempts by the state to replicate this model.

Yet in the sixteenth- and seventeenth-century period in which Chinese medicine was standardized in Japan along Song, Yuan, and Ming models, there was little to no attention to the role of the state, and little state involvement. As the Tokugawa period progressed, however, independent Confucian scholars, as well as the state under Confucian influence, began to show interest in the Confucian ideal and looked to realize integration of the realms of knowledge and governance in various ways.

Confucianism and state institutionalization of knowledge

Between the early eighteenth and early nineteenth centuries, the Tokugawa shogunate began to take a more active approach to knowledge. This approach began under the rule of Shogun Tokugawa Yoshimune in the Kyōhō Reforms (1716–1745) and was reinvigorated and considerably expanded under the rule of Matsudaira Sadanobu during the Kansei Reforms (1787–1793). The Kansei government's institutionalization of this state approach to knowledge meant that there continued to be a meaningful state engagement with knowledge through the course of the early nineteenth century. Below I will divide discussion of the development of state intervention in the knowledge field in two periods: the 1720s to 1780s period beginning with the Kyōhō Reforms, and the 1780s to 1850s period beginning with the Kansei Reforms. I see these two periods being divided by differing approaches to the institutionalization of knowledge, which I argue was a far more expansive and sustained strategy in the second period of reform.

1720s–1820s

Shogun Tokugawa Yoshimune's Kyōhō Reforms were motivated primarily by a need to set the finances of the Tokugawa shogunate in order, thereby putting the shogunate in a better position to deal with national emergencies, notably famine, where shogunal leadership was expected. Economic historians agree that by the beginning of the eighteenth century, the Tokugawa state finance system's reliance on rice taxation was causing a structural decline in real state revenue (taxation revenue as a percentage of overall economic activity). This was because from this period, rice's share of the overall economic activity of Japan had begun to shrink dramatically, as both the population leveled and the production of other goods rapidly increased. Shogun Tokugawa Yoshimune's reforms in large part tried to address this problem. Some of the wide range of measures attempted, however, had significant consequences for the state's engagement with knowledge.

Firstly, Yoshimune attempted to reform taxation and other bureaucratic instruments to gain a more reliable flow of funds for the state. Some of these financial reforms, for instance the taxation policy of *agemai*, proved serviceable in the short term, but they were not sustained and therefore proved ineffective in the long term (Hayami and Saito 2004: 192–200). Secondly, the reforms looked to prop up the value of currency, partly by limiting the export of bullion outside Japan. To achieve this second aim, Yoshimune looked to replace imports with indigenous production. This led to the establishment of state-led, supervised, and/or encouraged industries in silk, tobacco, sugar, and ginseng during the Reform period. Until this point, these products had often needed to be imported into Japan in exchange for bullion, notably Japanese mined silver and copper. The industry policies stimulating the production of silk, tobacco, sugar, and ginseng were sustained for long enough to establish industries, so that by the end of the century, imports had indeed been significantly reduced, often to zero (Toby 2008: 167–82).

This reform agenda is often associated with Confucianism because the general trend of these policies emerged under the growing influence of

Confucian political advisors in the shogunate. Yoshimune was the first shogun to include professional Confucians among his inner circle of policy advisors. Much has been made of the significance and effects of the advice of Arai Hakuseki in particular during this period (Nakai 1988). Other famous Confucians like Muro Kyūso were also consulted on political economy issues during this time. Indeed, Muro is regarded as responsible for the temporary attempt during this period to stop using currency devaluation as the prime financial policy, and instead introduce taxation reform (Hayami and Saito 2004: 198). Confucianism thus played a role in providing the knowledge professionals who set much of the policy agenda of these reforms.

Medicine again provides a good example of the role of Confucianism in these early eighteenth-century reforms. Of the main commodities targeted for local production under the reform, several were associated with medical efficacy. The economic policy of import substitution was thus related to another branch of the Kyōhō Reform agenda: that of social welfare. The general Confucian contours of the reforms called on the rectification of government finances in large part so the government would be in a position to successfully fulfill their obligations in times of famine: both through providing monetary relief to local areas affected by famine and other disasters (as they did particularly effectively in 1732) and also through direct provision of medical care (Hayami and Saito 2004: 206).

The creation of local production capacity for commodities associated with pharmaceuticals and the direct provision of medical care by the shogunate were both supported through Yoshimune's establishment of shogunal pharmaceutical production facilities in the form of herb gardens at Komaba and Koishikawa in 1721 and the establishment of public hospitals in shogunal-controlled territory, notably the Yōjōsho, a public hospital established in 1722 also at Koishikawa in outer Edo.[8] This hospital was established primarily to care for those ill as a result of extreme impoverishment. On the outskirts of Edo, this group was largely made up of famine refugees coming in from the countryside. The herb gardens were productive and played a role in replacing imports. The hospital was an important symbol of state responsibility for the health of commoners and would also prove an example for later state institutionalization of medicine, in particular, and overseas knowledge, in general (Andō 2005).[9]

The state's choice of establishment of herb gardens as an initial point of intervention in the medical field was also related to a vision of pharmaceuticals as a particularly practical field of medicine, and a general tendency of state interventions in medicine to be designed to encourage more practically oriented and functional systems. This push toward practicality was voiced most clearly by Neo-Confucian inclined doctors and articulated in Confucian terms. For instance, Kagawa Shūan in the introduction to his book on pharmaceuticals, *Ippondō yakusen* [Pharmaceutical Selections of the Ippon School], wrote,

"The artisan who wishes to do his work well, must first sharpen his tools."[10] These are undoubtedly the words of the sage. There has never been anyone in all history who has managed to do their work well without first sharpening their tools [thereby making them more effective]. Therefore, medical doctors who wish to practice well must first select their pharmaceuticals (KISS 68: 321).

The Kyōhō Reform engagement with medicine, however, was limited. The herb gardens and the hospital were the only major examples of medicine-related institutions run by the state before the Kansei Reforms (before the 1780s). Moreover, the state during the first period of intervention relied for the staffing of these institutions and their management on non-state structures and personnel. For instance, the hospital was staffed by so-called town doctors (*machi'i*) not trained, regulated, or permanently employed by the state. Although there was a state official overseeing it (a magistrate *bugyō*), the administration was left in the hands of the town doctors who also carried on their own private medical practices as their main forms of business. New institutions like the herb gardens and hospitals were thus established using hereditary lineage structures of administration, with the shogunate from the beginning putting a certain clan in charge of each of these institutions.

This resembled the state's institutionalized systems for the management of information at first contact in the port city of Nagasaki through which almost all Chinese and Western medical texts and techniques were imported. The management of information in the port areas had since the seventeenth century been left predominantly in the hands of the shogunal offices of the Chinese Interpreters (*tōtsūji*) and Dutch Interpreters (*oran-datsūji*). These offices were officially part of the Shogunate administrative structure, controlled under the Shogunal office of Nagasaki City Magistrate. But like the "town doctors" working in Edo, they operated predominantly independently, and also had their own private businesses which took up most of their time and energy. The head positions in the interpreters offices were inherited and the offices were administered on a day-to-day basis through family structures. The knowledge attained in the work of these offices (for instance about Dutch medicine) was employed by these clans primarily for their own commercial interests – for instance, through the sale of drugs and drug recipes. Their private schools, charging tuition, were a further important part of many clans' businesses, using knowledge gained through their privileged public position primarily for private gain (Honma 2009: 112–13).

Annick Horiuchi has argued that Edo-based scholars of "Dutch Learning" deliberately underplayed the role of Nagasaki interpreters, and that is why their role in providing Dutch medical knowledge is seldom acknowledged (Horiuchi 2003: 166–70). This is true, and it further also seems likely that the Nagasaki interpreter families themselves contributed to this situation by not publicizing the information on Dutch medicine they had (Honma 2009). The reason for that is simple: making knowledge public in the manner of so-called "Dutch Learning" scholars would break Nagasaki interpreters' monopoly on control of information as a commodity. The interpreters' position in the Tokugawa state system meant that their control of special foreign knowledge was famous, which is why people from Kaibara Ekken onwards went down to Nagasaki to get it from them. The Nagasaki interpreters had no need to build up an image of themselves as the Dutch Learning experts as Sugita Genpaku did. I would suggest this is why they were not identified as names in that movement: they already had reputations built on their position which enabled them to sell knowledge so long as that knowledge was exclusive enough to be sellable. In a sense, this was a function of the combination of them having state position, but no related requirement to provide information to the state.

Knowledge of Chinese language and trade conditions, vital for shogunate-controlled trade with China, was similarly initially left in the hands of certain families of "Chinese interpreters" (*tōtsūji*) who served the Tokugawa shogunate as interpreters, low-level diplomats, and customs officers. Other shogunate institutions did not have regular, sustained, or systematic access to the significant knowledge and information raised by the Chinese and Dutch Interpreter Offices in Nagasaki. In this early Tokugawa system, including during and after the Kyōhō Reforms, the state did not actively manage the knowledge professionals who were nominally in its service. They were not structurally integrated into any larger state-sponsored knowledge networks, nor were there any other administrative structures which could exploit the knowledge they attained.

The large Confucian and medical academies in Edo associated with the state were, until the Kansei Reforms, under even less control. In the case of medicine, the shogunate had since the early eighteenth century come to be associated with the Seiju School of Medicine of the Taki clan. For most of the eighteenth century, however, this school remained in the hands of that family, continuing to be run, all be it with shogunal patronage, for the private profit and continuation of the Taki clan itself. This paralleled the model of the position of the Hayashi clan school as the "official" shogunate Confucian school. It was still a private school, open to all paying customers, independent, simply with a history of shogunal patronage. This exemplifies the rather strange situation, by modern standards, where even though receiving shogunal patronage and vassal stipends, servants like the Hayashi and the Taki would spend most of their time attending to other private clients in their schools, in a business which the shogunate did not control, and with little sharing of information or any other significant practical cooperation with other state agencies. This situation had been openly criticized by Confucian scholars in popular published work already in the early eighteenth century, for instance in Ogyū Sorai's "Discourse on Government" (*Seidan*) (NST 36: 439–40).

Employment of knowledge professionals, including in the vital business of successfully turning knowledge into technique, thus occurred on a case-by-case basis. Sometimes, like under Shogun Tokugawa Yoshimune, on a relatively large scale, but not within a long-term institutionalized structure. There were some institutions created, for instance the Koishikawa Botanical Gardens, but they were not linked to other institutions in an overarching framework. This meant that when Yoshimune left power, and the advisors he had patronized left office or died, then the trend to employ knowledge in this way lapsed. Yoshimune's far-reaching reforms still worked primarily within the Tokugawa feudal system of lordly patronage. They were not institutionalized beyond the person of the liege lord. As a result, state reforms or innovations in the knowledge field under feudal rule were susceptible to quick reversal.

1780s–1850s

Attention to the institutionalization of knowledge within reformed structures of the state had to wait until the end of the eighteenth century. They began in earnest with the Kansei Reforms of Tokugawa Yoshimune's grandson, the shogunal regent Matsudaira Sadanobu in the 1790s. Beginning with the Confucian Academy, and moving on to medical and other academies, the Kansei Reforms (1787–1793) sought to systematically standardize, regulate, and expand state knowledge institutions. The shogunate under Matsudaira Sadanobu, and in the decades after he stepped down as shogunal regent, established direct state control over family schools which had traditional associations with the shogunate. As we will see later, state takeover often involved replacing the heads of the academies, displacing the hereditary leaders to introduce new practices. These reforms also ordered restrictions on the student population of the academies, creating more exclusive institutions whose education was directed toward serving the state's interests in creating a cadre of trained state doctors and administrators for public service. In short, the academies were directed toward public rather than private aims.

The first target of institutional reform was the Hayashi family Confucian Academy, which would come to be turned into an officially shogunate-controlled state Confucian Academy using the new official name of Shōheizaka Gakumonjo. In 1790, Matsudaira Sadanobu forced the Head of the Hayashi clan and school, Hayashi Kinpō, to employ Shibano Ritsuzan and Okada Kanzen as "assistants." From this point, these men of humble background were in a position to dictate terms to Hayashi Kinpō when it came to matters of academy management. Official shogunate proclamations from the period, while on the one hand presenting a rose-tinted historicization of the Hayashi clan, simultaneously publicly undercut Hayashi political control of the contemporary academy by demanding that Hayashi Kinpō "consult carefully" his "veteran" colleagues Shibano Ritsuzan and Okada Kanzen.

From His Lordship Governor of Etchui Matsudaira To Rector of Education Hayashi [Kinpō]
Inasmuch as the learning of Zhu Xi has enjoyed the confidence of successive generations of the ruling house since Keichō [1596–1614], and inasmuch as your house has for successive generations been charged with maintaining the aforementioned academic tradition, it might be expected to allow no remissness in its application to the orthodox learning and in the advancement of its students. However, in recent times a variety of novel doctrines have been preached abroad, and in some cases the prevalence of heterodoxy has ruined public morals. If this is really due to a decline of orthodoxy, it is altogether inexcusable. It has come to our attention that even among your students some are found occasionally whose scholarship is impure in the manner described above. What is the explanation for this? Now you are commanded to exercise a strict control over the Sage's Hall; and since Shibano Hikosuke [Ritsuzan] and Okada Kiyosuke [Kansen] have also been commanded to perform this task, you are to consult with them carefully on the content of this order and sternly forbid heterodoxy to the students. Further, you shall not confine it to your own school but shall make every effort to reach an agreement with other schools to pursue the orthodox learning and to advance men of ability. Kansei 2 [1790], 5th month, 24th day (Backus 1974: 118).

This letter is a good example of how Matsudaira sought to use new appointments to usurp Hayashi family authority in the Confucian Academy. As Makabe Jin has shown, not only through reference to the above letter but also a line of follow-up correspondence between Matsudaira and Hayashi Kinpō thereafter, through the early 1790s, Matsudaira Sadanobu systematically usurped Hayashi clan authority over their old school (Makabe 2007: 12, 108).

In 1793, when Kinpō died, as the last Hayashi family head and without progeny, Matsudaira Sadanobu seized the opportunity to position a young scholar from a leading samurai noble house, in fact one of his own relatives, as the newly appointed head of the Hayashi Academy. Matsudaira had this young man, born in 1768 as Matsudaira Norihira, the third son of the Iwamura domain lord Matsudaira Norimori, officially adopted as the new heir to the patriarchal leadership of the Hayashi house. Norihira then became known as Hayashi Jussai, and acted as figurehead leader of the Academy over the next half century. In reality, as the recently published daily records of the Academy in this period make clear, Shibano Ritsuzan, Okada Kanzen, and later appointees like Koga Seiri carried out the actual management and active reform agenda of the academy (Hashimoto 2007).

In 1788, soon after being appointed as regent, Matsudaira Sadanobu had the fifty-three-year-old Shibano Ritsuzan installed as Confucian advisor to the shogunate. Until about three years before then, Shibano had been based in the Kansai, where he had run private schools in Kyoto and Osaka. His only previous government experience was a brief stint as a Confucian advisor to the domain lord of Tokushima in the 1760s. Matsudaira Sadanobu knew him through his scholarly reputation in the private sphere, notably from his influential *Memorial* (*Ritsuzan Jōsho*), an unsolicited policy advice document which appears to have been reasonably widely distributed in manuscript form (Paramore 2012b; Takimoto 1914). Although much has been made of Shibano's later profile as an advocate of Neo-Confucian orthodoxy, he had a diverse array of associates in Osaka and Kyoto who are often associated with unorthodox and/or eclectic forms of Confucianism.[11] Matsudaira was appointing someone who was very much an Edo outsider, but deeply connected with the dense networks of private learning and political debate through the rest of the country, particularly the networks in Western Japan centered around the Kansai area.

Matsudaira Sadanobu saw this newly reformed Shogunal Confucian Academy as one element in a national plan for research and education intended to shake up Japan and push learning to the center of government administration – both in the shogunate and in the domains. As we see in the edict on heterodox learning quoted above, Matsudaira articulated the hope that the form of curriculum standardization carried out at the Shogunal Confucian Academy would also be picked up in the many domainal government academies. The line about "advancing men of ability" relates to the role of schools in government appointment, and therefore implies something made clearer in other writings, that he hoped domainal government academies would follow the central Confucian academy not only in academic practice but also in playing a key role in government appointment (Tsujimoto 1990: 207).

In addition to trying to influence domainal academies indirectly, Matsudaira's reforms also directly targeted the non-Confucian shogunal academies with reform agendas almost identical to those he carried out in the Confucian Academy. One example is the medical Academy. In 1791, in parallel with what was happening to the Hayashi academy, the Seijukan Academy of the Taki clan was brought under the direct administrative control of the shogunate and renamed the Igakukan (literally: the Hall of Medical Studies). The teachers of this medical academy became part of the bureaucratic structure of the shogunate, with a high-level shogunate official, a *Metsuke* (Inspector – equivalent roughly to a departmental undersecretary), in charge (Mori 1933: 209). Just as in the case of the Shogunal Confucian Academy, the establishment of this Shogunal Medical Academy as a state institute saw an influx of newly appointed teachers from outside the Edo establishment, primarily former "town doctors" from Western Japan. As with the likes of Shibano Ritsuzan in the case of the Confucian Academy, these medical imports from the Kansai were also often given Tokugawa retainer status and thus elevated not only into the capital and state service but also into the samurai caste and the retainership of the ruling Tokugawa family (Machi 1999a: 359; *Kan'ikafu*). Just as in the case of the Confucian Academy, the nationalization of the Medical Academy also brought with it the exclusion of private students from day classes or special dormitories, with the academy instead concentrating on the education of those who would directly serve the shogunate, and thereby the public. Examinations were also introduced following a system similar to that used at the Confucian academy (Mori 1933: 213, 224).

Another shogunal academy favored and reformed under Matsudaira Sadanobu was the Astronomical Institute (*Tenmonkata*). Unlike the medical and Confucian academies, the Astronomical Institute had been a unit under direct shogunal control since the seventeenth century. However, it had been in repeated conflicts with the *Onmyō* (Yin and Yang) office of the imperial aristocracy in Kyoto. The conflict was about which institution should compile the official state calendars. As in many other traditional societies, creation of calendars was considered a core duty of the state in Tokugawa Japan. Astronomical knowledge allowed calendar makers to make more accurate predictions of celestial events, and thus more effective calendars. Matsudaira Sadanobu intervened decisively in favor of the Shogunal Astronomical Institute in this conflict and ordered the use of the newest Western techniques in the creations of the Kansei calendars. To this end in 1795, he had Takahashi Yoshitoki (1764–1804) appointed to take over running the Astronomical Institute. Takahashi Yoshitoki was one of the first scholars in Japan to study, apply, and publish upon Johannes Kepler's theories. Matsudaira also had the Astronomical Institute carry out more and wider research roles. This began a trend which eventually led to Takahashi Yoshitoki's son, Takahashi Kageyasu (1785–1829), founding the *Bansho wage goyō* (barbarian [Western] documents translation service) in 1811, an institute specializing in the translation of Western knowledge.

Tokugawa state knowledge institutions and Westernization

Astronomical Institute scholars like Takahashi Yoshitoki and Takahashi Kageyasu were appointed into state offices only in part to carry out their primary job of making more accurate predictions of celestial events. Their ability to read Western texts was also regarded in and of itself as an important and useful form of knowledge – not just for science, but also from a military intelligence perspective. Through the turn of the eighteenth into the nineteenth century, the shogunate paid increasing attention to geopolitical developments relating to Western expansion and imperialism. Astronomy Institute scholars were often the first port of call for translations and analysis of documents, maps, and other objects from the West – which came not only directly through the Dutch but also quite often through China. In order to directly service this requirement, Takahashi Kageyasu in 1811 presided over the creation of the *Bansho wage goyō* (barbarian [Western] documents translation service). The appointment of the Takahashis in the Astronomical Institute, the way they were utilized in that institution, and the way they in turn developed it demonstrate the importance of Western knowledge in the Confucian-inspired shogunal knowledge reforms of the late eighteenth and early nineteenth centuries (Mitani 2006: 30–6).

Another similar perspective can be seen in the way the shogunate administered the Medical Academy and standardized the teaching of medicine once it took control. In the eighteenth century, the Taki clan medical school had already standardized their medical education along the lines indicated by orthodox works of the Ming scholar Xue Ji, using his medical textbooks as base. "Ancient Learning" approaches to medicine championed by Gotō and Kagawa in the early eighteenth century were strong, but they were integrated into a canon of texts with a diverse range of scholarly approaches seen in late imperial Chinese medicine and reflected and developed in Japan.[12] However, shogunate control also called for the integration of Western medical techniques in the education offered by the Shogunal Medical Academy. Under state control, the Shogunal Medical Academy thereby came to teach a standard Chinese medical curriculum, beginning first with study of the Neo-Confucian Four Books and Five Classics, before moving on to study classic medical texts from the Han period onward, but then also supplemented with Western technique. Even the *Igakukan gakuki* rules of the school alluded to this approach.

Of course the *Suwen* (Basic Questions), *Lingshu* (Spiritual Pivot), *Bencao* (Herb Canon) and the *Nanjing* (81 Nanjing) are the ancient medical classics, and thus must be honored and studied. The *Shanghan lun* (Treatise on Cold Damage Disorders) and the *Jingui yaolue* (Essential Prescriptions from the Golden Cabinet) belong to the teachings of the ancient sages and like the Six Confucian Classics, *Confucian Analects* and *Mencius* they should be read thoroughly. However, because the nature of illness constantly changes, if one does not add to this other effective measures found far and wide, then one may lack detailed knowledge of excellent treatments. With this in mind, alongside [the classics] one should consult books from the Jin, Sui and Tang dynasties, as well as those of the Song, Yuan, Ming and Qing. If we follow developments in the world and consider changes in medical trends then we can ever expand our knowledge, and in the words of Sun Zhenren, our medical knowledge will never be stagnant (Mori 1933: 217–18).

The importance of the ongoing study of Western technique at the Shogunal Medical Academy is attested to by their production of Dutch medical and Dutch-language texts, like medical dictionaries (Aoki 2012). Examination of the nature of these dictionaries, in particular their manuscript form and phonographic script, suggest that these dictionaries were prepared by Japanese with knowledge of spoken Dutch – possibly Nagakasi interpreters.[13] The dictionary, compiled and kept in the Shogunal Medical Academy, the *Igakukan*, shows the *Igakukan* had an interest in a book emphasizing ability to comprehend spoken Dutch pronunciation of pharmaceutical terms (including common Dutch pronunciation of Latin). Although there are reports of spoken Dutch being used in some Western Learning and medical schools in Japan, the only place where Dutch was being spoken at this time by someone who did not also understand Japanese medical terminology was Nagasaki – the only port open to Western shipping, and of course that Western shipping was Dutch. The nature of the dictionary thus indicates it likely to have been produced by Japanese with good knowledge of Chinese medicine and Dutch medicine, based in Nagasaki, and with regular access to spoken Dutch. The most obvious candidates are thus the Nagasaki interpreters.

And intriguingly, here lies the connection with the Confucian institutions of the state. Nagasaki interpreters were indeed regularly present in

Edo from the early nineteenth century – under shogunal orders. Surprisingly, they were not assigned in Edo to serve in the Medical Academy, the Astronomical Institute, or the office of barbarian translation which has arisen out of the Astronomical Institute. Rather, they lodged in and offered classes at the Shogunal Confucian Academy (Figure 4.1) on the Shōheizaka (Hashimoto 2007). This casts light on the increasingly pivotal role that the Confucian Academy came to have in the analysis of foreign intelligence in the years after the nationalization of the academy. Makabe Jin wrote an important book in 2007 in which he devoted over 600 pages to consideration of the role of the Shogunal Confucian Academy in foreign affairs and research. He did this primarily by tracing the service of three generations of Koga family members through the Confucian Academy: Koga Seiri (1750–1817), his son Tōan (1788–1847), and his son Kin'ichirō (1816–1884). Kin'ichirō even learned Dutch. The interest in the West, however, had begun already with Seiri.

Koga Seiri wrote an influential treatise warning of possible encroachment on Japan's autonomy by foreign, Western (particularly Russian) imperial ambitions, and advising the shogunate what action they should take to prevent it. *Kyokuron jiji fūji* (*A Secret Memorial on the Urgency of Current Affairs*) was one of the first political treatises to systematically address the Western threat issue.[14] It fits in with a range of other texts on this issue produced around this time such as Miura Baien's *Hekijahitsudoku Samidareshō* (1784), Hayashi Shihei's *Sangoku tsūran zusetu* (1786) and *Kaikoku heidan* (1787), and the Mito scholar Fujita Yūkoku's *Seimeiron* (1791). Koga Seiri's thesis, like Hayashi Shihei's works, was an advice on how to hold back foreign incursions. The manner through which Koga advised the shogunate to do that, however, is striking in its reformist nature. Koga recommended a diplomatically and militarily expansive policy including engagement with Western technology, arguing that the shogunate should "employ the barbarians to assault the barbarians" (Takimoto 1914: 185). This was his recommended approach to the problem of potential Western threat as early as the end of the eighteenth century. His third son and later head of the Shōheizaka Academy, Koga Tōan (1788–1847), continued this work, becoming a major writer on coastal defense alongside his Confucian duties.[15]

In his 1778 treatise on the Western threat, Koga argued that the most urgent reform was to "open the channels of communication" (Koga in Takimoto 1914: 170–2). This was also one of the most important elements of his advice for general reform of the shogunate bureaucracy contained in his most famous political work *Jūjikai* (Koga in Takimoto

1914: 157). In both works, he is referring primarily to communication between different levels of government and society in Japan. In *Jūjikai*, it is clear that what he calls for is a dynamic opening in the capacity of the upper levels to hear the advice of those lower in the hierarchy. In *Kyokuron jiji fūji*, Koga uses this Confucian idea to go further than he does in *Jūjikai* by suggesting the opening of the channels of communication not only as a tool of inter-agency governance but also to imply that the shogunate should seek intelligence and information from outside Japan and outside Asia. This is clear in his recommendation for the development of cannon technology and naval forces (Takimoto 1914: 174–7). Fascinatingly, the textual basis upon which he calls for this "opening the channels of communication" (Ch. *kai yanlu*, Jp. *kai genro (genro wo hiraki)*) is none other than a citation from Cheng Yi, the Song philosopher who, together with his brother Cheng Hao and Zhu Xi, is regarded as one of three founders of Neo-Confucianism (Takimoto 1914: 172; Zhu 1983: 290, 1985: 2449). This early call for Westernization was thus not only quintessentially Confucian, but it was quintessentially Neo-Confucian.

This Confucian base to Koga Seiri's ideas on Westernization is related to the image of China current in Japan at this time. The model at this time for his expansive vision of empire appears to have been not the West, but rather Qing China. Recent publications on the history of the Manchu empire have pointed out how successful it was until quite late in the piece in its program of territorial expansion – or what some have labeled "imperialism."[16] In opening his advice on how to deal with the Western threat in the north by "employing the barbarians to assault the barbarians," Seiri indeed refers to this approach as "the Chinese model" (Takimoto 1914: 185). Koga borrows the "employing the barbarians to assault the barbarians" phrase from the *Book of the Han*, a period in Chinese history often compared to the Qing in terms of the extent of expansionist activity (Fan 1985: 1576, 2281). Indeed, contemporaneously, the Manchu Qing empire was "defending" China exactly through this kind of dynamic territorial expansion bringing it into initially victorious military conflict with Russia – the very same foreign threat that Koga was worried about (Perdue 2005: 138).

The influence of not only classical, Han, Song, and Ming, but also of reasonably contemporary Qing political thinking and writing in the ideas of Koga Seiri is also an interesting point when considering the global manner in which he thought about the political issues facing the shogunate. While on the one hand Koga's openness to Western technologies and recommended policy of competing externally with the Western powers militarily is strikingly different to the image that is usually presented of orthodox Neo-Confucians, it is also interesting to note that

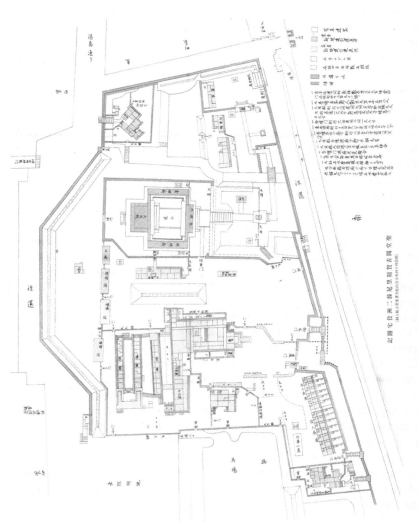

Figure 4.1 Floorplan of the Shogunal Confucian Academy, early nineteenth century (Shibunkai collection).

many influences on this approach to political advice appear to come from an at this time still aggressive and expansive (and Neo-Confucian) Qing China.[17] Unlike in the writing of other early nineteenth-century Japanese Confucians emphasized in secondary literature (for instance, the Mito School), Seiri and his colleagues in the state academy did not at all perceive China as weak, but rather associated Qing China and its Neo-Confucian tradition with global power.

The particular way the influence of late imperial China played out in the writings and advice of the Shōheizaka Academy scholars was in large part determined by their own critical and complex approach to Chinese government and scholarship. Shibano Ritsuzan in his *Memorial*, for example, praised Japanese scholars for translating Tang political treatises and the Ming legal codes as a great contribution to just government on one page, and then condemned mindless copying of Chinese ways on the next (Shibano in Takimoto 1914: 135–6). Shōheizaka Academy scholars on the one hand clearly favored terminology and ideas from Han texts, like those of Ban Gu, regarded as having marked the change in examination curricula from Ming to Qing, while also using Qing-era criticism of evidential learning to condemn the Sorai-ist scholarship in Japan which demanded a return to sole reliance on Han and pre-Han texts. In other words, scholars like Shibano Ritsuzan and Koga Seiri constructed their stance from a mix of positions picked out of the late imperial polemics on Confucian literary and political theory. They were happy to recommend Qing-favored Han dynasty political treatises and histories alongside Ming commentaries on Song Neo-Confucian theory that had been recommended by Korean envoys (Takimoto 1914: 137). Their tastes were diverse, transnational, and trans-dynastic, but clearly primarily late imperial Chinese influenced.

Critically, the approach to knowledge institutionalized at this time, and represented in texts produced and distributed privately, like Shibano Ritsuzan's *Memorial*, but also texts officially associated with the State Academy, like the *Shōheishi*, was two pronged (Kurokawa 1977: 21–3). On the one hand, there was the introduction of a standardized, shared curriculum of ethical education carried out through evidential argument. This was based on a standardized approach to Neo-Confucian learning influenced by Song, Ming, and Qing commentators and providing the "orthodoxy" often mentioned in relation to the Kansei Reforms – the standardization of knowledge necessary for communication across different sections of society and the cooperative implementation as technique.

As Shibano made abundantly clear, however, this shared corpus of a standardized body of base ethical knowledge was designed to create a shared ethic, an underlying sense of solidarity among the bureaucratic strata, over which would be lain the development of a range of their own specialist areas of knowledge. This emphasis on developing specialist knowledge among the members of the bureaucratic strata, in fields as diverse as traditional fighting techniques and the reading of Dutch texts, was the other important strand of the reformers' educational doctrine. Specialist knowledge, and thereby specialization, was something emphasized by Ritsuzan in his initial memorial to the shogunate, taken up in the organization of the academy, strengthened by its evidential approach to knowledge, and best exemplified by the championing of non-Confucian knowledge by Seiri's Koga family descendants in the Shogunal Confucian and Western learning academies.

The natural development of this outlook was clearly visible in the role Shogunate Confucian Academy scholars after this generation continued to play in informing the international outlook of the Shogunate. Koga Tōan, Seiri's son, published famous texts on naval defense as well as advising the shogunate (Maeda 1996: 396–440; Mitani 2003: 30–40). His son, Koga Kin'ichirō (1816–1884), was educated in Dutch as well as Confucianism and would go on to serve in the Confucian Academy a similar capacity as his father, partly as an expert on external affairs, before in 1856 being appointed the first Head of the Barbarian Documents Research Center (*bansho shirabesho*), which shortly thereafter became the Shogunal Institute of Western Learning.

Confucian knowledge institutions and Meiji modernization

Research on modern Japanese history often highlights the role of the Shogunal Institute of Western Learning. Officially first called the "Barbarian Documents Research Center" (*bansho shirabesho*), and in 1863 renamed the "Practical Learning Center" (*kaiseijo*), it was far more than a translation center. This shogunal institute and school was the main point of advice for the government on foreign affairs, provided interpreters and translators for all official tasks, and established a number of departments for the study of different aspects of practical learning from the West. The first major treaties between Western powers and the Japanese government were negotiated with advisors and interpreters from this institute. The major role of many graduates and teachers from this academy in the modernization and Westernization of Meiji Japan is often commented upon. Leading educators, scientists, bureaucrats, and politicians of Meiji Japan who trace lines back to the Barbarian Documents Research Center include the early Meiji Finance and External Affairs Minister Terashima Muneyori (1832–1893), the naval reformer Akamatsu Yoshinori (1841–1920), the chemist Kawamoto Kōmin (1810–1871), the statistician, bureaucrat, and legal scholar Sugi

Kōji (1828–1917), the scholar-bureaucrats Nishi Amane (1829–1897) and Tsuda Mamichi (1829–1903), the later President of the University of Tokyo and Privy Councillor Katō Hiroyuki (1836–1916), bureaucrat, politician, and President of the House of Councillors Tsuji Shinji (1842–1915) as well as many others.

Yet modern historians often overlook its Confucian roots. The Barbarian Documents Research Center was a direct outshoot of the Shogunal Confucian Academy, its director and early staff being appointed out of it. Most of the major figures associated with the Barbarian Documents Research Center in the Meiji period, including later appointments, were educated first in Confucian academies. Indeed recent studies into many of these figures' activities in the modern period have emphasized the role of Confucian thought in their interpretations of modern techniques and Western political systems (Sugawara 2009). The roles of some of these people post-1868 will be discussed further in the next chapter. Most members of the influential Meiroku group of scholar bureaucrats in the 1870s, for instance, were former students of either the Shogunal Confucian Academy or the Barbarians Documents Research Center (Kōno 2011).

Another effect of Tokugawa Confucianism in Meiji modernization, however, was simply institutional. The expansion of state academies and the new approach to state involvement in knowledge led by the Shogunate in the Kansei Reforms was replicated in the domains, as had been Matsudaira Sadanobu's intention. The late eighteenth and early nineteenth centuries thus saw not only an important expansion in the number of domainal state academies but also saw them increasingly conform to a unified approach of tuition set by the Shogunal Academy in Edo (Figure 4.2) (Ishikawa 1960: 258–9). This simple act of dissemination of state academies and standardization of language and method of instruction was an important precedent. Later Meiji state schools would have students use English to study Western technique, displacing Chinese. But the basic method of having students learn a foreign language to process technique and information was similar. There was also an even more direct institutional link between the Confucian domainal academies and the modern system of education: the modern Normal Schools often occupied the buildings of the former domainal Confucian academies, often also appropriating parts of their staff. These Normal Schools, teacher training colleges, were the lynchpin of the modern Meiji infrastructure of education and the base from which knowledge of English and capacity to use Western scientific method was spread in the Meiji period (Duke 2009).

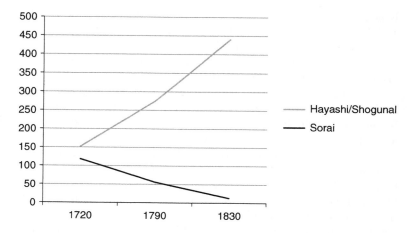

Figure 4.2 Graphic representation of the number of domain state academies associated with different Edo Confucian schools during the Tokugawa period.
Source: Ishikawa 1960: 267–8.

The shogunal institutionalization of knowledge which followed the Kansei Reforms meant that by the mid-nineteenth century, Japan possessed an informal, but standardized and state-supported infrastructure of knowledge institutions, academies, and schools which linked state and non-state centers of knowledge to each other across the country. This infrastructure centered around the shogunal Confucian and other academies and fanned out in the provinces through the domainal schools and academies as well as many private schools. This infrastructure of knowledge was primarily Confucian, not in the sense that Confucianism monopolized the content of learning, but rather because: (1) generalist learning, what we might call the liberal arts basis of learning, including the way it was politically colored, was Confucian, (2) state academies sitting at the center of the web of knowledge institutions identified themselves as Confucian, and (3) the primary language of learning (including the destination of translation for most Western works) was a form of Classical Chinese which in the Japanese context of the time could not be disentangled from the Confucian tradition. In this sense, a broad Confucian knowledge network was in place, and this network provided the basis for the reception of Western ideas, politics, science and technology.

This infrastructure of knowledge had moreover produced a cadre of thousands of educated Japanese who would be the human conduit through which the onslaught of Westernization and modernization after the 1850s would be mediated. These people did not all identify themselves as Confucian, but they all shared a Confucian education and thereby expressed themselves in a vocabulary reflecting that background. One could argue, and many good scholars have, that they mediated the reception of Western modernity through the lens of the eclectic Confucian knowledge framework in which they had grown up (Matsuda 2008; Ōkubo 2010; Sugawara 2009; Watanabe 2012). As we will see in the next chapter, the Confucian imprint in this mediation and reception, particularly when related to politics, was palpable.

5   Confucianism as liberalism

> Money is provided and medicine, clothes and food sought for the
> sustenance of vagrants. Ah, here [Massachusetts] benevolent govern-
> ance surpasses that of China or Japan!
>
> (Niijima Shimeta (later Niijima Jō) in an 1867 letter to his father (Niijima
> 1977: 17))

Modern academic writing has a long tradition of portraying
Confucianism as inherently opposed to the politics of Western modernity. Writing on modern Japanese history often locates Japanese resistance to political Westernization, notably including democracy and
liberalism, in the Confucian tradition (Hall 1955; Ooms 1985). Yet the
earliest positive Japanese assessments of Western governance in general,
and democracy, liberalism, and egalitarianism, in particular, were made
through Confucian lenses and argued in Confucian terms by Confucian
scholars. These positive Japanese Confucian assessments of Western
governance were even sometimes arrived at through the mediation of
Qing Chinese writing. The Chinese scholar Xu Jiyu (1795–1873) put
forward a positive Confucian assessment of modern Western civilization
in a tract already published in China in 1850. It was popular enough in
Japan to warrant reprinting there in 1861 (Xu 2000). Just like the scientific and strategic analysis discussed in the previous chapter, Japanese
ideas on governance as late as the Meiji Restoration were arrived at
through a transnational transmission of ideas based in the language of
Classical Chinese and the vocabularies of Confucianism. China was still
the intellectual mid-wife, even at the birth of Meiji Japan's process of
Westernization – a process which would quickly become deeply anti-
Chinese.

  This chapter will focus on the way the legacy of Tokugawa
Confucianism shaped the emergence of the Westernized modern order
in Japan. The basis of late Tokugawa intellectual education was
Confucian and the core of the Confucian message transmitted was political. It should therefore come as no surprise that the field of human

activity over which Confucianism demonstrated the most sustained influence through the dramatic transformation of Japan to a modern Western-style society was politics. In particular, Japanese approaches to liberalism, the dominant political ideology of late nineteenth-, twentieth-, and twenty-first-century global capitalism, was heavily inflected by Confucianism. This chapter will focus on this Confucian role in the development of Japanese liberalism, looking at how some of the most quintessentially Western and modern models of political thought and institutionalism were reimagined in Japan through Confucianism. Later in the chapter, I will also discuss how Confucianism mediated understandings of the link between liberalism and capitalism, and in conclusion, I will touch briefly upon how Confucianism even played some role in the initial reception of socialism. This chapter will thus consider the role of the Confucian legacy in shaping Japanese reception and acceptance of Western political modernity, as well as its role in influencing early Japanese imaginations of forms of resistance to the global capitalism with which Western modernity was and is so closely intertwined.

The following three chapters will thus portray a Confucianism which functioned to some extent as a form of Tokugawa shogunate memory, inspiring critical engagements with modernity and capitalism, just as Confucianism had earlier served to inspire critical engagement with the feudal system under the Tokugawa shogunate. In both cases, Confucianism was used both to imagine resistance to the dominant paradigms of the time, while simultaneously providing the frameworks for understanding and thereby integrating those paradigms into Japanese society and culture.

Western statecraft as Confucian system

Japan's forced opening of ports to the Americans and other Western powers from the mid-1850s onward was accompanied by a rising tide of nationalism. This nationalism was connected with the Confucian tradition through Mito Learning, but by the 1850s rallied around National Learning figures like Hirata Atsutane who identified themselves as anti-Confucian and saw Confucianism as a collaborative ideology with Westernization (Burns 2003; Koschmann 1987; McNally 2005; Wakabayashi 1986). In this sense, Confucianism during this turbulent period was not perceived as particularly anti-Western. Anti-Western sentiment and politics was instead increasingly identified with National Learning, which in turn pitted itself against Confucianism. By contrast to the particularism of National Learning, Confucian universalism, as touched on in the previous chapter, provided a basis for positive engagement with Western science and sociology. Pro-Western sentiment during the 1850s and 1860s period in which anti-Western xenophobia was at its height also tended to be expressed in Confucian terms, and often by Confucian intellectual figures. The positive engagement with Western Learning led by Confucians from the 1850s onwards increasingly led to the West being perceived as the locus of a set of sociological, political, and technological systems conducive to the realization of the Confucian Way in modern society.

For instance, Yokoi Shōnan's *Kokuze Sanron* (Three Theses on State Policy), one of the most famous pro-Western tracts written during this period, a tract which eventually got the author murdered by xenophobic nativist fanatics, presented Western countries as the embodiment of idealized Confucian states.

In America three major policies have been set up from Washington's presidency on: First, to work towards ending all wars on this earth in line with the will of Heaven, because nothing is worse than violence and killing in the world; second, to broaden enlightened government by learning from all the countries of the world; and third, to entrust the power of the president to the wisest instead of transmitting it to the son, to not have ministers bound in service to the ruler, but instead to work with complete devotion for the peace and general welfare of the people. Laws, administrative practices, and all other arts and instruments, all considered good and beautiful on this earth are adopted and made their own and thereby the cultivation of benevolence and righteousness is advanced. In England the unity of governance is rooted in the sentiments of the people, the actions of officials, great or small, take the people into account. The most beneficial action is decided upon, and an unpopular program is not forced upon the people. War or peace is decided thusly. When there were wars lasting several years against Russia and against China causing countless deaths and costing millions in cash, all taken from the people, not one person complained against them. Furthermore all countries, Russia as well, have established state academies for the civil and military arts as a matter of course, but also hospitals, orphanages, and schools for the deaf and dumb. There is nowhere where they are not rushing to enact governance and education based on moral principles and for the benefit of the people. It almost conforms to the governance and education of the three dynasties (NST 55: 448–9; Watanabe 2012: 330; de Bary et al. 2005: 644).

The "three dynasties" referred to here are the Xia, Yin, and Zhou, which for early modern Japanese Confucians represented the golden age of perfect sagely Confucian rule in ancient China, the epitome of a society and governance in line with the Confucian Way. Yokoi judged policy clearly along the universalist "intention of Heaven" that is for the benefit of "all the countries in the world." He emphasized the value of education to be employed in governance and argued for a meritocratic approach to appointment valuing such an education. He further praised the states's intention to work for "general peace and welfare" (*kōkyō wahei*). In Chinese and Japanese, this phrase suggests more than just peace and welfare. *Kōkyō* in Japanese (*gonggong* in Chinese) today means "public." In Yokoi's day, this word suggested governance in harmony with the people. The word can be found in Confucian texts like the "House Records of Confucius" (included in the *Book of the Han*) (Fan 1985). The emphasis on the connection between English governance and the sentiments of the people uses similarly egalitarian aspects of the Confucian tradition to assert a Western–Confucian nexus. The state's role in education is held up again as indicating its proper Confucian benevolence, with institutions a Japanese audience could understand being provided as concrete examples. The first institution highlighted in this list of examples, "the state academies of civil and military arts" were in the Japan of the time, as outlined in the previous chapter, represented by the state Confucian academies.

Yokoi wrote this tract in the context of a discussion over whether Japan should "open" itself to interaction with the Western powers and conform to the norms of Western interstate relations. The West emphasized that their call for recognition was based on the principle of equality of nations (ironically enough given the historical context). Immediately after the oft-quoted "three dynasty" line above, Yokoi continued on to argue that the Western powers' attempts to open Japan should be perceived on the basis of "the Way of publicness" (*kōkyō no michi*) – *kōkyō* (publicness) here being used traditionally in contrast to "private" or "selfish" governance.

If Japan then decides to continue to take the old isolationist way of looking at things, refuses to understand the principle of common discourse, and instead prefers private [selfish] governance, then how can this not be called stupid. Just look at China (NST 55: 449)!

Yokoi thus contrasted rational, renewing, and publicly engaging governance (in mythical ancient China and the contemporary West) against government which isolates itself against both foreigners and its own people (the contemporaneous, defeated Qing China). But even in discussing China, the renewing and enlightening effect of early Qing rule was contrasted against the stagnation of China in the past century. The recent mistakes of the Qing dynasty are quoted to show bad governance, but earlier manifestations of the Qing dynasty, notably under the rule of Emperor Kangxi (1654–1722), were also used to provide an example of relatively good governance (NST 44: 449). Importantly, therefore, the Japanese discourse was thus not yet overwhelmingly anti-Chinese or even anti-Manchu.

The prime role of rationality and reason as universalist concepts seen in Japanese Confucian responses to the West at this time was not only a matter of reception but was also linked to the new approach taken to Japan by important emissaries of the Western world, notably the United States. As Watanabe Hiroshi has pointed out, US President Millard Fillmore's letter to the shogunate which directly preceded Commodore Perry's military intervention to open ports in Edo Bay (Tokyo Bay) was framed in a different way to many earlier Western missals to Japan. It did not request relations as a favor of noble privilege, but rather demanded equal diplomatic standing on the basis of equal standing as civilized nations (Watanabe 2010: 371–2). In other words, the letter did not employ the classic feudal or premodern language of asking for royal favor and privilege, as had been successfully employed through the seventeenth and eighteenth centuries by the Dutch and Koreans (and unsuccessfully in the nineteenth century by the Russians, Dutch, and British). The American letter was rather rooted firmly in a modern enlightenment parlance. This parlance was able to find resonance with critical Confucian thinking in Japan which imagined governance based on universal principles of ethics contained in Confucianism.

The language used in the official Classical Chinese translation of Fillmore's letter made by shogunate authorities gives an insight into this resonance. Translated back into English, it reads: "Our country's subjects are also governed by the [Confucian] Five Virtuous Relations." In the years immediately afterward, there are many examples of government and intellectual figures in Japan who saw this request as conforming to Confucian ideas of natural reason and ethics. Even among the feudal lords, Maeda Nariyasu, Lord of Kaga, Uesugi Narinori, Lord of Komezawa, Matudaira Yoshinaga, Lord of Fukui, Mizoguchi Naoaki, Lord of Shibata, all recorded that opinion in writing at the time (Watanabe 2010: 372–3).

There was thus a Confucian-inspired (and expressed) political base which was receptive to the discourse through which the Americans packaged their demand for political and commercial engagement. This nineteenth-century Western message of a universal value of national difference departed from the idea of universalism delivered by the Jesuits in the sixteenth and seventeenth centuries. It did not imagine ideal ethical governance being realized by a single religious hierarchy, but rather in the context of a multipolar political world order which shared certain universalized administrative and legal systems providing structures for ethical interactions between states, peoples, and individuals. This was thus a vision which resembled that of Confucianism and the traditional forms of government idealized in its mythical ancient Chinese past as understood by Japanese in the late Tokugawa period.

Key then was that the West, through this Confucian lens, was perceived as offering not primarily a set of *new* moral standards, but a set of rational and effective systems that would deliver just and moral governance conforming to the traditional standards. The emergent Western modernity was thus able to be grasped as a set of administrative and legal systems and processes aiming to create a stable and just order: an aim inherently attractive to Confucians. The idea of what today in northwestern Europe is called the *rechtstaat*, a system of governance and law designed to create a fair and ordered state, was thus a universal underpinning of the way Japanese intellectuals and politicians approached the various ideologies that were rising in late nineteenth-century Western political thought and practice (Goerlitz 1970).

This was certainly the way that early Japanese official visitors to Europe and the United States perceived the West when they went there on diplomatic and study missions through the 1850s and 1860s. Many figures who would go on to play major political roles in modern Japan had the opportunity to visit Western countries early and mix in elite government and intellectual circles through their participation in embassies of the late Tokugawa state. Fukuzawa Yukichi, the father of Japanese liberalism, and Katsu Kaishū, one of the key trans-Restoration statesmen of Japan, both first traveled to America in 1860 in concert with the Tokugawa state embassy to the United States to ratify the Treaty of Friendship, Commerce and Navigation. Fukuzawa also spent time in Europe in 1862 as part of a Tokugawa government embassy, and Shibusawa Eiichi (the founder of the first stock company and first modern bank in Japan, often called the "father of Japanese capitalism") spent nearly two years in France studying as the escort of the heir to the Tokugawa shogunate Tokugawa Akitake in the mid-1860s. Itō Hirobumi, later prime minister of Japan, at the time a Chōshū domain samurai, also traveled to London in 1863. The longest engaged work by Tokugawa officials in a Western country, however, was the posting of Nishi Amane and Tsuda Mamichi to the Netherlands between 1863 and 1865.

Nishi Amane and Tsuda Mamichi were dispatched for two years to Leiden in 1863 with the explicit mission of studying Western statecraft. This was the most serious, sustained, institutionalized, and influential Japanese attempt to engage and understand the West before the Meiji Restoration. Nishi and Tsuda were both officers of the shogunate's prime academy for the study of the West, the Barbarians Documents Research Centre (*bansho shirabesho*) – the offshoot of the Shogunal Confucian Academy discussed in the previous chapter. They had been selected by the shogunate for dispatch to universities in the United States, but because of the outbreak of the American Civil War this had to be deferred. Eventually they were instead dispatched to Leiden University in the Netherlands, accompanying the shogunate naval officers going to Rotterdam to participate in the construction of modern warships for the shogunate. As opposed to the technological and engineering aims of their shipmates, and the similar emphasis on engineering seen among the Chōshū Five, Tsuda and Nishi were rather dispatched to study what we might call the social technologies of Western governance and administration. Their aim, as recorded by them in Japanese, was to study *chikoku-gaku* – literally: "the learning of national governance."

The Dutch government arranged for them to be tutored privately by Simon Vissering, a professor in the Law Faculty at Leiden. Vissering, who would shortly thereafter be appointed Finance Minister of the Netherlands, was the prize student of J.R. Thorbecke (1798–1872), a major early nineteenth-century European liberal thinker and author of the Dutch Constitution. Vissering personally formulated a five-subject regime for Nishi and Tsuda including natural law, national law, international law, statistics, and economics. It was an integrated series of private lectures on Western legal frameworks, the philosophy underlying them, and the finance and accounting practices that made them work (Ōkubo 2010; Watanabe 1985).

Underlying this system as Vissering presented it was natural law. As Nishi later translated into Japanese from his Dutch-language notes of Vissering's early lectures: "Natural law is rooted in man's nature, that is why it is called natural law" (Nishi 1879: 1–4). The word Nishi chooses for "nature" is (Jp. *sei*, Ch. *xing*), the Confucian term for one's inherent, and following the Mencian and Neo-Confucian traditions, inherently good, nature. Natural law, however, was different to human nature, in that while human nature was a moral state that related to one's own conduct, natural law related to one's relations with others, and was therefore concerned with what was just or unjust. Morals and law were therefore divided, and the ultimate status of natural law was described by Vissering as allowing freedom to the extent that the freedom of another is not hindered. Assisting people in poverty or sickness, or saving others in danger, was "a matter of morals, not of natural law" (Nishi 1879: 7–8).

The systems of natural, national, and international law all held in common along this line that they were instruments for the management of human society. As Tsuda put it in eloquent Confucian terms, "different from legal morality, Confucian morality is deeply concerned with benevolence, righteousness, rites and education, but law only discusses the right and wrong of a matter" (Tsuda 2001: 228). Nishi, like Tsuda, concurred with the division between law, governance, and morals.

Crucially, however, he actually saw that as conforming to the Confucian Way. For Nishi, it was only the Neo-Confucians post-Zhu Xi who had seen "making true one's intention and rectifying the mind as wanting to equalize all under heaven" by making morality and governance contiguous (Nishi 1962: 1: 236–8). Earlier, purer forms of Confucianism, on the other hand, resembled the Western liberal system he was learning. As Nishi himself pointed out, and modern scholars like Ōkubo Takeharu, Sugawara Hikaru, and others have noted, in this analysis (seeing the division of morality and governance as quintessentially Confucian) Nishi was following the teachings of Ogyū Sorai (Ōkubo 2010: 50). If Confucianism was efficient and objective governance, as the powerful Sorai-ist tradition of Confucianism in Japan had suggested, then surely this perfectly ordered world of Dutch law, society, and economics was a Confucian order. In this way, Nishi and Tsuda used Japanese Confucianism – and particularly the Sorai tradition – to mediate one of the core problematics of late nineteenth-century Western legal and political thought (not only for East Asians but notably for European Christians as well) – the place of morals.

Statistics and economics also blended seamlessly into this world of rational social right and wrong. Statistics were perceived by Nishi and Tsuda, as they had been in earlier writing by Fukuzawa Yukichi, as a system for grasping the nature of society as a whole. Rather than the world of individual subjectivity, morals, or action, statistics were the means by which the entire totality of a society could be measured and thereby understood. They were the unifying principle underlying the diversity of human society.[1] For Nishi and Tsuda under Vissering's influence, statistics became even more a tool not only for understanding society but for driving it. "Statisticians can record the reality of social life and in so doing can comprehend the natural laws that regulate our lives and actions" (Tsuda 2001: 228). The implication was that this would facilitate governance which increases utility and welfare. Similarly, economics was seen as a tool for unearthing underlying principles in society which can assist in its just governance (Ōkubo 2010: 121).

Laws and regulations were the fundamental building blocks of this system, but it was managed through statistics, and underlying all of this was a philosophical world view. The nature of that philosophical outlook was very much a function of the particular moment of Dutch (and broader northwestern European) social and political history into which Nishi and Tsuda had been dropped. The mid-nineteenth century saw the rise in respectable northwestern European society of liberalism and positivism. In Holland, Vissering sat at the center of a well-organized and connected group of liberals closely connected to power. Thorbecke, the

greatest icon of Dutch liberalism, and creator of the reformist 1848 Dutch
Constitution, had been Vissering's professor. Vissering now occupied the
professorial chair his teacher had vacated, while Thorbecke served as
Prime Minister. In 1879, Vissering himself would serve as Finance
Minister of the Netherlands. In other words, Nishi and Tsuda were not
just being tutored by a renowned university professor, but by someone at
the center of the public intellectual and political networks of European
liberalism.

Liberalism

Already at this early stage of the Japanese importation of Western systems
of law, politics, economics, and their administration, liberalism thereby
sat center stage. Vissering was connected into an intra-European movement of liberalism in awe of the recent works of Bentham and J.S. Mill.[2]
British liberal ideas in particular were on the rise in the Holland that Nishi
and Tsuda came to inhabit. This naturally meant that Vissering, Nishi,
and Tsuda were also heavily influenced by the philosophical outlooks that
flanked this rise of British liberalism – notably utilitarianism. Because
they were so deeply embedded in this liberal milieu in Europe and had
had such excellent critical Confucian educations in Japan, Tsuda and
Nishi were surprisingly adept at bridging the gap between Confucian
morality and utilitarianism.

There were a number of factors to their advantage in this struggle. One
was the role of Christianity in nineteenth-century liberalism. The pro-
found Christianity of many nineteenth-century British liberals is nowadays often forgotten, but the Christianity of English liberal texts was
immediately noticeable to Japanese Confucian intellectuals, and the
attempts to bridge Christian morality with philosophical utilitarianism
likewise. In fact, because Christianity was still banned in Japan when the
rush of translations of English liberal texts began around 1869,
translators like Nakamura Masanao had to jump hoops to try to rework
texts like J.S. Mill's On Liberty to remove the Christian references. The
result was a text that looked even more Confucian than it would have
otherwise (Mill and Nakamura 1872). The Christian content, legally problematic and therefore very noticeable in the contemporaneous Japanese
context, was replaced and replicated with Confucian terminology.

What really made it easy for Nishi Amane in particular, however, to
accept the utilitarian outlook of Bentham, his followers, and indeed many
aspects of northwestern European political philosophy and statecraft was
the fact that one of the most influential forms of Japanese Confucianism
in his own education, Sorai-ism, also deftly mediated potential conflict

between moralism and a Sorai-ist Confucian outlook that had much in common with utilitarianism. Already in this first engagement with nineteenth-century British liberalism, a newly emergent and crystallizing ideology, Japanese thinkers found parallels available in the Confucian tradition to mediate transmission. This fascination with liberalism, and utilization of Confucian frameworks to package, transmit, and understand it, continued through the fall of the Tokugawa shogunate and into the construction of modern Japan in the Meiji period. This was the case not only for figures who had backgrounds in the Tokugawa state academies and were open about the effects of Confucianism on their thinking, like Nishi, Tsuda, and Nakamura Masanao, but it was also true of figures who in their rhetoric harshly criticized, rejected, and condemned the Confucian tradition, notably Fukuzawa Yukichi.

Fukuzawa Yukichi chose to package his advocacy of liberalism as an antithesis to Confucianism. Yet he also often couched his views in Confucian terms and used certain Neo-Confucian ideas centrally in his own writing. For instance, Fukuzawa explicated his version of how to achieve Mill's idea of "a sense of dignity" by to some degree accepting Confucian values, not as inherent values but as means of "playing at the game" of life.

Having been born into this world, even as maggots, we must show considerable conviction. And what is that conviction? It is the determination that even though we know life to be but a game, and a brief one at that, we shall not treat it as such. We shall work hard to avoid poverty and suffering and shall aspire to wealth and pleasure, pursuing our own contentment and happiness to the extent that they do not interfere with those of our fellows. Telling ourselves fifty to seventy years is a ripe old age we will honor our parents, love one another as husbands and wives, provide for our children and grandchildren, work for the public good beyond our front doors, and strive to lead a life perfect in every respect (Watanabe 2012: 406–7).

Service to this Confucian-sounding litany of social relationships was, according to Fukuzawa, the way to "stay sober," another idea of religious practice spanning Mill's protestant liberalism and Neo-Confucianism. Watanabe Hiroshi sees Fukuzawa's conception of the individual as rooted in something similar to Neo-Confucian "human nature." Fukuzawa also, like both English liberals and Confucians, emphasized the place of the family at the center of social organization (Watanabe 2012: 408).

The most striking Confucian influence in the oeuvre of Fukuzawa, however, is the idea of "civilization." Civilization was of course one of the key elements in the nineteenth-century ideology of Western imperialism. Invasion and colonization of "less advanced" nations both within Europe and North America (Ireland, the Sioux), but especially beyond (in New Zealand, Australia, Indonesia, China, and Japan), was justified by appeal to a universal concept of civilization. This concept, although possessing particularly powerful characteristics in the modern period that intersected with the trajectories of global capitalism and racism, of course had a much longer premodern European history going back to the Romans. As we saw in Chapter 1, ancient East Asian empires possessed a similar idea of civilization, and the Chinese history of this term's use in politics, political ideology, and religion was intimately intertwined with the history of Confucianism (Zürcher 2000). Fukuzawa's reading of Western civilization, which he used to trash Confucianism, was also actually reliant on and ran parallel to Confucian ideas. This influence of ideas of a hierarchy of civilizations determined through material success, mediated through the matching Confucian ideology of civilization, also assisted the rapid acceptance of social Darwinian ideas in Japan, as will be discussed in the next chapter. So even in the most self-avowedly anti-Confucian thinker of early Japanese liberalism, Confucianism still played a mediating role.

Nishi Amane and Tsuda Mamichi were much more open about the interaction between traditional, liberal, and utilitarian influences in their thinking. As we saw earlier, the grounding they were given in Western statecraft and political economy in Holland was based in a liberal outlook and occurred in a highly politicized liberal milieu. Nishi from the outset identified many aspects of Dutch statecraft, including the liberal outlook, with Confucianism. His way of making sense of the disparities was to see Western statecraft and liberalism as inherently anti Neo-Confucian, but conforming to other Confucian outlooks, notably those of Ogyū Sorai.

Despite the individualism and property-centered nature of the liberal system, Nishi, following Vissering, made sure to emphasize the overall social function of the system of governance, and the ultimate ideal utility of laws – to assist all.

In relation to our people [the commoners], it should cultivate their livelihoods, mitigate against their demise, assist them in having a happy life, and stop them from worrying about what comes after death (Nishi 1962: 1: 237).

A core concept for Nishi is one he takes from Vissering, the Dutch "*matschappelijke leven*," which in English translates into something like "social life." Nishi and Tsuda agreed to translate it as the very Confucian sounding "*aioiyashinai no michi*" which we could translate back into English as "the Way of mutual cultivation."

Nishi uses this phrase constantly in his translations and original philosophical, political, and economic work to denote society. In some uses, it takes on a markedly Confucian tone, as in one example where he explains the term in relation to human nature: "People live socially so they can help the distressed, in this way they fulfill their [inherently good] human nature" (Nishi 1962: 1: 219–20). The Confucian antecedents of the phrase are clear. Han Yu (768-824CE), one of the main forerunners of Neo-Confucian theory, uses the term in his commentary of the *Doctrine of the Mean*, "once there is life, then there must arise the Way of social life." Ogyū Sorai also used the phrase in his most popular Confucian treatise, "Discerning the Way" (*Bendō*), where he wrote: "The way of people is not solitary, there must be millions of people together for this Way to arise ... bringing millions of people together and cultivating their caring and productive nature is the Way of the Ancient Kings" (NST 36: 17–18). So the social aspects of the liberal system emphasized by Vissering resonated with a long Confucian tradition that Nishi was aware of, and he used that tradition to interpret this important (if nowadays often overlooked) aspect of liberalism.

There were, however, also elements in Nishi's liberalism which clearly did not interact well with Confucianism, notably the central role of property. Nevertheless, the important position of property in the liberal system was packaged by Nishi with familiar terminology. Nishi started his explanation of property, again following Vissering, with nature. Nature, which in Nishi's Japanese became the Confucian term for human nature (Jp. *hito no sei*, Ch. *ren zhi xing*), had above it "the autonomous self-interested mind," from which came "self-directing and self-standing rights" and, as another form of right, "private property." These were then to be regulated within "social life" by "rights and duties" (Nishi 1962: 1: 273, 282–4). So although the foreign (from a philosophical perspective) idea of private property sits at the center of the system as the core right, the system begins with the familiar Confucian-like term of "human nature" and ends in mediation or practice through the similarly familiarly Confucian "rights and duties."

Interestingly, the way Nishi chose on return to Japan to defend the idea of private property was a little different to Vissering. Vissering emphasized simply that private property was part of natural law, and that therefore any attempt to rid the world of private property, such as communism, would "oppose the natural rules of human society on this earth" (Ōkubo 2010: 112). Nishi, however, although beginning with human nature, gives a more detailed argument in *Hyaku isshinron*.

Humans are all in possession of the same shared human nature, but it is not possible for them to all realize this nature as "the Way." So if we look then to find where is the shared sameness, we discern that it is in their desires and hatreds. These desires and hatreds, whether you have a thousand men or ten thousand they will be the same. No one can change this. Now if there is someone and they suddenly hit me, or cut me down dead with a sword, or even if they don't do that, if they just curse me or look down upon me, should someone like me think that is acceptable? Or should I think I hate them? Of course I am going to hate them, and this emotion arises in the same way it arises in a beast. There is no one in this world who wants to be punched and kicked. This is thus the well-spring from where comes the existence of peoples' autonomous independent rights ... Furthermore, if someone comes and cheats me out of something that is mine, or steals something of mine while I am not looking, what kind of emotion will arise in someone like me? Of course, the emotions of anger and hatred will arise against that person, and once they arise they will be plain to see and impossible to conceal. This is where peoples' right of private property arises from. Once this arises and is seen, then the just state of affairs arises where no one else says it is theirs or tries to touch it. These two are human universals. Even in the most barbaric country no one thinks it is acceptable to hit or steal. Ultimately, this is the root of all law (Nishi 1962: 1: 282–3).

Law then, the underpinning of Nishi and Tsuda's outlook on political economy, was rooted in protection of the individual and private property. Economics, the second important element in the political economy outlook, also relied on the accumulation of property to increase social welfare, and thereby better society. Thus through the Confucian mediation of the introduction of liberal law, political thought and political economy to Japan, property, and by association wealth and capital, were positioned centrally and justified. What then of capitalism itself?

Capitalism

Interestingly, in the post-Meiji Restoration period, successful capitalists were some of the most ardent advocates of Confucianism. The most famous example is Shibusawa Eiichi (1840–1931). Shibusawa was the first person in Japan to establish a joint stock company, the first Governor of the Bank of Japan, one of early Meiji Japan's financial government reformers, and from the 1870s onward one of Japan's major capitalists. Shibusawa saw Confucian education, literacy, and the ability to think clearly as key to success in the modern world. In the disorder of the fall of the Tokugawa shogunate and rise of the new Meiji government, Shibusawa seems to have lamented most of all the lack of education and moral fortitude of leadership figures, both samurai and merchant. Of samurai, he noted their general lack of morals and courage. Of some merchants, their stupidity, and lack of education. He disparaged one of the leading figures in the Mitsui Corporation of the time, Minomura Rizaemon (1821–1877), by focusing on his lack of education and coarseness, concluding that "the man could barely read" (Shibusawa 1994: 55–6, 137).

Born a commoner in Musashino, Shibusawa's own rise began with his 1861 enrolment in the Confucian Academy of Kaiho Gyoson (1798–1866). His quick abilities in administration and bookkeeping were noted and led to a meteoric rise into the samurai class as a vassal of the Tokugawa shogunate, and, during 1867–1868, as escort to the shogunal heir Tokugawa Akitake during his studies in Paris. When he came back from France at the end of 1868, the shogunate had been removed, but he continued to serve the former shogun Tokugawa Yoshinobu in Shizuoka. It was there that he established the first joint stockholder company in Japan based on examples he had seen in France. Using domainal finance, he set up the company to encourage enterprises in Shizuoka, and also tapped into the account to speculate based on a number of central government decisions, allowing him to considerably increase economic activity in the domain while simultaneously increasing the value of the domainal state's income. His experimentation in Shizuoka came quickly to the attention of the new government, who had him brought into the new Finance Ministry in Tokyo in 1869. There he worked closely with some of the most powerful figures of the Meiji oligarchy: Okuma Shigenobu, Itō Hirobumi, and Inoue Kaoru. In 1873, he left the ministry and formal government service, going on to a long career in business leading the nation's biggest banks, companies, and financial organizations. From 1910 he began to relinquish most of his corporate positions to focus the last twenty years of his life on private diplomacy, social, and publishing projects. Most of these projects Shibusawa framed as forms of Confucian activism, all part of his attempt to advance a Confucian revival in modern Japan.

A unique element in Shibusawa's Confucian activism was his framing of Confucianism in relation to a critical outlook on capitalism. Shibusawa, despite being the "father of Japanese capitalism," was highly critical of certain aspects of the capitalism he inhabited. Throughout his writings and other activities he seriously problematized the preeminence of the individual he saw in capitalist society and liberal thinking (Shibusawa 1918: 48). He believed the excesses of individualism which capitalism encouraged had to be countered. The infatuation with individual interest in the rapid-growth capitalism that Shibusawa was witnessing created a situation where "competition can be too rough," excessive, ultimately causing corruption (Shibusawa 1918: 70–1, 78–9). Fairness could not be based simply on competition between individuals or on individual interest – the basic methods of capitalist accumulation. This critical analysis of capitalism and competition even informed Shibusawa's approach to property. Shibusawa, unlike the liberals, was prepared to acknowledge the problematic role private property could play in supporting the anti-social features of capitalism. The fact that some people had more property than others, and that the others would want it, was a "Heavenly principle" sure to cause resentment and thereby probably a violent counter reaction (Shibusawa 1918: 69–70). The premier capitalist of modern Japan thus rejected the idealization of private property that sat at the philosophical base of modern liberal capitalism.

Shibusawa Eiichi's analysis of the problems of capitalism, and his ideas on how Confucianism, and Confucian practice, in particular, could assist in overcoming these problems, illustrate a number of problems in the social positioning and effective practice of Confucianism in modern Japanese society. As well as organizing and funding a wide range of Confucian activities, Shibusawa wrote prodigiously about the position of Confucianism in modern Japan, both in relation to the Tokugawa tradition and more interestingly in relation to the social context of rapid development capitalism which he was living within. In the second decade of the twentieth century, Shibusawa authored two books which seem to have been intended as vehicles for expressing his outlook on Confucianism's relation to past tradition and contemporary competitive society: *Record of Rakuō* (*Rakuōkōden*) – a biography of the shogunal regent Matsudaira Sadanobu; and *Seminar on Self-Cultivation in the Struggle for Truth* (*Shisei doryoku shūyō kōwa*), a treatise on the role of Confucianism in contemporary capitalist society (Shibusawa 1918 – referred to below as *Seminar on Self-Cultivation*).[3]

Record of Rakuō was a scholarly biography and collection of source documents about Matsudaira Sadanobu. Despite its at times hagiographic nature, it became the standard academic reference work on Matsudaira Sadanobu from the time of its publication in 1937 (posthumously in the name of Shibusawa Eiichi) until many decades thereafter. *Seminar on Self-Cultivation*, however, was a much less scholarly, yet in many ways more historically interesting work. This is partly because *Seminar on Self-Cultivation*, despite being billed as the personal advice of Shibusawa, appears to have been modeled on another guide to self-cultivation authored a hundred years earlier: Matsudaira Sadanobu's "Record of Spiritual Exercises" (*Shugyōroku*) discussed in Chapter 3. In its overt claim to represent a form of Confucian practice, in its arrangement, and in its use of personal stories and focus on "spiritual betterment," Shibusawa's *Seminar on Self-Cultivation* clearly took Matsudaira Sadanobu's 1823 *Shugyōroku* as a model. But Shibusawa's book also fitted neatly into a very different, much more contemporary and global literary context – that of the modern self-help book. Shibusawa's *Seminar on Self-Cultivation* was influenced in both form and content by the genre of Western self-help books which enjoyed huge popularity in Meiji Japan, starting with the very influential book by Samuel Smiles *Self Help*, which was even referenced by Fukuzawa Yukichi and other serious intellectuals (Kinmoth 1981: 10–20, 260–70). Shibusawa's book therefore provides a nice way of seeing how Confucianism was mediated between its traditional Tokugawa role and the rampant individualism, materialism, and capitalism which emerged in nineteenth- and early twentieth-century global modernity.

One of the main themes running through Matsudaira Sadanobu's *Record of Spiritual Exercises* was an aversion to physical, particularly sexual, temptation, and discussion of methods to avoid it. Shibusawa also has a whole chapter which, with the title "Disciplining the Flesh," sounds very similar in inclination. In comparison to Matsudaira, however, Shibusawa's asceticism had a more modern character. Shibusawa's "Disciplining the Flesh" focuses disappointingly more on the culinary than the lascivious (Shibusawa 1918: 571–84). There is also a seventy-page chapter devoted to "Looking at Merit Through Personal Examples" – a typical chapter in Confucian moral primers giving examples of virtuous persons, in this case drawn mainly from the imperial household and the late Tokugawa family (Shibusawa 1918: 503–70). The last 150 pages are devoted to filial piety, including the necessary moral tales from history (Shibusawa 1918: 600–750). So much for the last one-third of the book, a modernized, but nonetheless in most respects relatively faithful rendition of a Confucian moral primer.

The first half of the book, however, complicates the matter. Here we see influences which are much more reminiscent of the liberalism of Fukuzawa, Mill, and Vissering, the positivism of Comte, and the utilitarianism of Nishi and Bentham. But we also see a clear counter reaction against the liberal and individualist sentiments which by the time this work was published in 1918 had found firm footing in Japanese society. A major and intriguing ongoing theme in Shibusawa's work is his criticism of people's focus on success and failure. Judging people and things based on success and failure, according to Shibusawa, fails to grasp the "Principle of Heaven and Earth." Similarly incorrect was any obsession with "money and wealth," which Shibusawa considered "equal to sake lees" (Shibusawa 1918: 3). In other words, according to the great modern Japanese capitalist, money was no more precious than the byproduct dregs of the sake brewing process.

People should instead follow "Heaven's will." For Shibusawa, the idea of Heaven's Will (Jp. *tenmei*, Ch. *tianming*), was so central that he summed up his view of Confucianism as "bringing the mind to peace through realizing [Heaven's] mandate" (Jp. *anshin ritsumei*, Ch. *anxin riming*). This is a term from *Mencius* that was also picked up on by Zen Buddhists (Shibusawa 1918: 5). The central place of Heaven in Shibusawa's understanding of Confucianism, and its almost sentient character, is reminiscent of Ogyū Sorai (Kurozumi 2003: 351–3). Conforming to Heaven's Will would also determine fate: "Fair and unselfish Heaven will definitely assist one to develop one's fate" (Shibusawa 1918: 4). So what is Heaven's Will concretely? Traditionally, this was a question Confucians normally avoided. Shibusawa, however, was happy to define "the principle of Heaven" very clearly as "the development of the nation-state" and "living a life for society" (Shibusawa 1918: 4–5). In other words – it was social and national. The strong social outlook Shibusawa takes in many parts of the book leads him to a very different view on individualism than that favored by his contemporaneous liberals. Shibusawa directly rejected Fukuzawa Yukichi's idea of "independent self-respect" (*dokuritsu jison*, sometimes translated into English less literally as "personal independence") stating that he found the idea simply impossible to realize.[4] Shibusawa saw people as inherently social animals. Individual humans all naturally "stand in society." "People gathered together form a society and this organizes a nation-state" (Shibusawa 1918: 66).[5]

Shibusawa's Confucianism and social commentary thus walked a tightrope. On the one hand, the book calls for the individual to realize her/his "*honbun no sei*," their original, Mencian, inherently good human nature. But for Shibusawa that nature was also *inherently social*. The quintessential model in Shibusawa's writing for an ideal human character was the Imperial Rescript on Education. He particularly emphasized the Confucian Five Relations outlined therein which delineated the nature of good social relations between husband and wife, friends, siblings, parents, and children (Shibusawa 1918: 52–3). On the other hand, Shibusawa repeatedly hammered home the importance of strong individual will, self-belief, self-motivation, daring (Shibusawa 1918: 36–40). People should be willful enough not to follow the crowd, but to stick with their convictions "like a magnet" (Shibusawa 1918: 44). Within this mix, emotionality is considered a core value (Shibusawa 1918: 60–1). Desire is an absolutely essential quality in people – not only acceptable, but compulsory.

Desire is natural and necessary, but needs to be channeled. Thus the need for the spiritual exercise and practice that the book calls for: "Along with advancing one's knowledge, one must at the same time advance spiritual practice" (Shibusawa 1918: 49). People's emotions "should not be calm like ash" (Shibusawa 1918: 81), but needed to be "moderated," as described in the *Doctrine of the Mean* (Shibusawa 1918: 81–4). Shibusawa saw Confucian practice as the key to resolving the tension between these two seemingly incompatible motivations of individual will-fulness and sociality. Through Confucian education and practice, people would be able to relativize the individualist, competitive aspects of modern society. Society in its current state invited overly individualistic, uncontrolled desire, extreme individualism: thus the pressing need for Confucian practice, or "spiritual exercise" in Shibusawa's terms.

So if this was the social analysis, what then of the nature of Confucian practice outlined by Shibusawa. Beyond the doctrine and posturing, how did the actual practice he advocated sit in relation to these problems? As outlined in Chapter 4, the nature of practice outlined in Matsudaira Sadanobu's *Record of Spiritual Exercises* had a uniquely social character. Practice, although carried out with the aim of cultivation of the self, was conducted in the context of physical jujitsu practice between two opponents. The self was thus conceived, "cultivated," in relation to another. The unique features of this kind of practice, as opposed to other contemporaneous practices like quiet sitting, or indeed ascetic abstentionism, were its relational, socially embedded nature and its utility.

Many parts of Shibusawa's *Seminar on Self-Cultivation* similarly discuss the tension between the individual and social. The overall framing of the book and the problem it identifies and seeks to resolve are thus similar. Surprising then that the actual practice outlined is completely individual, and moreover rather boringly materialist. Despite Shibusawa on many occasions in *Seminar on Self-Cultivation* talking about sociality, when it comes to the actual details of how to conduct practice, all the methods outlined are individualistic, and many of them are even related to consumption. In fact, the most "spiritual" that Shibusawa's outlined practice gets is his morning routine:

Waking up at 6am I wash my feet and take a stroll in the garden, for 15 minutes I get in touch with the natural things like trees and flowers, at this time I have nothing on my mind, I make my mind and body as one, and after that I take a bath (Shibusawa 1918: 572).[6]

Most of the rest of Shibusawa's advice on practice is nothing more than mild asceticism. "Of course if one has too much sex or eats or drinks too much this will be damaging, the important thing is that each individual listens to their own body and judges their actions accordingly" (Shibusawa 1918: 578). In the sub-chapter entitled "Health and Spiritual Exercises," there are just two points of advice offered: make sure to sleep enough and go to the doctor if you feel ill (Shibusawa 1918: 581–3). This is thus definitely the modern, material, and rather stale world of Samuel Smiles, not the ecstatic spiritualism of Ignatius of

Loyola, nor indeed the dynamic hand-to-hand Confucian combat practice of Matsudaira Sadanobu. In fact the only social aspect in the "spiritual exercises" advocated by Shibusawa is his advice "not to stay indoors too much and not avoid talking to people" (Shibusawa 1918: 581).

Shibusawa is a powerful symbol of the position, role, and potential of Confucianism in modern Japan. Shibusawa intelligently and sensitively analyzed problems in the nature of capitalism around him. He was confident enough to critique elements of liberalism, notably the liberalism of Fukuzawa, which failed to address these problems, and perhaps even exacerbated them. He saw in the Confucian tradition, concretely even, through examples like Matsudaira Sadanobu, potential antidotes to these problems through a more social but also more individually controlled, measured approach to life. He engaged his advocacy of Confucianism with contemporary society not only through citing the Imperial Rescript but also through authoring a book in a style fashionable at the time and in line with works like Smiles.

Yet when it came to the actual action of practice, the creation of a regime of practice to satisfy the spiritual requirements as he outlined in his book, or to the formulation of social systems or institutions which similarly might mitigate the anti-social features of capitalism which he himself had identified, he was lacking. The version of practice outlined by Shibusawa had little to no Confucian or indeed religious content of any kind. Light asceticism is the only even remotely religious element, and this seems a shadow of the Protestantism of Smiles and the other self-help gurus more than anything else. The solution to capitalism imagined by Shibusawa is ultimately as completely individualistic and completely materialist as the problematic he identified. Confucianism was thus a useful framework for analysis, even of things like the role of property in modern society, but it seemed to offer no direct answers, at least not at the level of daily practice.

Socialism

The social problems associated with high capitalism, and the contradictions of capitalism itself, also fueled more radical movements in modern Japan. The formations and early histories of these movements were also intertwined with the nineteenth-century legacies of Confucianism. Katayama Sen (1859–1933), often claimed as Japan's first socialist activist, unsurprisingly had an even deeper problem with private property than Shibusawa. Even before having ever encountered Marx or Engels, Katayama saw the right of private property as the core instrument of capitalist dispossession.

Capitalists do not acknowledge the results of labor, they continue to take unearned income, and they are able to take all of this completely because of the existence of the right of private property. In this way this profit gained without being earned is basically equal to what the worker should receive and the capitalist is forcibly stealing (Katayama 1904: 4).

Studies on early Meiji intellectual and political history often spend little time on socialism because it arrived so late on the scene and had, notably in comparison with liberalism, a relatively limited effect on the development of mainstream political structures, institutions, and practices. Indeed, Katayama confirms this reality. Katayama was a full generation younger than Shibusawa. Only an infant at the time of the Meiji Restoration, Katayama's intellectual formation occurred in a Japan even further along the rapid trajectory of change that integration into the global capitalist economy had brought. The first self-affirmed Japanese liberals had already become developed thinkers and influential scholars in their own rights fully within the pre-Restoration order – complete with its comprehensively Confucian institutionalization of learning. Katayama instead graduated into secondary-level education in an academic world where the state-run schools at the top of the educational hierarchy had already gone over to completely Western syllabi. In 1880, Katayama got his first big break when he gained entry to Okayama Prefecture Normal School. The Normal Schools were the main ladder up out of the provinces for the bright young Japanese of the time, but their nationally set curriculum was completely Western and heavy on technical learning.

Yet for Katayama and many critical political thinkers like him in the 1880s, Confucian learning was still an important background to politics. This was for two main reasons. Firstly, simply because the generation directly above them used Confucianism so centrally in their mediation of Western political, philosophical, and economic ideas. Secondly, and more directly, because by the 1880s, the traditional private Confucian schools had come to occupy a new, and sometimes radically political, position in Japanese society. Private Confucian schools, or Chinese learning academies (*kangaku juku*) as they were normally known at the time, were still popular in the 1870s and 1880s. During this period, the state was simply not able to provide enough state schools to cater for the demand. This meant that the private Confucian schools found a new role as preparatory schools for the state system. Despite the fact that the content and aims of the education were in general completely different, the one overlapping element was the development of advanced literacy.

State schools often used Chinese or *kanbun* literacy, intimately linked to study of the Confucian Classics, to test general literacy upon entry. To become literate in educated, technical Japanese is not easy. To be able to read and write good academic Japanese, even now, but particularly then, one needed a solid grasp of not only many Chinese characters but also enough understanding of literary (in the broadest sense of the word) context for the use of this kind of language. Confucian learning offered that contextually embedded literacy (Ōta 2013: 57–8). So the Confucian schools did not at first die out, but ironically enough actually enjoyed a brief two decades of high popularity as the literacy training grounds for a Westernized state system not yet sufficiently expanded to universally spread literacy itself. The introduction of the state education institutions and examinations which linked to quasi-meritocratic appointment systems for government position thus increased the overall value of learning as never before. During the initial period when the new regime was still setting up its educational apparatus, this created an opportunity and boost for enrolment of the private Confucian schools – if only for that first twenty years after the Restoration.

The fact that these schools during this period attracted a large number of the most ambitious Japanese from all walks of life who had designs on social mobility moreover made them hotbeds for political discussion. We have as a source for this no one less than the first prime minister of Japan, Itō Hirobumi, who lamented the politicization of Confucian school students at that time in the following terms.

As to the training of college students, science should be roundly encouraged, and they should be discouraged from debating politics. Having too many students of politics will not be to the benefit of the people . . . Students of today usually emerge from the Chinese learning schools [kangaku juku – private Confucian academies]. When a student of Chinese Learning opens his mouth, he immediately starts talking about politics, rolling up his sleeves and debating matters of the realm. For that reason when they change over to reading Western books they are incapable of calmly and methodically studying and applying themselves to the mastery of encyclopedic knowledge. . . . In order to correct this vice, engineering, technical and encyclopedic studies should be promoted . . . (Yamazumi 1990: 83).

This meant not only that these institutions were the physical setting for critical political discussion but also that this discussion continued to follow Confucian linguistic, discursive, philosophical, and political forms. Or as the scholar Kurozumi Makoto has put it, Confucianism continued to "provide the expressive vocabulary" of political critique (Kurozumi 2003: 177).[7]

So Katayama, as a student assistant in a private Confucian school in Tokyo during 1882 and 1883, was centrally positioned in this field of resistance. However, while maybe a hotbed of political discussion, the private Confucian schools of 1880s Tokyo were certainly no centers of socialism. Katayama Sen discovered socialism only after moving to the United States. He was introduced to it through his involvement with left-wing Congregational Christians in the United States in the late 1880s and early 1890s. In fact, the careers of many of the early Japanese socialists show a similar trajectory of moving first from Confucianism to Christianity, then from Christianity to socialism. Much research on early Meiji Christians notes the fact that samurai with a strong Confucian educational background were overly represented among early Meiji converts to Christianity. Similarly, most early Japanese socialists in the late nineteenth century had a Christian background. There are thus several indirect links between Confucianism, Confucian school institutions, and early Japanese socialism. But they are only indirect. In fact, while in America, and even after his initial return to Japan in 1896, Katayama would have better been characterized as a social-democrat labor activist than a radical socialist.

Radical socialist ideas only surfaced in Katayama after his return to Japan, mainly in reaction to the violent state suppression of democratic labor activism. Socialism was too late a comer in Japan to be directly influenced by the Confucian tradition. By the time Katayama was manning the barricades at steel plants in Tokyo, Confucian academies, private or otherwise, had all but vanished from urban Japan. Unlike Katayama, his slightly younger followers had never been taught Sino-Japanese *kanbun* and thus could not even read most Confucian texts. Nonetheless, in Katayama's case at least there was some connection. In his memoirs, he mentions the *Zuochuan commentary of the Spring and Autumn Annals* and the education he received on this text while studying in Confucian academies as the "constructive knowledge" through which he engaged later (Western) logic and philosophy, eventually including Marx (Katayama 1931: 114–20).

The example of socialism thus, while showing the indirect influence of Confucian ideas, systems of education, and informal institutions, even this late, is nonetheless primarily an example of the limits of traditional Confucian influence in the development of critical Japanese politics after the 1880s. Confucian influence was limited primarily because the Confucian institutional base of the Tokugawa period had been in various respects decimated as a result of the Meiji Restoration. The Confucian research institutions were coopted into modern state educational facilities that had Western curricula, or just abolished like many domainal institutions. At an educational level, the private schools held on for one generation, but by the end of the 1880s the state system had expanded and stabilized to an extent that it could offer most ambitious students what they needed completely within the Westernized state context. The Confucian academies died. This meant that centers for Confucian practice, be it the self-cultivation of the Neo-Confucians, or various other methods by other tendencies, vanished. The Confucian influence looked at in this chapter was a legacy of Tokugawa Confucianism, the actions of those trained within its institutional structures. To understand Confucianism's history after the late nineteenth century, we therefore have to look at the dynamics around the destruction of Confucian institutions and practice during and after the Meiji Restoration of 1868.

6   Confucianism as fascism

> Considering the achievements of our long national history, the fate of
> the world some centuries from now may well be to see our nation
> assimilate and refine even Western culture. I firmly believe this is our
> nation's great aspiration and indeed its manifest destiny.
>
> – Hatoyama Ichirō, Minister for Education and Culture, 27th January, 1934,
> at the inauguration of the Association for the Propagation of Japanese
> Confucianism (Nihon Jukyō Sen'yōkai 1934: 15)

The transformation of Confucianism into an ideological tool of totalitarianism ironically began with authoritarian state suppression of
Confucianism. The Meiji Restoration of 1868 was followed by a con-
certed state attack upon Confucianism. That attack began with abolition
of former Tokugawa and domainal institutions of Confucian religious
practice and education and was followed by the new state comprehensively displacing Confucianism from the field of education. That displacement, however, was accompanied by a more sinister and deliberate
suppression of religious activity across the board. For a number of specific
reasons which will be discussed later, Confucianism was particularly hard
hit by the broad anti-religious policy of the early Meiji state. Confucian
institutions and practice almost completely disappeared from Japan by
the late 1880s. By the 1890s, however, some elements of elite Japanese
society would begin to see the advantages of a partial resurrection of
Confucianism. The nature of that resurrection, however, would maintain
the suppression of the religious elements of the tradition, recasting
Confucianism within the cold frame of Western philosophy. That philosophical bias, in turn, would lay the foundations for the later linking of
Confucianism with fascism.

The early Meiji suppression of Confucianism

In many divergent parts of the world, the rise of modern nationalism has
been accompanied by a period of suppression of religion, usually followed
by a reorganization of the place of religion in the polity along new nation-

state-centered lines. The French Revolution and its aftermath is the classic example of this process, but similar processes also occurred in China and Japan. The religion question was particularly central in Chinese and Japanese processes of Westernization and modernization because the Western imperial powers used the trope of religious freedom centrally in their suppression of local sovereignty – the core element of the rosy-sounding "openings" of China and Japan. Religious freedom (meaning free access and legal privilege for Western Christian missionaries) was a key demand in the treaty negotiations which institutionalized the unequal trade and diplomatic relationships between Western powers and China and Japan.

The idea of "civilization," key to the Western empires' arguments of justification for their unequal treatment of Asian countries in nineteenth-century trade and diplomacy, was also heavily reliant on religious ideas. Furthermore, the communication of this idea to the Chinese and Japanese elites during the nineteenth century was mediated by religious institutions, notably Christian missions. This meant that Chinese and Japanese statesmen, for instance the famous Chinese reformers Kang Youwei (1858–1927) and Liang Qichao (1872–1929), or the first constitutional prime minister of modern Japan, Itō Hirobumi (1841–1909), came to conceive of religion as a key element of Western statecraft. As Itō Hirobumi made perfectly clear in his famous speech opening the Constitutional Convention of the Japanese Empire in 1889, from his perspective, the model of the Western nation state was reliant on religious elements for control and mobilization of the citizenry, so the structure of the Japanese state must therefore also deploy religion centrally (Kokuritsu Kōbunshokan 1984: 156–7; Kuo 2013: 235–64; Paramore 2012a: 19–30).

This perspective of Itō was not at all new in Japan. The Mito Confucian Aizawa Seishisai's *New Theses*, one of the key political texts of the nineteenth century, and an inspiration to Meiji Revolutionaries and Tokugawa loyalists alike, had strongly argued that because the religious dimension was key to Western statecraft, the Japanese state must deploy the religious charisma of the imperial house to play this role in the Japanese polity (NST 53; Wakabayashi 1986). This outlook fed into the mid-nineteenth-century growth in Shinto propagating National Learning, particularly the mass Shinto National Learning movement centered around Hirata Atsutane which was a major intellectual and organizational base of support for Meiji Revolutionaries in their struggle against the Tokugawa shogunate through the 1850s and 1860s. When the Meiji Revolutionaries came to power, they thus began with an idea of establishing Shinto as a national religion for Japan. They set up a ministry within the government charged with administrating the religion, and put Shinto institutions in charge of local places of worship (Hardacre 1989).

This attempt to establish Shinto as a kind of state religion inherently required the repression of other religions. There has been much written on the repression of Buddhism which accompanied these reforms (Ketelaar 1990). The most notable form in which the attacks on Buddhism took place during this period was state appropriation of property, and thereby religious place and space. Then, as now, Shinto Shrines were often located in Buddhist temple grounds, or vice versa. The practice of rituals that appear Shinto or Buddhist were/are often integrated with one another. The attempt to make Shinto a national religion therefore had to firstly disentangle Buddhism and Shintoism, mainly by denigrating Buddhism. This needed to be done on various levels: institutional, liturgical, practice, place, and property. But the most noticeable was the appropriation of space and the consequent banishing of Buddhist religious and lay people and practice from certain spaces and sometimes consequent destruction and desecration of Buddhist objects and buildings in those spaces.

Confucian institutions and religious spaces faced a similar repression through the appropriation of space around the same time. The Meiji government attacked the old state Confucian academy and the attached Yushima shrine, the center of state Confucian worship under the late Tokugawas. In 1871, the academy was shut down. The buildings became a museum and events space, and the book collection was moved around various different local and national government authorities (Figure 6.1). In this way, the institution was stripped of its knowledge-related elements, its books and teachers, and the space was changed from a religious/knowledge usage to one of cultural exhibition and exoticization. Most notably, the objects of religious worship in the complex, for instance the statue of Confucius, were stripped of their religious role, firstly through the transformation and secularization of the space around it, and secondly through state bans on the practice of Confucian worship – strictly enforced in the old state academy grounds (Makabe 2007: 23–7).

This all indicates that the new state saw Confucianism in general, and the old shogunate state academy in particular, not only as a threat but as threat conceived of primarily in religious terms. The appointment of National Learning scholars to challenge Confucianism in the Academy demonstrates that the new government saw the Academy as a representation of an alternative religious ideology more than it saw it as a knowledge institution. The ban on Confucian worship deepens the impression that it was this aspect – worship, religious practice – which the government sought to limit in Confucianism. So we could perceive attacks on

Figure 6.1 The former Confucian Academy transformed into an "Exhibition Hall" – early Meiji period (Shibunkai collection)

Confucianism in the first years of Meiji rule simply as one element in a general state repression of religion that occurred at this time.

The Meiji government, however, also had particular reasons to want to suppress Confucianism specifically. As outlined in Chapter 4, the late Tokugawa state employed Confucianism in a wide array of areas, and utilized Confucian institutions to create state infrastructures and networks of knowledge, medicine, science, and education. Confucianism thereby came to be very closely associated not simply with any particular ideology of the Tokugawa state, but moreover with that state's practices, institutions, and personnel. This caused figures in the early Meiji state to be inclined against Confucianism in general, and particularly against the central Confucian institutions of the old Tokugawa state. This inclination was reinforced by the fact that the forces of the Meiji Revolution, in the conflict with the Tokugawa state which brought them to power, used the anti-Confucian rhetoric of nativism and National Learning as ideology. This provided another motivation for the Meiji government to attack and undermine Confucianism, particularly its nodes of social, political, and institutional engagement – notably the old Tokugawa-aligned institutions.

The Shogunal Confucian Academy was thereby an immediate target for the Meiji forces upon entering Edo/Tokyo. They carried out a reform of the Academy in the first year which required it to submit to the control of National Learning scholars from Kyoto. This created two factions within the Academy, the original Confucian and Western Learning specialists, on the one hand, versus the National Learning scholars who had been put in by the new Meiji government, on the other. The refusal of the Confucian and Western Learning scholars to submit to the authority of the nativist zealots from Kyoto was the catalyst for the wholesale closing of the Academy in 1871. Meiji state suppression of Confucianism, in general, and the former official organs of the state Confucian academies, in particular, continued through the course of the 1870s, including through the deliberate exclusion of senior Shogunal Confucian Academy figures from admittance to the new prestige knowledge institutions of the Meiji state. As outlined in the previous chapter, many former mid-level and junior researchers in the Shogunal Confucian institutions, usually after a couple of years of hiatus, found important employment in the knowledge infrastructure of the Meiji State – working at mid- to increasingly high levels in the bureaucracy and educational institutions. However, as Makabe Jin has shown, in the establishment of the Imperial Academy (a Japanese version of the Royal Academy), the Meiji government exerted considerable political pressure to have Koga Kin'ichirō, the former head of the Bansho Shirabesho, excluded against the wishes of all other founding scholar members (Makabe 2007: 17–19). It also applied pressure on other major intellectuals to make sure that there was no resurrection of the scholarly networks associated with the former Tokugawa state.

This neutralization of the old official shogunal Confucian academies and their most senior leaders was mirrored in the treatment of most domainal Confucian schools, particularly as the new Western education system of the Meiji state began to be rolled out.[1] The first line in the Westernization, nationalization, and universalization of education that occurred in the early Meiji period was the establishment of Normal Schools to train the teachers to be employed in the planned universal education system. In many parts of Japan, the Normal Schools took over the buildings of the Domainal Confucian Academies. This meant that treatment of space, personnel, and property followed similar trends to that seen in Tokyo. The spaces of the old domainal academies were completely transformed into centers of secular Western education – the only religious element allowed being the elements of Shinto used in national rituals. This is one reason why the early Meiji state's repression of religion had a much more sustained and damaging impact on Confucianism than on Buddhism. Most Buddhist temples and other institutions were restored to Buddhist sect control after the initial years of repression, whereas most Confucian academies were irreversibly transformed into state-controlled centers of Western-style education. The Buddhists usually got their spaces back; the Confucian spaces, however, were lost forever.

Confucian as the anti-modern

Confucianism was also challenged by the inherent nature of the Meiji's Westernizing reform not only of religion, education, and governance but also of the state's way of thinking about interaction between these fields. The Western state model being foisted upon Japan called for a separation of politics and religion. The position of Confucianism in the Tokugawa state appeared to completely contravene that doctrine. The modern separation and compartmentalization of the fields of religion, philosophy, and academic knowledge bifurcated the central axis of Confucian practice in late Tokugawa Japan. Confucianism, which had been central to the state, was now the antithesis of the state. Confucianism, which had been the seat of knowledge, was now redundant knowledge. Confucianism, which had combined knowledge, philosophy, and religion, was now forced to identify within only one of these categories: was it a philosophy, or a religion?

Most importantly, Confucianism's former domination of the educational infrastructure was not compatible with the totally Westernized technical education system that the early Meiji government imagined. The Meiji state conceived of knowledge completely through new Western disciplinary frameworks. Confucianism was thus not seen as a branch of knowledge, but of religion. The full-scale reform of the education system to make it completely based on Western models required the displacement of the Confucian academies' (notably including the private Confucian academies) central place in the infrastructures of learning and knowledge – thereby removing one of the key points of usefulness and social integration of Confucianism in Japanese society. This was to be the downfall of the large network of private Confucian academies that since the early Tokugawa period had underlain the increasingly central social position of Confucianism in Japanese society.

As discussed in the previous chapter, the private academies in Chinese learning continued to function through the first twenty years or so of the Meiji period, often becoming nodes for radical political debate. But the construction through this period of a universal and completely Western-based state education system slowly but increasingly pushed them out of the knowledge field. Meanwhile, the banning of Confucian worship through the first years of the Meiji period, and the neutralization and/or secularization of important spaces for worship like the Yushima Seidō, also affected the sphere of private Confucian learning. Crucially, the nexus between Confucian and Western Learning which had been established in the late Tokugawa period, particularly in the state institutions, was broken by the attraction of Western specialists into the new Meiji state system, and the denial of Confucian learning an academic status.

This meant that Confucianism in its private academy manifestation lost its best card in the competitive game of attracting students: its traditionally close association with the field of Western knowledge. This association was first denied by the Meiji state, and then methodically undercut by the expansion of that state's universal education infrastructure. Instead, through association with China, which under Western influence Japanese began to increasingly identify as the antithesis of Western modernity, Confucianism began to be perceived as backward and reactionary. This all led to a sharp trend in decline in Confucian learning and literacy. For many scholars, the Meiji period thereby actually marks the end of meaningful Confucian influence in Japan. As the near complete absence in academic writing on modern Japan of discussion on Confucianism in any form other than cliché demonstrates, most historians and religious studies scholars working on modern Japan have regarded Confucianism as dead in Japan from this point on. Confucianism, the assumption goes, was not compatible with Western modernity. Therefore, as the antithesis of Western modernity, Confucianism had no place in the story of Japan post-Westernization and modernization other than as a rhetorical tool in nationalist ideology.

Intriguingly, however, it was exactly this increasing representation of Confucianism in Japan as the antithesis of Western modernity which heralded the beginnings of its resuscitation. Ever since the mid-Tokugawa period, a major issue for Japanese intellectual and state engagement with Western modernity was the position of Christianity in Western systems of thought and governance – from constitutional monarchy to liberalism. The wholesale adoption of Western education, academic, and knowledge systems as the basis of Meiji modernization brought with it the problem of how to replace the role of Christianity in these systems. This was particularly pressing in the case of the national universal education system, notably in its connection with national ethics and national ideology.

Many late nineteenth-century thinkers across the globe agreed that one of the major challenges posed by modernity, or global capitalism, was the maintenance of morality and/or ethics. Even for liberals like J.S. Mill, ethics was a necessary element in successful social organization – which needed to be rooted in the nuclear family and informed by Christian morality (Mill 1989). Japanese liberals like Fukuzawa Yukichi also emphasized the role of the nuclear family in providing an ethical core for the new society, while at the same time rather unsuccessfully trying to relativize the Christian origins of this ethics (Fukuzawa 1973: 97). Most thinkers and government officials, however, looked to emulate more culturally embedded models of national morality from places like Germany. For those looking to emulate German-style models of national morality, the Christian element was simply too central to be ignored. It had to be dealt with directly, discussed, and either accepted or replaced.

There were indeed people who seriously advocated the wholesale appropriation of Christianity as part of the modernization of Japan. The central position of National Learning in the Meiji Revolution, however, and the long anti-Christian tradition in Japan, made this all but impossible. For some Japanese from the 1880s onward, the solution was clear: replacement, not simply with the cult of the imperial family, but with the ethical systems of Confucianism. From the late 1880s, German-educated figures like Inoue Testujirō (1855–1944) came to argue for a new utilization of Confucianism in this way to replace the role played by Christian values in underpinning German ideas of national morality. This then became Confucianism's new role, and new point for reentry into mainstream Japanese society. That, however, required significant changes to the social contextualization and subsequent meaning of Confucianism in Japan. It had to be made compatible with modern nationalism, and this was to be achieved by rhetorically disengaging it from the religious realm, and reintegrating it socially as political philosophy and ethics – a process which occurred mainly through the 1890s.

Confucianism as philosophy

Traditionalist figures like Motoda Eifu (1818–1891), personal tutor to Emperor Meiji, had already begun to call for a Confucian revival as early as the late 1870s. The "decline in morals" brought on by the rapid rate of change in the country was addressed by Motoda through calls for a return to the Confucian ethics of "humaneness, righteousness, loyalty and filial piety" (Motoda 1939). Calls like these from figures like Motoda, however, initially gained little traction. This was partly because they made little sense in the context of early Meiji Japanese modernization. There was wide consensus among members of the Meiji oligarchy that, following the trend current in Western statecraft, and as dictated by Western powers in the nature of treaty negotiations, politics and religion must be separated. For Meiji oligarchs like Itagaki Taisuke (1837–1919), Confucianism was the epitome of the "mixture of politics and religion" which was unacceptable to his Western partners and an antithesis to the ideal of modernity (Smith 1959: 43). Motoda, despite his privileged position as imperial tutor, did not succeed in his calls for Confucian revival because he never clearly offered a vision of Confucianism which could neutralize these criticisms. He was able to get Confucian slogans included in official proclamations and rescripts, but he was not able to originate a way for them to be used within the modern political context. For slogans like "loyalty and filial piety" in the Imperial Rescript on Education and other ideological documents to have a meaningful social and political effect in Japan, they had to be reworked and repackaged in a modern framework. A modern nationalist version of Confucianism could only gain hold once it had been reworked into a form whereby it was no longer seen as antithetical to the political, intellectual, and academic systems of modernity and material progress. What was required was a reworking of Confucianism which both allowed it to vent sentiments critical of the excesses of Westernization and modernity, while also fitting within the new parameters of political, intellectual, and religious discourse dictated by the (originally Western) paradigm of the modern nation state.[2]

This was achieved primarily by Inoue Tetsujirō through completely repositioning Confucianism's place in the Western academic schema, no longer as a religion, but as a philosophy. In this endeavor, Inoue used not only traditional Asian thought but also some of the latest Western philosophical and sociological paradigms to reposition Confucianism in Japan. Unlike figures such as Motoda Eifu and Sakatani Shirushi, who reveled in Confucianism's traditional position bridging the realms of governance and religion, Inoue sought to make Confucianism comprehensible within the modern constellation of academic categorization by denying that Confucianism was a religion, and arguing that it was instead a philosophy.[3] He used this definition to position Confucianism not only outside the politically problematic realm of religion but also against the traditional religious symbol of Western culture: Christianity. Confucianism as philosophy, according to Inoue, offered an ethical system adaptable to a program of modern "national morality," while simultaneously not in any way undermining the "scientific" basis of modern secular education. In this respect, Confucianism was superior to Christianity because it did not undermine science and rationalism in the way which Christianity, according to Inoue and the Western scientist writers he quoted, did. He publicized this position widely through a prodigious production of articles and books and multiple public speeches. They influenced not only Japanese reformulations of Confucianism but also those of China. For instance, the excerpt below comes from a speech Inoue gave at the Japanese Society for Philosophy in 1906, a speech attended not only by influential Japanese but also several key Chinese thinkers, including Liang Qichao (1873–1929), who would later go on to become influential intellectual voices in the politics of the Chinese Republic.

It is good if we have something like Confucianism [in education] because the aim of Confucianism is pure morality in its broadest sense. Moreover, there is no impediment to teaching Confucianism in schools because [unlike Buddhism and Christianity] it does not contradict the natural sciences (Inoue 1944: 806).

In this way, Confucianism could both replace the role of Christianity as the basis of national morality, and in fact even do a better job by both being more secular and scientific, and at the same time representing Eastern cultural values. Inoue's identification of Confucianism in this way as philosophy rather than religion had several antecedents. Jesuit missionaries in China and Europe in the seventeenth century had attempted to argue that Confucianism was not a religion so that they could justify to the Catholic hierarchy their decision to allow elite Chinese converts to continue to carry out the Confucian rites necessary for them to hold office in the Chinese imperial bureaucracy (Mungello 1994). Although Inoue had almost certainly heard of these European conceptions of Confucianism when studying in Germany, there was a more immediate example to hand for Inoue's ploy of identifying Confucianism as philosophy: modern Japanese Buddhism.

Through the 1880s, many European-educated Japanese Buddhist intellectuals also attempted to modernize Buddhism by identifying it as a kind of philosophical religion rather than a "superstitious" religion. This was done precisely so as to help identify their religion against Christianity and the West, while at the same time allowing Buddhism to appear in line with the sociologies of Western knowledge and science. One of the most successful advocates of this line was Inoue Enryō, a friend, collaborator, and early publisher of the young Inoue Tetsujirō directly after the latter's return from Germany (Paramore 2009: 107–44).

Inoue Tetsujirō followed this Buddhist example but went further by denying any religiosity to Confucianism at all. Confucianism was to be regarded purely within the realm of philosophy. This empowered Confucianism even more than Buddhism to stand against Christianity as a symbol of Eastern ethics. Confucianism's remodeling along these lines as a symbol of indigenous East Asian, and particularly Japanese, philosophical morals and ethical politics allowed Confucianism to then be deployed centrally and aggressively in modern society. It allowed Confucian slogans in the ideological texts of the state to be brought to life in political argument, giving them real social meaning and political impact.

Inoue played a major role in beginning this kind of employment of Confucianism in political society through his authorship of *Chokugo Engi*, the official government commentary on the Imperial Rescript on Education. Although the content of the half-page-long Rescript itself was the result of negotiations between figures like Motoda Eifu and Inoue Kaoru, its interpretation and particularly the politics it came to represent was very much determined by Inoue Tetsujirō's over one-hundred-page commentary which was distributed to all schools in Japan together with the actual rescript in 1891 (Inoue 1942).

Even more importantly, in late 1892, Inoue put Confucianism for the first time in decades on the center stage of mainstream political debate through his personal inauguration of what became one of the major political debates in mid-Meiji Japan: the so-called Debate on the Clash Between Education and Religion. This debate has come to be known by this name after the title of an article written by Inoue in late 1892 which attacked Christianity and egalitarianism as antithetical to the Japanese imperial state and its project of scientific modernization, education, and development. It sparked a major reaction with thousands of articles appearing over the next two years in major popular journals and newspapers in Japan, dominating public debate at certain moments during this period.[4] This debate was key to a public repositioning of the Imperial Rescript on Education as a document which advanced Confucian morality as a bulwark against Christianity, egalitarianism, and anti-developmentalism. The result of this positioning was brilliantly innovative in that it put Confucianism on the side of conservative moral politics, but at the same time also on the side of science, philosophy, the nation, and modern national education. It was a force of tradition and conservatism, but one which stood against the (perceived) anti-modern forces of religion (read Christianity) and egalitarianism.

In this repositioning of Confucianism, Inoue expertly deployed a range of recent developments in European academia – using Western secularism and science to entrench Confucianism as representative of a national secular morality. For instance, he pointed out the similarity between elements of Japanese Confucianism and aspects of Neo-Kantian philosophy, and he deployed Herbert Spencer's social organism theory (what is sometimes today colloquially if incorrectly labeled "social Darwinism") to argue for the rationalism of the hierarchical structures of Confucian ethics.

Inoue Tetsujirō thereby reinvented Confucianism in Japan through masterfully influencing developments in three separate fields: academia, the state, and public discourse. He influenced a new academic imagination of Confucianism through his role as Professor of Eastern Philosophy at the University of Tokyo. He engineered a new place for Confucianism in the official ideology and discourse of the state through his advisory role in the creation and official interpretation of the Imperial Rescript on Education. And he launched a new popular conception of Confucianism through his role as an influential political commentator in major public debates of the early 1890s.

This meant that by the outbreak of the First Sino-Japanese War in 1894, although still religiously and institutionally marginalized in Japanese society, and far removed from its socially central position in the late Tokugawa period, Confucianism had nonetheless been rehabilitated not only as one element in the national ideological framework but as a central element for deployment in real mainstream political debate. Furthermore, because figures like Inoue and indeed most other exponents of Confucianism – Shibusawa, for instance – had taken pains in their explication of Japanese Confucianism to demonstrate how it had changed course from the Chinese tradition during the Tokugawa period, the Japanese Confucianism they advocated was understood as not Chinese (Shibusawa 1918: 65–75). This was important, because it meant the rehabilitation of Confucianism was insulated from the regular outbreaks of anti-Chinese sentiment which occurred in Japan at times like the First Sino-Japanese War. The new modern Confucianism of Inoue was, in this respect at least, politically superior to Tokugawa Confucianism – it was no longer susceptible to charges of "Chineseness."

However, this institutionalized position for Confucian doctrine in key ideological documents of the state, and new role for Confucian content in political argument, did not stop the decline of Confucian academies, organizations, and the practices associated with them. By the 1890s, the private Confucian academies had all but vanished from the public sphere of modern Japan and had little to no relevance to either the education system or politics. A number of Confucian clubs and organizations had been set up during the Meiji period to promote Confucianism in their steads, but none of these were popular. They were all mainly literary organizations which had only very small, although sometimes extremely exclusive, memberships. New clubs and associations organized around an interest in Confucianism included the Shibun gakkai (founded 1880), Nippon Kōdōkai (1884), Kenkei kai (1899), and Tōa gakujutsu kenkyū-kai (1909). They came to have an increasingly literary and objective scholarly character during this period. In other words, Confucianism through the period from the 1880s up until World War I experienced a hiatus: Confucianism had been resuscitated as an element of state ideology, but there were no Confucian schools, activities, worship, or activism on any significant scale. Interest in Confucianism was polite, objective, distant, and all but totally upper class.

Confucianism's reinvigoration as conservatism

World War I changed everything. Confidence in Western modernity was profoundly shaken not only in war-devastated Europe but also in the East Asian nations watching from the sidelines. In China, negative cultural reactions to World War I provided part of the background for the May Fourth Movement, catalyzed by the injustices of Versailles (Fitzgerald 1996). In Japan, images and writings from Europe depicting the barbarism of the Western Front challenged the association of Western modernity with civilization and order. At the same time, World War I ironically brought wealth and a new economic confidence to Japan through increased trade revenue in war provisions. Part of this economic expansion was linked to the rise of aggressive Japanese imperialist expansion in China. This in turn reinforced self-imaginings of Japan as a regional mercantilist imperium over East Asia, notably including China. For Japan, World War I, as well as displacing the myth of European civilizational superiority, also boosted domestic military and political confidence as Japan earned cash through military supply production and export and took the world stage along with the Entente Allies and America on the winning side through limited military actions against German colonies in the North Pacific and annexation of German outposts in China (Dickinson 1999).

Not surprising then that 1918 ushered in a change of fortunes for the new Confucianism of modern Japan. 1918 saw the merging of most pro-Confucian scholarly associations into a more activist organization called the Shibunkai, which would preside over a rise in the popularity and social integration of Confucianism in Japanese society and beyond over the coming decades. The Confucian perspective was the perfect standpoint from which to condemn the ugly face of Western modernity exposed by World War I. As Hattori Unokichi wrote in the very first edition of *Shibun*, the journal of the new organization, the German militarism of World War I was equivalent to the *hadō* (Ch. *Badao*), or "Usurper's Way," the way of violent warrior rule that Mencius and Confucius criticized as the opposite of the Confucian "Kingly Way." Ironically, although using Confucian discourse condemning a by nature violent state in this passage, the overall intent of the article was to justify Japan's participation in the War on the side of the Entente (*Shibun* 1:1 (February, 1919): 19–36). This reveals the new integrated dual role that Confucianism came to play, as a lens for understanding the deficiencies of Western modernity, but within a modern nationalist paradigm also used to justify nationalist goals – including war. Of course, it is possible to conceive of this as a contradiction, but it is a contradiction underlying many forms of twentieth-century conservatism, be they Japanese, European, or other.

The increased wealth, freedom, and for a while relative democracy of Japan in the World War I and immediately post-World War I period also brought to the surface other elements of modernity and capitalism which had become globally problematic in the late nineteenth and early twentieth centuries: notably, industrial conflict between capital and labor. In the 1910s and 1920s, the elite in most industrial countries came to associate industrial conflict with the experience of World War I, the break down in the social order caused by the war, and the rise of revolutionary socialism. Labor conflict was thus perceived by the Japanese non-laboring classes, as by similar interests in other countries, as a problem inherent in high modernity. A return to a non-Western and pre-industrial ethics therefore seemed a logical solution in Japan as elsewhere. One of the major figures in the 1918 launch of the Shibunkai, Shibusawa Eiichi, the following year launched the "Conciliation Association" (*Kyōchōkai*), an organization with the express purpose of preventing labor conflict. The membership overlapped to a significant extent with membership of the Shibunkai, and the Conciliation Association's approach to labor relations was overtly Confucian – the key concept being the *Wang dao*, or Confucian Kingly Way. According to Shibusawa Eiichi, "If Capital deals with Labor according to the *wang dao* and vice versa, believing that their interests are common to each other, there will be no strife" (Obata 1938: 166).

This approach, of course, was not unique to Japan. In Europe and America, conservative traditionalist movements also arose seeking to overcome both the anti-social features of liberal capitalism and the radical leftist reactions against it. Warren W. Smith in his masterful post-World War II study of early twentieth-century Japanese Confucianism at several points notes the parallel between conservative Confucianism in Japan at this point and Catholic corporatism in Europe (Smith 1959: 124). Indeed, rhetoric like that of Shibusawa quoted above closely matches those used by "Christian Democratic" or "Catholic People's" parties and organizations in Europe through the mid-twentieth century. Like Catholic corporatists, the Confucian activism in 1920s Japan sought to counter socialistic tendencies partially by trying to compete against them for anti-capitalist sentiment. Through a partial criticism of materialism and modern economics, these movements portrayed themselves as standing at least partially in opposition to capitalism. For these Confucian conservatives, however, unlike the socialists, the problem of capitalism was not the nature of its distribution of material wealth, but rather the social relations which in their view underlay materiality. In this sense, they reversed the materialistic outlook of both doctrinaire socialists *and* free-market capitalists. In 1920, Koyanagi Shigeta expressed this outlook in the second edition of *Shibun* by quoting Confucius, "I do not worry over scarcity, but I am anxious over inequality. I do not worry over poverty, but I am anxious about not being at peace" (*Shibun* 2:2 (April 1920): 89–94).

Shibusawa Eiichi's enthusiastic promotion of Confucianism, and particularly his role in promoting "self-cultivation" and the ideal of "the self-made man" examined in Chapter 5, was primarily advanced through the organizational infrastructure of the Shibunkai. It occurred within the context of this early twentieth-century search for a conservative means to moderate capitalism, and thereby counter socialism. Yet, as argued in Chapter 5, Shibusawa seems to have failed in his attempt to formulate a credible modern practice of "self-cultivation." This ultimate failure to match his Confucian analysis of the problems of capitalism with an effective Confucian system for its mitigation is an example of the kind of emptiness which has led many commentators to consider early twentieth-century, religiously inspired conservative movements, including this Confucian movement, as not much more than a cloak for corporate-led proto-fascism (Smith 1959).

In defense of figures like Shibusawa, however, it is important to note that at this early stage of revived Confucian political activism the conservative position was clearly couched in support of democratic frameworks. A rejection of materialism, by Confucians or Catholics, just like the ambivalent approach to materialism taken by many socialists, did not necessarily mean or lead to a rejection of other elements of political modernity like democracy. Figures like Hattori Unokichi, at least in 1919, while condemning socialism, also clearly defended democracy, and even argued that the egalitarian nature of Confucianism made it particularly suited to democracy and vice versa (Harrell 2012; *Shibun* 1: 4 (August 1919): 327–34). One of Shibusawa Eiichi's close collaborators in the Shibunkai, and a co-author of *Shūyō Zensho* (Collected Works on Cultivation) in 1918, the capitalist Yasuda Zenjirō (1838–1921), was even assassinated by ultra-nationalists for refusing to financially support them (Shibusawa and Yasuda 1918). Confucianism, like Catholic corporatism in Europe, had a conservative anti-labor bias, but also had egalitarian tendencies and in some formulations seemed an honest attempt to understand and react to the serious social disorder arising from late industrial capitalism. It is too easy an option to simply equate such sentiments automatically with proto-fascism.

That given, however, it is equally important to note that the histories of corporatist anti-socialist groups, notably Catholic action groups, often had interconnections with the rise of fascism (Brown 2014). In Japan, the rise of this new conservative Confucianism developed characteristics which made it susceptible to later authoritarian and fascist cooption. The first problem was the lack of an ability to originate a form of practice giving Confucianism any meaningful and regular form in Japanese life, as outlined earlier. A second, related problem was the imposition of a layer of state and imperial rituals over Confucian practices, and the consequent packaging of this new wave of Confucianism within the structures of the state imperial cult. This notably involved the development of new Confucian rites and rituals alongside state Shinto ones, and Confucianism's consequent linkage to the emperor cult, and thereby to the military. As the Shibunkai and its activities continued to grow in popularity, influence, and confidence, Confucianism's association with national morality, the state organs, and notably the military increased. In 1927, the Minister for Education, Mizuno Rentarō, who took an active interest in the resuscitation of Confucianism through the 1920s, articulated his views that Confucianism needed to be less bookish, more practical and focused on teaching morals, and therefore should involve more ceremonial practice – and this practice, Confucian ceremonies in particular, should be carried out in Shinto fashion (*Shibun* 9:12 (December 1927): 721–6).

By the end of the 1920s, Confucianism had therefore been repositioned in Japan much closer to the interests of the state, but with an active and popular public association promoting it. The state and Confucian associations, notably the Shibunkai, were linked in multiple ways. For instance, the state made available Yushima Seidō, the Confucian shrine of the old shogunal academy, and therefore traditionally the Confucian shrine of the Japanese central state since the late 1700s, as a site for a major revived Confucian calendar of rituals. These rituals were then attended by cabinet ministers including the prime minister, imperial princes, and senior members of the general staff. Under state pressure like that of Mizuno, the nature of the rituals was changed to intersect with imperial Shinto ritual. In this way, the Confucian ritual scheme was reestablished as an official ritual of the Japanese state, but was also affected by that state's politico-religious predilections. This state dominance, and in some respects control (for instance in relation to ritual practice), made this new Confucianism particularly susceptible to being caught up in the ideological confusion and systematic structural failure which was about to befall the Japanese state itself.

Confucian fascism

The 1930s saw Confucianism, like the rest of Japanese society, move onto a new footing. The 1931 Manchurian incident began a long period of military conflict in China and severe economic and later military conflict with the United States: the so-called Fifteen Years War (1931–1945), beginning with the Manchurian incident, moving through the full-blown Second Sino-Japanese War from 1937 and into the Pacific Theatre conflict of World War II from 1941 to 1945.

The transformation of modern twentieth-century Japanese Confucianism from an albeit conservative movement to one with explicit fascist tones occurred in this context and can be clearly marked off by the formation in 1934 of Japan's own Confucian missionary society, the Association for the Propagation of Japanese Confucianism, *Nihon jukyō senyō kai*. The founding congress of this organization, attended by dignitaries from the Prime Minister down, was addressed by politician and head of the State Academy of Oriental Culture, Katō Masanosuke

(1854–1941) who made a speech which well illustrates the new radical tendencies of Confucianism represented within this organization.

Capitalists exploiting the flesh and blood of laborers while laborers band together and strike in opposition. Landlords and tenants each wishing their own share to be large, so tenant disputes arising constantly. Politicians taking advantage of their positions and yearning for unfair profits ... Communist influence at Kyoto University ... these are the poisons of following material culture (Nihon Jukyō Sen'yōkai 1934: 7).

Katō's position as head of a state institution of oriental studies is indicative of the synergy that came to arise between the expansionist war aims of the military on the (predominantly Chinese) mainland, the colonialist orientalism of the Japanese empire's Area Studies scholars (predominantly Sinologists), and the new expansive missionary zeal of the Confucian associations, who came to see their project, just like that of Japan, no longer as only one of national redemption, but of civilizational and perhaps even global redemption in an imperial context.[5] The quote that opens this chapter, where Minister of Education Hatoyama, at the same event where the above quote from Katō comes, predicts a Japanese Confucian cultural takeover of the world, illustrates the almost millenarian tone that began to inhabit the Confucian discourse of fascism in Japan.

Ironically, Confucianism's long historical relationship with Christian Mission had come full circle. From Confucianism's definition in Jesuit texts of the seventeenth to nineteenth centuries as an object of Christian Mission in China, Confucianism had now transformed into an almost perfect copy of the imperialistic Christian missionary movement of the nineteenth century, and with the same primary geographic target of mission and colonization: China.

Confucianism as colonizing mission

Confucian associations and leaders were coopted into the project of imperialism and colonialism just like other religions in Japan. It is important to note here that the transformation of Confucian groups into "missionary" societies followed the same model the state dictated for all the other competing Buddhist, Shinto, and even Japanese Christian groups. Religion in all these guises was deployed in the empire. This then also shows that despite the rhetoric of the likes of Inoue Tetsujirō, by the 1930s Confucianism was again ultimately being treated by the state as a religion alongside other religions.

Intriguingly, but also rather understandably, Japanese Confucianism in its export version in the empire was quite different to the increasingly radical and fascistic manifestation in Japan proper. The radical message, in particular the anti-capitalist rhetoric, was gone. After all, the capitalists in Manchuria were predominantly Japanese, many with close institutional links to the military. The message of Japanese-delivered Confucianism in Japanese-occupied greater Asia was rather predominantly cultural conservative, resting firmly on the idea of the Kingly Way, the central plank of the post-1918 conservative political message of Japanese Confucianism. In other words, despite Japanese Confucian missionary expansion to occupied Asia being a result of and related to the radicalization of the Japanese state toward fascism, the message of Japanese Confucianism outside Japan proper was not the post-1934 fascist one but the earlier conservative manifestation associated with the kind of activism we saw from Shibusawa in the 1910s and 1920s.

This was innately related to the primary utility Confucianism had for the Japanese in their East Asian empire. Confucianism was used by Japan in occupied East Asia to claim the Asian credentials of modern Japan, particularly in contrast to their only two even remotely competent Asian political rivals: the Chinese republicans (the KMT and their Republic of China) and the Chinese communists (the CCP and their various territorial manifestations in occupied North China). By holding up Confucianism as the identifier of Asian culture, Japanese authorities were easily able to claim themselves as the real stewards of Asian tradition in comparison to the republicans and communists because both of these groups initially rejected Confucianism as an antithesis to their imagination of a strong, modern China. In other words, Japanese utilization of Confucianism in occupied East Asia played on a strategic weakness of Chinese republican and communist ideologies: their rejection of major elements of their own cultural heritage, a rejection which inhibited their ability to construct a form of nationalism which followed standard models.[6]

The argument that the Japanese state rather than the Chinese state was the defender of the Confucian tradition and therefore East Asian values was reinforced by Japanese academic and political assertions that true Confucianism had already died in China long before the twentieth century. According to the Japanese line of intellectual history, Confucianism had only meaningfully been carried on and developed in Tokugawa Japan. Inoue, for instance, saw Hayashi Razan as having transformed the nature of Confucianism already from the early Tokugawa period (Inoue 1905). For many other scholars, it was Ogyū Sorai's rejection of Song Learning and emphasis on the idea of the Kingly Way, and more importantly the Mito School's linkage of this Kingly Way to the glorious history of millennia of continuous rule by

Japan's god-like imperial house which gave Japan a more pristine and logical version of Confucianism than that of China. It was Japanese Confucianism which thanks to this "Kingly Way" was able to withstand the pressure of the Western threat (Kiyowara 1944: 726). This allowed Japan not only to use Confucianism to identify itself as representative of Asia but to do this in contrast against its republican and communist political and military enemies in China. That then allowed Japan as the champion of the Confucian ethic which represented Asia to represent itself, its state, its capital, its war – primarily as the champion of the Orient in its conflict with the Occident (Shibunkai 1999: 19). Confucianism was thus a central prop in the ideology which allowed Japanese militarists to obscenely claim the war against China as, in the words of General Doihara Kenji, "a war for the renaissance of Oriental culture . . . to lose this war will mean the eternal defeat and subjugation of the Orient to Western civilization" (Smith 1956: 209).

The use of Confucianism to justify such assertions, however, did not go unanswered. In the 1930s, ideologues of the Chinese Republic like Hu Shih (1891–1962) engaged in academic exchanges of fire with Japanese ideologues like Inoue Tetsujirō over the simple question: who represents Confucianism – the Chinese Republic or the Japanese Empire? Hu Shih's engagement with this argument along these lines also reveals the devilish long-term (including postwar) influence of the Japanese Empire's ideological use of Confucianism. It invited the Chinese state to identify with Confucianism and coopt Confucian conservatism into the nationalist program as the Japanese were doing. In the course of constructing a rebuttal, the ideologues of the Chinese Republic began to accept and employ this instrumental link between the Confucian tradition and modern nationalism similar to that established by the Japanese. This in turn influenced a new appropriation of Confucianism by authoritarian ultra-nationalists in the Chinese states.[7] Chiang Kai-shek's regime, starting as a lurch to conservatism in 1927 became, at least in ideological terms, increasingly fascistic through the 1930s and 1940s. Japanese rightist utilizations of Confucianism thereby provided a kind of example to this later authoritarian Chinese Republic's similar engagement with the tradition, an example which some might say has also been informing recent ideology construction in the People's Republic. Of course, how Japanese military and civil officials utilized Confucianism varied considerably between the different occupied territories.

Puppet Manchuria

Manchuria, the Japanese puppet state established in northeastern China in 1932, undoubtedly exemplifies the most overt use of Confucianism by the Japanese government in its East Asian empire. Manchuria was set up officially as a Confucian state, as the founding and defining ideological document of the state, its establishing proclamation, made clear.

Statecraft should be founded upon the principle of the Way and the Way founded upon Heaven. The principle on which this new state is based is to follow Heaven that the people may have peace and security. [The state will] ... promote and popularize education, respect the teachings of Confucianism, and apply the principle of the Kingly Way, and practice its teachings. These, we believe, will enlighten the people to maintain the honor of perpetuating the peace of the Far East and thus set an example of model government to the world (Manchoukuo Dept. Foreign Affairs 1932: 5).

This was not simply a Japanese invention, but was also enthusiastically advanced by the Qing loyalist Confucian scholars who formed the back-bone of the puppet regime's cabinet, notably the first Prime Minister Zheng Xiaoxu (1860–1938). The Confucian message there was similar to the conservative corporatism seen in Japan in the 1920s, initially similar to the comparatively mild approach of Shibusawa, and in the early stages free of the fascistic flourishes of some 1930s ideologues in Japan proper.[8]

Occupied China

The use of Confucianism in Manchuria was thus perceived as a good ideological model to emulate after Japan invaded the remaining northern provinces of China in 1937. The so-called Provisional Government of the Republic of China (PGROC) was set up by the Japanese four months after the full-scale invasion in 1937. It was very similar to the Manchurian administration in that it was "led" by a former Qing bureaucrat, in this case, Wang Kemin (1879–1945). He was backed up by other Chinese figures opposed to the nationalist and revolutionary ideology of the Republic, and instead emphasized an anti-nationalist universalist and corporatist message. They established civil associations and organizations to promote their approach of a revival of Confucian statecraft and mor-ality under Japanese leadership in China. One of the members of one such organization, the Xinminhui, explained their position in a speech to primary school teachers.

Western methods of progress are not natural, as are oriental. The West uses scientific methods to correct and control natural development. This is the method of conflict. The Kuomintang adopted this and destroyed the old family and the old religion. The Japanese are shedding their blood in order to help restore Chinese civilization which was dying because the revolution destroyed Confucianism (Smith 1959: 205).

Here we see a message very similar to the message of conservative Japanese Confucianism of post-1918 Japan, but then with the artifice of the West linked to the program of the KMT. The activities of these organizations can thus be seen to have fulfilled the primary ideological objective of associating Japan with a modern, effective manifestation of East Asian tradition, and the Chinese Republicans with the disorderly and inherently anti-social aspects of Western modernity.

Unfortunately for the Japanese and their Chinese collaborators, however, this ideological concoction and organization failed to stem the tide of Chinese resistance in North China, especially that emanating from the rural villages and fueled by CCP activism. Smith has provided an interesting analysis of the failure of Confucian conservatism to take hold in northern China at this time. For him the location of the old gentry elite in the cities meant that there were no collaborators on the ground in the countryside to advance the case for conservatism. Those who might have actually been open to an argument attacking Western modernity and capitalism from a traditionalist perspective, the landed gentry, were themselves located in the modernizing cities, while those still in the conservative rural areas were the peasants to whom the land-reform message of the CCP was eminently more appealing (Smith 1959: 214–17).[9]

By the end of 1938, this puppet regime and its anti-KMT rhetoric had been replaced by a new one led by former KMT stalwart Wang Jingwei (1883–1944). Wang appropriated wholesale the nationalist and republican ideological rhetoric of the Chinese Republic rather than rejecting it. Wang's regime was thus formulated to be not only an alternative Chinese government but an alternative KMT. This new puppet government was therefore not interested in trying to appeal to the population through an alternate ideology of Confucian universalism. They were happy just to try to use the same republican ideology of the KMT, but with the offer of peace with the Japanese and a possible end to the violence as an added motivator. The message of Japanese Confucianism as the epitome of a universal Asian resistance to Western modernity therefore failed to work in China, mainly, if we accept Smith's analysis, because of the nature of the social and political situation on the ground.

Colonial Korea

Confucianism was much more effective for the Japanese in Korea. Korea was fertile ground for the deployment of Confucianism, if only because it was the only country in East Asia where the modern Japanese regime took over directly from another regime which employed Confucianism centrally (Buzo 2007: 7, 30). Confucianism was not only the ideology of the Choson state (1392–1910), it also underlay the institutions of state, religion, and education (Grayson 2002: 177). The central place of Confucian institutions and their utility was recognized by the early colonial government. For instance, although attempting to implement a Western-modelled academic system of schools as in Japan, the colonial administration retained traditional local Confucian schools (*sŏdang*) in places where Western/Japanese schools could not be established. It then used these schools' connections with the local traditional gentry to gain influence in the countryside.[10] They appropriated wholesale the institutions of state Confucianism, notably the state academy of the Choson dynasty, the Sungkyunkwan, which was renamed the Keigakuin, but otherwise in many respects continued on much unchanged – for instance, with many of the same staff, and holding Confucian state ceremonies for the colonial regime. Major Korean Confucian figures, notably the leaders of the official academies and shrines, were rather successfully courted by Japanese state-aligned Confucians, particularly by the Shibunkai, which hosted visits to Japan by groups of major Korean Confucians of the academy in Seoul, men who often also held high position in the colonial government (Shibunkai 1999: 34–56).

Japanese state-supported Confucian institutions and their rituals attracted considerable support and participation in Korea. In 1928, there were reportedly nearly a quarter million Korean members of the state-aligned Korean Confucian organizations. There were still an estimated 100,000 participants at state shrine rituals even in 1937 after Japanese administration had taken a brutal turn for the worse. This indicates that Confucianism may have had some effective force in motivating Korean people to participate in the ideologies and institutions of the Japanese colonial state. However, Confucianism was only able to function effectively for the Japanese government in Korea, as in Manchuria, so long as it continued to represent conservative values, symbolizing an alternative to the radical rupture of the Westernizing modern.

Ironically, Confucian's utility for colonial rule in Korea was undermined primarily by the Japanese colonial administration itself through its failure to hold to the basic conservative values it claimed to represent. The Japanese administration identified itself with Confucianism primarily by claiming to uphold the key universal Confucian virtues of loyalty and filial piety. But in 1937, the Japanese government decided to force all Koreans to change their family names – to abandon the Korean house name of their ancestors and take up an artificial Japanized name. Many Koreans perceived this as a request to reject their family lineages. This then set the Japanese administration directly at loggerheads with one of the central ethical tenets of Confucianism: filial piety. By making Koreans reject their family heritage by changing their surnames, the identifier of their ancestral lineage, the Japanese government was forcing Koreans to be un-filial, while at the same time requesting their loyalty.

The 1937 Japanese state attacks on this vestige of Korean cultural identity, therefore, symbolize Japan's inability in the fascist turn to accept the multi-ethnic and multicultural reality of their empire, even in one of the few non-Japanese parts of the Japanese empire where their rule was secure. This represented not only the beginnings of the end for Japanese rule in Korea, but also an end to any real utility of Confucianism in bolstering the imperial project in any form other than cynical propaganda. The incompatibility of the cultural homogenization policy of the state from 1937, and the promise of Confucian universalism, perhaps ultimately represented an inherent mismatch between fascism and Confucianism at a deeper level.

Trans-war Asia

On the other hand, other aspects in the political usage of Confucianism developed under the fascist regime of the Japanese empire were surprisingly enduring in the trans-war period – particularly in postcolonial Asia.[11]

In Japan, leaders of the fascist regime used Confucianism as a plank of their defense in the Tokyo Trials. The opening address of the united Japanese defense at the trial, for instance, contains the following example which is indicative of how fork-tongued the rhetorical usage of Confucianism had become in Japan by the end of the war.

The intrinsic content of the idea of the new order as used in Japan is the "Kōdō" [Kingly Way] or "Imperial Way," as it is sometimes translated. The gist of the "Imperial Way" is benevolence, righteousness and moral courage. It respects courtesy and honor. Its ideal is to let everyone have his or her own part, and fulfill his or her duty. It envisions ruler and ruled to be of one mind and the affairs of state to be administered by the sincere aid of the whole people. It is just the opposite to the idea of militarism and despotism [Jp. *hadō*, Ch. *badao*]. It is extremely difficult to express such ideals in language other than Japanese, but as far as the respect for individual personality is concerned, there is no fundamental difference between the "Imperial Way" and democracy. It is unusual to adduce evidence to prove such abstract ideas in a court of justice, but we must do this in the present case. We shall offer a speech made by one of the accused in the Imperial Diet showing the difference between the "Imperial Way" and the totalitarianism of Germany and Italy (Kobori 1995: 38–9).[12]

The confused nature of the use of Confucianism within the context of ultra-nationalist fascism is clear even in this defense document. It tries to

Figure 6.2 South Korean military dictator President Park Chung-hee fighting the communists in an earlier manifestation as uniformed officer of the Japanese Imperial Army

position Confucianism as a universal East Asian cultural value to defend the establishment of the East Asian Co-Prosperity Sphere, but it also includes multiple references to Japanese exceptionalism – be they in regard to the position of the emperor or the capacities of the language. It goes without saying that this kind of employment of Confucianism in the postwar did the reputation of the tradition no good among the Japanese people. References of this kind were reminiscent of a cynical fascist cooptation of Confucianism which left most Japanese with an extremely negative image of the place of Confucianism in their own recent history.

In China, as touched on earlier, major figures, even liberals like Hu Shih, had been driven into a discourse on Confucianism's role in politics which saw them in many ways appropriating elements in the Japanese empire's politicization of Confucianism, even as they tried to rebut it. Taiwan under the authoritarian rule of Chiang Kai-shek after 1945, and thereafter right up into the 1980s, would see Confucianism used as part of a state ideology that shared many features with fascism. In Korea, just as the Confucian Academy of the pre-Japanese occupation Choson state had continued serving the state under the Japanese, so too the Confucian institutions went on to stay close to the authoritarian US-backed South Korean state after "liberation," and to use Confucianism in a similarly conservative culturalist way. As in the Choson to Japanese transition, so too in the Japanese to US/South Korean transition, there was plenty of continuity of Confucian personnel. Yu Ŏk-kyŏm, for instance, appointed head of the Department of Education under the United States Military Government in South Korea between 1945 and 1947, had been a Confucian rhetorician for the Japanese, even making anti-US speeches. His brother, Yu Man-gyŏn, another Confucian academy figure, was a provincial governor under the Japanese. As Michael Seth has outlined, Yu Ŏk-kyŏm collaborated just as well with the Americans and he had with the Japanese, serving their interests loyally (Seth 2002: 36–8).

In China and Korea, the Japanese utilization of Confucianism during the occupation had been mainly conservative rather than fascist. Nonetheless, the brutal authoritarianism that flourished in these countries post-1945, often supported by US forces in the Cold War context, created regimes in South Korea and the ROC on Taiwan that through the 1950s, 1960s, and 1970s most definitely carried on fascistic ideological elements which, if not inherited from the Japanese occupation, then were at the very least reminiscent of Japanese imperial practices during the war (Figure 6.2). From the perspective of the increasingly secure, economically comfortable, and democratic Japanese of these same post-war decades, however, the fascistic vision from across the sea was discomforting to say the least. The disturbing knowledge that the origins of these authoritarian monsters just over the water may have had something to do with "we Japanese" only served to bring back the uncomfortable memories of recent history. Unlike the rest of East Asia, Japan itself had made a clean break with fascism and most of its causes – or at least, that was the new ideological narrative. In Japan, Confucianism, like everything else associated with the fascist past, was best forgotten.

7   Confucianism as taboo

We resolve to pave the way for a grand peace for all generations to come.
Emperor Hirohito quoting Song Confucian Zhang Zai (1020–1077)
during his radio address to the Japanese people announcing surrender
(15 August 1945)

Postwar Japan was a new country. At least that was the message leaders and intellectuals wanted to give after 1945, and have kept giving ever since (Koizumi 2005). In that new country Confucianism quickly became taboo. Meiji had destroyed Confucian institutions and practice; fascism and World War II destroyed Confucianism's reputation. Associated closely with the fascist politics which had brought about the devastation of the war, it was tainted. The sole social field Confucianism had occupied with influence post-Meiji, ethics teaching in schools, was totally remodeled, with US-originated civics education completely replacing Confucianism. The only place that any Confucianism appeared at all in standard Japanese education post-1945 was a couple of passages of *Confucius Analects* used for grammar teaching in the small classical Japanese element of the high school language curriculum. There was no structural positioning of Confucianism in general society in any way which would have people reflect on its ethical meaning or history of social and religious practice. The changes to the education system reduced its presence in normal life experience to a couple of sentences from an antique foreign text philologically dissected to understand some finer points of a redundant Japanese grammar. Interest in Confucianism was now restricted to the ivory towers of elite academia, and most of the very limited social impact it had on postwar society was delivered through the mediation of that academic context. Confucianism's limited influence in postwar Japanese society was thus delivered top-down through the ideas of academics who functioned as public intellectuals.

The immediate postwar period saw the meteoric rise of some public intellectuals and high-profile academics whose work used Confucianism centrally. This chapter will thus begin by looking at Maruyama Masao (1914–1996) and Tsuda Sōkichi (1873–1961), two contrasting examples of public intellectuals who influenced the public life of immediately postwar Japan. I will both contrast their influence with more fanatic vestiges of the prewar formulations of Confucianism, for instance in the actions of Mishima Yukio (1925–1970), and also look at the influence of figures like Maruyama and Tsuda on the more sustained but cloistered academic study of Confucianism which continued through the late twentieth century. This later academic study was initially restricted to the universities but in the past decade has begun to become more oriented toward debate in the public sphere. The chapter will conclude with a consideration of the place of Confucianism in this later academic engagement with the public sphere, as well as review the activities of what civil society Confucian organizations remain in Japan today.

Making Confucianism taboo: Public intellectuals and fanatics in the postwar

Undoubtedly the most famous post-World War II Japanese figure associated with Confucianism is Maruyama Masao. Certainly no Confucian himself, Maruyama was a University of Tokyo professor of political science and the history of political thought who idealized Western liberalism. In wartime, Maruyama, although unlike others not dismissed from his position at the University of Tokyo, nevertheless suffered under the repression of the security services. In the postwar, however, he became Japan's premier liberal public intellectual. He wrote leading opinions in newspapers and magazines and addressed political rallies of hundreds of thousands protesting against Japan's remilitarization under the United States–Japan Security Treaty. Although participating as a leading figure in rallies of this magnitude against conservative governments, he was nonetheless loathed by many in the influential socialist left of postwar Japanese politics for whom his openly liberal bourgeois political agenda was nearly as offensive as that of the conservative LDP government they both opposed (Karube 2008; Kersten 1996).

As well as being the most influential public intellectual of the postwar, and its leading liberal, Maruyama was also the preeminent academic expert on the history of Japanese Confucianism. Maruyama's two most famous works are both products of the 1940s and 1950s – one produced during the war and the other in the postwar period. *Studies in the Intellectual History of Tokugawa Japan*, written through the war years, published as journal articles during the last years of the Pacific War and finally as a book in Japanese in 1952, is a history of the political philosophical role of Confucianism in early modern Japan, focusing particularly on its effects on the formation of the modern Japanese nation state and its political ideology. Although presented thus as a history of Confucian thought, the book's points were deeply political and present. As Maruyama himself wrote in an introduction to a later printing, the book was his answer and resistance to the "overcoming modernity" and "national morality" ideologies of the wartime fascist state (Maruyama 1974: ix, xxx, xxxi). He thus used the history of Confucianism in Japan as the central plank in his argument against fascist nationalism.

By comparison, his postwar works barely mention Confucianism at all. *Thought and Behaviour in Modern Japanese Politics*, a collection of political essays written and widely publicized in the late 1940s and early 1950s, was first published as a book in Japanese in 1957 and translated into English with later additions in 1963. The word "Confucianism" only appears once throughout *Thought and Behaviour in Modern Japanese Politics*, and then only to retort an argument made by Tsuda Sōkichi (Maruyama 1963: 5). Maruyama considered his struggle in the postwar, as during the war, to be against fascism. Yet although choosing Confucianism as the central vehicle of his wartime struggle, in the postwar he would not even name Confucianism. The reason is intimately related to Confucianism's postwar association with fascism, an association Maruyama had stressed in his earlier work, and which now saw not only Maruyama, liberals, and socialists but also most conservatives in Japan avoid any reference to Confucianism in the public sphere. The initially central and then completely absent role of Confucianism in Maruyama's career and oeuvre is the best example of the establishment of the Confucian taboo in postwar Japanese society. Despite their lack of direct reference to Confucianism, however, Maruyama's postwar political writings also give important insights into the thinking that led to Confucianism becoming taboo in the postwar.

The fascist past towered over the consciousness of immediately post-World War II Japan and particularly over its intellectual elite. The avoidance of a recurrence of fascism was an obsession for many, chief among them Maruyama. After the collapse of a brief coalition government under Socialist Party Prime Minister Katayama Tetsu (1887–1978) in 1947–1948, conservatives returned to power. The anti-communist imperatives of the United States in Japan caused the US Occupation's earlier support for the labor unions, social democrats, and left liberals to flail, allowing former wartime leaders to come back into power. Meanwhile, the rise of McCarthyism in the United States itself presented Japanese progressives with a frighteningly familiar vision of fascistic political repression, reminding them of the fragility of democracy, even in the country which claimed to represent democratic values to Japan and the world. Maruyama equated McCarthyism with fascism as early as 1952

(Maruyama 1963: 157). For him it was a reminder that "parliament [parliamentary democracy] presents no serious obstacles to the development of fascism" (Maruyama 1963: 162). It appears that Maruyama saw the return of fascism through the parliamentary system as a real possibility in the LDP-governed Japan of the 1950s and 1960s.

Certainly, the LDP included plenty of former militarist corporate and political leaders of the wartime past. Through the second half of the twentieth century their descendants were well represented among the LDP's parliamentary elite, as they still are today. Many LDP leaders, including Yoshida Shigeru early on, right through to Nakasone Yasuhiro in the 1980s, were reportedly sometimes advised by Yasuoka Masahiro (1898–1983), a self-proclaimed "Yangming Confucian" who was implicated in the trans-Asian policies of the fascist period and purged during the US Occupation. Yasuoka himself used his role in the editing of Emperor Hirohito's surrender broadcast to tote his pacifist credentials, but in most respects he represented continuity with the ultraconservatism of the prewar period.[1] Like Shibusawa, Yasuoka concentrated on the Confucian development of the individual and on the practice-centered development of individual "character." It was in this respect that Yasuoka's "Confucianism" influenced the Nobel Prize-nominated writer Mishima Yukio. Mishima died in 1970 by killing himself at a Japanese Self-Defense Forces base which he and his associates had seized attempting to inspire a fascistic military coup. By taking senior officers hostage, he forced junior officers to assemble hundreds of soldiers in front of the balcony of the base's main building. From there he gave a fanatic speech attempting to rouse them to coup. The soldiers just laughed at him. Seemingly unable to make himself heard through their jeers and the humming of helicopters overhead, he went back inside and committed *hara-kiri* (Figure 7.1).

Two months earlier Mishima had written and widely publicized a tract praising Yangming Confucianism. Printed in two different popular journals under the title "Yangming Confucianism as Revolutionary Philosophy," the piece praised the armed insurrection of Ōshie Heihachirō, repeating the common post-Meiji nationalist misrepresentation of this rebellion as a proto-nationalist uprising (Benesch 2009; Kojima 2006: 184–5). Four years previously Mishima had written to Yasuoka praising his practice-based approach to Confucianism in comparison to the miserable desk-jockey style of other Confucian scholars.

Reading and studying your works carefully I have come to harbor a great ambition to demonstrate the "unity of knowledge and action" [ethic] of Yangming Confucianism (Mishima 2005: 238).

Figure 7.1 Mishima addressing Self-Defense Force troops shortly before his suicide

Admittedly, Mishima's ultimate manner of "demonstration" was probably not what Yasuoka had in mind. Nonetheless, the association between Yasuoka and Mishima had been made. This meant that ultimately their connection only served to discredit Yasuoka even further in the eyes of many in mainstream Japan. Attempts in the postwar to revive the conservative practical Confucianism of early twentieth-century Japan seemed ultimately unable to disengage the laudable ideal of Confucian practice from the millennial aspects of mid-twentieth-century Japanese fascist nationalism. The lack of traction of Yasuoka's approach is best summed up by Mishima himself, who in "Yangming Confucianism as Revolutionary Philosophy" compared the position of Confucianism in his contemporary Japan unfavorably with that of Confucianism in America.

Other than among a small fraction of devotees, the general situation is that people [in Japan] know nothing more than the name of Wang Yangming. I hear that in America there are three scholars studying Yangming Confucianism, but in Japan there are only two or three scholarly houses continuing the Yangming Confucian tradition. Its basic merit as a philosophy inspiring practical action has been completely lost (Mishima quoted in Kojima 2006: 185).

Subtle activities like those of Yasuoka and the not so subtle interventions of Mishima did bring Confucianism back into occasional public view – but only very rarely and sporadically, and not in a way that cast Confucianism in a positive light. The perceived connection between Confucianism and the wartime fascist past was only reinforced. Unlike these peripheral figures, most mainstream conservatives were quite cautious and thereby very reticent to be associated overtly with Confucianism. Nakasone Yasuhiro (1918–), prime minister of Japan from 1982 to 1987, is a good example. Despite being one of the most nationalist of LDP politicians of his time, and allegedly a sometime associate of Yasuoka, he was careful not to openly associate himself with Confucianism. In his memoirs he makes little to no reference to Confucianism directly, nor indeed to Confucian figures, despite repeatedly referring to influences from Buddhism and even Marxism (Nakasone 1999: 230–1). As Minister of Defense at the time of the Mishima incident, he gave a statement implying Mishima was insane, labeling Mishima's conduct simply "deviant" (Kojima 2006: 192; Nakasone 1999: 165).

Like most of the symbolism of pre-1945 fascism, reference to Confucianism was avoided even by most conservative politicians, who at the time were reticent even to invoke the emperor system. Their strategy was to deny all the symbolism of the pre-1945 order so as to avoid any easy rhetorical link to their own sometimes dubious wartime pasts. They instead identified themselves with the postwar and pro-American order of democracy and liberalism, emphasizing their support for capitalism and anti-communism to differentiate themselves from both the contemporary socialist opposition and pre-1945 fascist past.

The left and the liberal center also avoided reference to Confucianism, but for deeper reasons. Not only had the label of Confucianism been tainted for the center and left by appropriation at the hands of fascism, more importantly Confucianism still represented for them the traditional premodern past. For Japanese liberals and leftists of the immediately postwar this was even more problematic than the association with fascism. This was due to the postwar Japanese left's extremely teleological and developmentalist outlook. Doctrinaire Marxism heavily informed the outlooks of not only the considerable section of the Japanese intelligentsia associated with the Japan Communist Party but also the larger group of both intelligentsia and general population associated with the Japan Socialist Party and even many postwar liberals like Maruyama. The teleological element in Marxism was particularly powerful in East Asian intellectual life. In postwar Japan major arguments which bitterly split both the Japanese Communist Party and significant elements in humanities academia revolved around interpretations of the teleology of Marxism (Anderson 1974: 435–505). Undisputed, however, was the enlightenment-rooted idea of the progress of human society, and analyses of society couched completely in terms of that teleology of progress. Confucianism, simply because it was seen to represent past, premodern tradition, and premodern Asian society, was thereby regarded as inherently "counterrevolutionary" and thus a negative social force (Maruyama 1963: 160).

Mainstream liberal outlook also worked within this same teleological model. Maruyama's critique of fascism, for instance, focused almost exclusively on its character as a reactionary tendency – acting against a teleological progress of history. Bizarrely, he compared the role of fascism in the modern world to the role of the counter-reformation and Jesuits in early modern Europe (Maruyama 1963: 159). This provides an insight into the interesting secular spiritualism of modernity which inhabited Maruyama and many other mainstream educated people in Japan at that time.[2] Conservatism was for them, like for the socialists, an inherently negative social force simply because it represented the past. Their progressive teleological vision of modernity engendered a secularist spiritualism: the "spirit of progress." It was on this basis that Maruyama criticized other scholars' approach to both fascism and premodern culture. Tsuda Sōkichi, one of the few intellectual defenders of premodern tradition left after 1945, had tried to defend the Japanese emperor system by claiming that its role in Japanese fascism was "exceptional" or "accidental." For Maruyama, this was a deep misunderstanding of the conservative roots of fascism. The emperor system consisted of a feudal and premodern spirit, and it was therefore a real and unavoidable cause of fascism – not just a rhetorical dressing (Maruyama 1963: 23).

Confucianism, as another element of the premodern societal past, was regarded in similar terms. Postwar Japanese intellectuals did not see Confucianism's role in fascism as simply a rhetorical appropriation. Conservative cultural ideologies, as Confucianism had become in early twentieth-century Japan, were regarded as real facilitators of fascism. This tendency was supported by Maruyama's belief that conservatism and fascism were essentially not different phenomena. For him, the claim that "fascism is necessarily reactionary, but conservative reaction is not necessarily fascism" was nothing more than "a mistaken notion actively propagated both now and in the past by fascist demagogues and other conservative reactionaries" (Maruyama 1963: 160). Whereas most commentators now are reticent to conflate conservatism and fascism,

Maruyama held a position today associated more with doctrinaire Marxists than liberal intellectuals. For Maruyama, however, this approach was in no way exclusively Marxist but simply conformed to the basic teleological outlook of the enlightenment. He quoted Hegel not Marx to justify this outlook, and he saw it simply as an indelible part of an enlightenment associated with Protestant reformation in Weberian terms.

The few writers who still engaged the role of Confucianism in Japanese culture post-World War II were usually intellectually incapable of overcoming the way Confucianism had been set in anti-Chinese Japanese nationalist contexts during the early twentieth century. The best example of this is Tsuda Sōkichi, a scholar who bridged the trans-war period and provided the intellectual roots of much of the serious non-liberal scholarship on Confucianism of the postwar period. Tsuda was a traditionalist who emphasized the separation between Chinese and Japanese tradition, implying the superiority of the latter over the former. This allowed him to present a conservative nationalist position acceptable to the prewar and wartime order, but also to differentiate himself from wartime ideology through his explicit rejection of the undertones of trans-Asianism. His position was clearly nationalist but also ambivalent toward the aims and ideologies of Japanese trans-Asian imperialism. Even at the height of the war in China he refused to accept the premises of a trans-East Asian order.

Of course, what Japanese people today [1938] praise as "East Asian culture" means nothing whatsoever to Chinese or Indian people (Tsuda 1970 [1938]: 199).

This ambivalence enabled Tsuda to continue to function post-1945 and be one of the few voices using the history of Japanese thought, including Confucianism, to advance a nationalist or traditionalist position in the postwar. The extent to which Tsuda was able in the postwar to carry on with pretty much the same academic approach he had taken through the 1930s is intriguing. One of his most famous books, *Shina shisō to nihon* (*Chinese Thought and Japan*), which first appeared in 1938 based on writings from the mid-1930s, was reissued in 1947 with virtually no changes. Only the militarist introduction written the year after Japan's full-scale invasion of China was altered. The 1947 preface to the postwar edition, however, rather than critically reflecting on anti-Chinese elements in his original work of the 1930s, actually emphasizes this anti-Chinese voice and has it speak to the contemporaneous context of the Chinese Civil War. He concludes his 1947 preface by quoting from part of his original gung-ho 1938 introduction.

Japanese have their own Japanese culture standing in opposition to China, and Chinese have their own Chinese culture standing in opposition to Japan. The necessity of correctly understanding this is today more urgent than ever (Tsuda 1970: v).

Throughout the book, including in the title and new preface, the Japanese word *Shina* instead of *Chūgoku* is used to refer to China. *Shina* is a word made popular by the radically anti-Chinese nativist scholars of the Tokugawa period to remove the connotation of "centrality" in the Japanese word *Chūgoku* ("middle kingdom"), the standard Japanese name for China. Although for a time neutral, through the course of conflicts with China in the early twentieth century the word *Shina* came to have a decidedly derogatory tone by the end of the war and soon after became taboo. Yet Tsuda was still using it there in 1947, despite xenophobic nationalism being very much out of fashion by that time. So why was this book able to still be well received in this comparatively enlightened period of modern Japanese politics? This can be attributed to other features of the book which were much more in tune with the progressive spirit of that time and place and are closely related to Tsuda's reading of Chinese culture's role in Japan, notably his book's: (1) egalitarian class outlook, and (2) embrace of the teleology of modernity.

Tsuda emphasizes, in general correctly, that Chinese culture's positioning in Japanese cultural history was rooted among the elite. He used this fact to then jump to the conclusion that this Chinese cultural influence, notably including Confucianism, was thus not relevant to the ordinary "everyday life" (*seikatsu*) of most Japanese.

In the knowledge of Japanese intellectuals of the past Chinese thought was valued, but this was simply imposed over the everyday life of Japanese, it didn't impact directly on everyday life (Tsuda 1970: ii–iii).

Although what was recorded in the Confucian classics was received in Japan as knowledge, it had no impact on the everyday lives of the Japanese (Tsuda 1970: 83).

Throughout the book, Tsuda continued to hammer this point home, also using it to differentiate himself from the more infamous anti-Chinese polemicists of the Japanese nativist tradition and thereby disentangle himself from the intellectual genealogy of Japanese fascism. The nativists, he argued, may have said they opposed Chineseness, but they were actually intellectual elitists themselves whose own ideology inevitably collapsed back into a Chinese-originated form of anthropocentrism and state moral ideology which was quintessentially Confucian (Tsuda 1970: 53–76). Tsuda thus criticized past nativists and Japanese nationalists on the basis of their elitism, then used that elitist aspect to charge even the anti-Chinese of the past as having actually been under the sway of elitist Confucianism. Tsuda thereby lined himself up with originally leftist trends in prewar Japanese scholarship: historians, anthropologists, and ethnologists who emphasized "real everyday life" of the Japanese people.[3]

Many Marxist historians and scholars in postwar Japan continued, for obvious reasons, to value this kind of nominally anti-elitist scholarship focusing on the common people. At the height of the war, in 1942, Tsuda had taken this position to extremes by critiquing the vision of Prince Shotoku presented in the *Nihon Shoki*. This led to him being convicted of lèse-majesté and sentenced to prison. This so-called Tsuda Incident, together with the general anti-elitism of his scholarly approach, endeared Tsuda to the postwar left on the one hand, while differentiating him from the more elitist ideologies of the war regime (and other past purveyors of anti-Chineseness) on the other. This was one factor which enabled him to survive the transition into the postwar through a murky but palpable association with a "people's history" appealing to leftists, and a consequent distance from the formal ideologies of the wartime regime, despite his embrace of a kind of primitive folk nationalism. To put it in simple terms, because Tsuda's anti-Chinese outlook was packaged as anti-elitism, and applied against Japanese elite figures in history, it was tolerated by those on the left and thus able to survive the postwar settlement.

Another factor which helped Tsuda's transition into the postwar was that he set his anti-Chineseness in relation to the teleology of modern progress and development. For Tsuda, Chinese classical culture was the science and academia of the past, of the premodern. In the last paragraph of this 1947 preface, in another auto-quote from his excluded wartime introduction of 1938 he called for (1) the elimination of all Chinese linguistic elements from the Japanese language, (2) a continuation of Japanese scholarship which criticizes Chinese culture, and (3) the elimination of all Classical Chinese language instruction from schools. All of this, he claimed, was necessary because Confucianism "does not conform to the spirit of modern science" (Tsuda 1970: vi).[4] In short, even for Tsuda, a self-proclaimed traditionalist, the ultimate problem with Confucianism, even beyond its Chineseness, was its premodern nature. Confucianism needed to be jettisoned primarily because it was not compatible with modernity. It was inherently regressive. In this sense, we can see an overlap in the underlying logic of the arguments of both Maruyama and Tsuda – an overlap shared by many Japanese thinkers of the postwar.

According to Tsuda, the knowledge field, the intellectual field exactly where he thought Chinese influence had flourished, was one area that should be Western, not Chinese. The spiritual and cultural fields should be Japanese, because they always had been. Here we see an interesting invasion of a notion of timelessness or essentialism into his thinking, but only as it related to culture. In this sense he was completely modern. The one field not allowed to show progress in the nationalist ideologies of modernity was culture, whose timeless nature underpinned the civic religion of secular nationalism (Paramore 2015). This cultural essentialism provided an important element of real intellectual infrastructure and justification for the reinvigoration of *nihonjinron* writing which occurred in the postwar, accelerating along with Japanese economic success and nationalist confidence through the 1960s and 1970s (Miyoshi and Harootunian 1999, 2002). It also informed much serious scholarship which continued through this period. Serious scholars who nonetheless ran similarly culturalist lines using "Japaneseness" as an analytical category through the 1960s and 1970s included major respected academics like Minamoto Ryōen and Sagara Tōru, who taught some of today's most progressive, and ironically enough also most pro-Asian scholars of Japanese intellectual history.[5]

A polite distance: Academism and cultural heritage

Through the half century after the war, scholarship on Confucianism thus developed in a more cleanly academic context and orientation, working through a range of multiple and contradictory influences. Unlike in the immediately postwar period, major scholars of Japanese intellectual, political, and cultural history who dealt with the Confucian legacy through the second half of the twentieth century did this almost exclusively in academic venues. They were certainly not public intellectuals, and few of them even aimed to position their work outside fields of specialized academic research. Discussion on the place of Confucianism in Japanese culture became more clearly academic, and out of this critical and scholarly context arose work which began to develop and break through the trans-war obsession with unique national culture.

Scholars like Abe Yoshio, Watanabe Hiroshi, Ogyū Shigenori, Kojima Yasunori, Kurozumi Makoto, Hiraishi Naoaki, Maeda Tsutomu, Sawaii Keiichi, and many others began to break new ground in the study of Confucianism in Japan and the rest of East Asia and also to return to focusing on the central role of Confucianism in Japanese political and cultural history (Abe 1965; Ogyū 2008; Watanabe 1997). Most of these scholars, however, shunned public intellectual activity, and all of them spurned what was left of the social infrastructure of Confucian activity. Their approach to the Shibunkai, for instance, one of the very few Confucian civil society organizations left over from the prewar period, is instructive in this respect. The Shibunkai seems a fairly benign organization these days. They run some small seminars on how to read classical Chinese texts which cater to a few hundred participants a year in central Tokyo (Shibunkai 2015). Many senior scholars, however, refuse to have anything to do with the Shibunkai. For them, the Shibunkai's prewar 1945 résumé and current utilization of Shinto ritual is enough to earn them the label "non-scholarly" (*gakumonteki ja nai*).[6] For these scholars, engagement with Confucianism in any form not completely restricted to the modern academic context of the university is still taboo. Academic engagement with the history of Confucianism thus remained a carefully restricted cloistered academic activity, not touching the public sphere or mainstream Japanese society.

Over the last couple of decades, however, academia in Japan has begun to change somewhat, notably on this point of public engagement. Some highly regarded professors now seek public profile for their scholarly work by repackaging it in increasingly publicly accessible forms. This has led to a situation where, in the last decade in particular, scholars specializing in aspects of cultural history deeply embedded in Confucianism have also sought to engage a broader readership in the public sphere, even sometimes having their work speak to contemporary political and social issues (e.g., Karube 2011, 2012; Sueki 2004, 2012a, 2012b; Kojima 2006, 2007; Koyasu 2002, 2003, 2007, 2009).

The best example of this is the work of Yonaha Jun, particularly his book *Chūgokuka suru nihon* (*The Sinification of Japan*) (Yonaha 2011). Born in 1979, Yonaha Jun has over the past five years become a major public intellectual in Japan. He appears on television and in a wide range of different print media, including regularly in the *Nihon Keizai Shinbun* (*Nikkei Newspaper*), where between 2012 and 2013 he even had his own monthly column, heavily publicized by the newspaper under the motto "One step ahead of history: historian Yonaha Jun" (Yonaha 2012–2013). Educated at the University of Tokyo under the renowned historian Mitani Hiroshi, and himself having already by 2010 authored a solid body of academic scholarship, Yonaha, of Okinawan ancestry, turned his sights to a new form of popular, highly political, highly postmodern and decidedly irreverent public intellectual activity.[7] *The Sinification of Japan* was a bestseller in Japan. In 2013, the book was translated and published in Chinese (Yonaha 2013). The secret of this book's success is its combination of cutting political commentary and humor. The entire book is presented as parody, a form Yonaha uses to effect Foucault's idea of "discursive disruption."

The core of Yonaha's thesis in *The Sinification of Japan*, and the structure of his parody, is a tongue-in-cheek suggestion that the last

millennium of Japanese history, and recent world history, can be perceived through an abstraction based upon an imagined history of a "clash
of cultures" between "Chinese civilization" and "Japanese civilization."
Yonaha constructs his abstraction of "Chinese civilization" out of the
intellectual history of post-Song dynasty imperial China, closely related
for him to the rise of Neo-Confucianism. He then takes elements from
this historic reconstruction of imperial Chinese civilization and Neo-
Confucianism and applies them in analyzing the "free market American
empire" which he thus portrays as the "Chinese civilization of today." His
construction of "Japanese civilization" is built upon the history of
Japanese society he sees emerging in the medieval period and crystallizing
in the Tokugawa period as the product of a rejection of the post-Song,
universalist model of "Chinese civilization." He then extends this
"Japanese civilization" into a similarly abstracted formula which he then
portrays as matching the post-Westphalian international order of competing nation states. Yonaha then narrates recent Japanese and world
history through the lens of this clash between these two "civilizational
models," portrayed as competing for dominance in global history.

It is clear from the start, however, that Yonaha is playing with
abstracted ideas of civilization, and that these two are not intended to
represent the reality of either China or Japan. Yet the conceptual frameworks are indeed built upon the foundations of critical Japanese academic
Sinological writing of both past and present, which Yonaha's argument
relies upon a great deal. Notably, he reconstructs the early twentieth-
century Japanese Sinologist Naitō Konan's linking of the rise of Neo-
Confucianism with a Song modernity thesis. He also cites liberally from a
contemporary critical Sinologist, Kojima Tsuyoshi (1962–), using his
ideas on the history of Confucianism in East Asia. In Yonaha's hands,
however, these cultural elements are not primarily associated with
Confucianism as a transnational tradition, nor named as Confucian.
Rather, he lifts concepts, abstracts them, and then links them to modern
global phenomenon like the Westphalian international order, or the rise
of US global hegemony. Although the conceptual framework is built in
large part on Japanese academic Sinology's analysis of Confucianism,
Confucianism as a concept and as a word is hidden from view and seldom
named. It appears that even a figure like Yonaha, even when deploying
academic analysis relating to Confucian culture in the most irreverent
manner, even when doing parody, must still package it in the mainstream
modernist categories of culture and nation in order to have it fly in the
contemporary Japanese public sphere. Most Japanese academic writing
which has managed to break out of the cloisters, although seldom as
creative or intelligent as Yonaha, nonetheless also usually conforms to

this general norm of nation-based cultural nomenclature in avoidance of the word Confucianism.

They thereby all follow what we could call the post-1945 "Maruyama rule" on Confucianism: avoid using the word completely and prefer alternative Western-originated culturalist conceptual packagings instead of Confucianism. The most notable package used is one originated by Maruyama himself: "Japanese intellectual history" (*nihon shisōshi*).[8] Most writers who deal with Confucianism's role in Japanese history package their work as representing "Japanese intellectual history," and for most, although not all, that then determines a subjugation of Confucianism's transnational aspects to notable points in Japanese cultural history emphasized in the national history curriculum. The methodology of intellectual biography favored by many practitioners plays into this trend.

Of course, there are exceptions. One notable exception is Kojima Tsuyoshi, a professor of Chinese thought at the University of Tokyo who in the last years has taken to writing predominantly on the history of Japan, including as it relates to contemporary political controversies like Yasukuni (Kojima 2007). Kojima does not restrict his activities to writing. In 2014, he even went into cooperation with Kaji Nobuyuki and Fuji TV to create a television series "Analects Leadership Seminar" aimed at encouraging young children to read *Confucius Analects*. This adventure, however, does not seem to have been successful. The television series never went beyond the very limited audience of Fuji TV's pay-to-view children's specialty channel (which most Japanese houses cannot access). An associated attempt to run tutorials for children collapsed. This exceptional attempt by Kojima to resuscitate Confucianism seems to have been a failure, again confirming the taboo status of Confucianism in general society.

What then of the realms of Confucianism outside this academic line. The only significant Confucian civil society organization left in Japan is the Shibunkai – the descendant of the organization discussed in the previous chapter. The Shibunkai is led today by retired Sinologists, respectable emeritus professors of ancient Chinese literature and culture who maintain Yushima Seidō, the site of the old Shogunal Confucian academy, and make sure that the seasonal Confucian rites continue to be practiced there as they have been since the 1700s. They also run a regular series of seminars each year at the same Yushima location on various elements of classical Chinese culture. Most of these seminars are given by retired professors of Sinology from various private Tokyo universities and attended by retired senior citizens in groups of about ten or so.[9] In 2015, they planned to offer sixty-one seminar courses. Even on the false assumption that all of these seminars occur, and that there is no overlap in enrolment, the maximum attendance they could expect for the entire year would be around 600. Combining that with the turn-out at the seasonal rites, again making the false assumption that there is no overlap in attendance, we could assess that over the course of the entire year around 1000 Japanese people maximum will have any interaction whatsoever with any activity run by the Shibunkai. That represents less than one in 125,000 Japanese, and the overwhelming majority of that tiny fraction will be elderly retirees.

The Shibunkai are thus certainly in no process of Confucian revivalism as one sees, for instance, in some parts of China today. Their aims are also then clearly very different to those of the pre-World War II organization. The contemporary organization is on no mission. Rather, over the past several decades it has successfully concentrated upon maintaining the basic seasonal rituals of Confucian practice at Yushima, looking after the buildings and making them accessible to the public, and thereby preserving the basic Confucian heritage of Japan. Last year I attempted fieldwork at Yushima Seidō and interviewed several members of the Shibunkai, including their President Ishikawa Tadahisa (1932–). The Shibunkai is one of the few places in Japan where one indeed feels Confucianism is not taboo. They are quite prepared to use the word Confucianism in describing their organization, if nonetheless also very cautious in how they use it. As Ishikawa pointed out to me, they use the word *jukyō* (Confucianism) expressly and deliberately to include the religious element of Confucianism, and indeed see their continuation of elements of the ritual scheme of Confucianism on Japanese soil as one of their prime duties. The overall impression I took away from the Shibunkai is one of an eminently decent organization led by decent people committed to the similarly decent and broadly laudable goals of cultural preservation, heritage, and knowledge. My impression of the Shibunkai, the last vestige of any organized, social formation representing Confucianism in Japan is something like a mini version of the Church of England – a group of respectable gentlemen and ladies from good families committed to preserving what they see as an eminent part of the cultural heritage of their country.[10]

Yet the rest of the country's lack of engagement only confirms how deeply the postwar taboo status of Confucianism runs in contemporary Japan. In thinking about the nature of taboo, however, it is important to also acknowledge one of its more positive roles – as a social device to avoid conflict. If we see taboo in this way, then the disparities in the arguments of Maruyama and Tsuda, their reception into the same pacifist-inclined postwar society, and the continuation of the taboo today, all begin to make sense. Maruyama and Tsuda sat at politically and culturally opposite poles, but both of them, by dismissing Confucianism in their consideration of Japan's contemporary problems post-1945, avoided the problematic of potential conflict between ideas of Japan and China, a conflict which, in the 1940s to 1980s historical context, would have likely sprung from any mainstream attempt to position Japanese modernity in relation to a traditional cultural form associated with China. Their visions of how Japan should progress – the Western liberalism of Maruyama or the romantic egalitarian folk nationalism of Tsuda – both made Confucianism taboo partly so that these visions did not have to collide with the elements of Japanese history seen as associated with Chinese civilization. Those in the postwar who did not conform to the rules of taboo, who directly engaged and named Confucianism as something Japanese, be they fanatics like Mishima, or respectable low-key institutions like the Shibunkai, were rejected by the mainstream as *haram*.

Although in the immediately postwar cooling off period such a taboo may have been politically useful, and certainly allowed the development of a removed academic discourse which produced a large volume of good comparative research on Confucianism, one wonders about its utility today. The taboo seems to inhibit attempts to look at the production of modernity across East Asia through shared cultural forms, which in turn perhaps also thus limits the cultural and discursive resources available to China and Japan dealing with each other in the new, challenging circumstances of the twenty-first century.

Epilogue
China and Japan: East Asian Confucian modernities and revivals compared

---

> Song dynasty Confucians used Buddhism to construct a new philosophy, a kind of "Buddhism in Confucian Clothes" which reached fulfillment in the Ming dynasty.
> – Liang Qichao (1873–1929), Chinese political thinker and modernizer, describing Neo-Confucianism in "Qingdai xueshu gailun" [General Discussion of Qing Dynasty Learning] (Liang 1985: 7)

Two modernities, two Confucianisms

Ever since the systematization and standardization of its textual apparatus in the Han dynasty, two contrasting inclinations have been consistently identified in Confucianism: (1) the idealistic Confucianism of individual moral betterment, which assumed innate human goodness, was associated with *Mencius* as a text and later Neo-Confucianism as a movement; and (2) the instrumentalist Confucianism of political realism, which emphasized the pragmatism of the "ancient" Chinese sovereigns, was associated with *Xunzi* as a text, but also with elements in the Old Text movement in Han China, their followers, and innovators in Qing China, and Ogyū Sorai and Japanese Confucianism from the 1700s onwards. It is important to note that these two different and sometimes contradictory inclinations are discernable through most of the history of Confucianism post-Han. The persistence of both inclinations through over two millennia of history indicates that the difference between them is not simply genealogical but also deeply epistemological.

The presence of these two differing approaches throughout Confucianism's premodern history also demonstrates the inherent plurality that the tradition possessed before modernity. Scholars of religion today tend to agree that most religious traditions tolerated greater plurality in their premodern manifestations than after religious modernization. Historical and theoretical writing on religion and political thought over the past decades has demonstrated that the processes of religious modernization usually reduced tolerance for internal pluralism. Religious

183

modernization, certainly in Asia, usually involved setting the parameters of a tradition in a more fixed and singularly defined manner. It was this religious and political modernization which led to the fluid plurality of Confucianism previously shared by both China and Japan being transformed into fixed, more singularly defined forms. And it was precisely in this process of modernist reconstruction that clearly differing forms of Confucianism crystallized in the two countries.

As pointed out in Chapters 5 and 6, in Japan it was the latter, politically realist inclination of Confucianism which informed the formation of the modern Japanese Confucianism of the early twentieth century. The Chinese construction of a modern version of Confucianism, on the other hand, rather emerged from the former idealistic Mencian inclination. This was the Confucian form favored by Kang Youwei (1858–1927), and from which emerged historiographical attempts by later political thinkers of the Chinese Republic like Liang Qichao to construct a version of Confucianism which paralleled their own vision of an idealistic revolutionary Chinese Republic. The establishment of the Republic of China and the People's Republic of China were both achieved through revolutions which articulated their objectives in terms of idealistic ideologies of both republicanism and revolutionary socialism. Modern Confucianism in China, through its idealism and emphasis on inherent human goodness thus reflected, encouraged, and conformed to the spiritual proclivities of republicanism and revolutionary socialism which constituted early Chinese political modernity.[1]

On the other hand, Japan, as discussed in Chapter 5, initially read Western political modernity through the influence of particularly instrumentalist interpretations of Confucianism. Nishi Amane and many other modernizers were clearly affected by influential late early modern Japanese readings of Confucianism as utilitarian, pragmatic, and realist. These *Xunzi*-like readings were not only those of Japan's most influential Confucian scholar Ogyū Sorai; they were also shared by the new nominally Neo-Confucian leaders of late Tokugawa state academism, as discussed in Chapters 3 and 4. This conception of the Confucian Way as inherently pragmatic is one reason why many nineteenth-century elite Japanese regarded Western liberal states, particularly comparatively progressive and yet also aristocratic places like Massachusetts, England, and Holland, as realms according to the Confucian Way. Although some Qing Chinese Confucians also associated Western state models with Confucian ideals, it was less common for late Qing Chinese to see actual Western politics as a realization of the Confucian Way. Perhaps this was partly due to the comparative brutality of Western imperialism in nineteenth-century China, but it also reflects the different modern Confucian settlements which were beginning to crystallize in the two countries.

Japan and China thus shared a history of having to navigate the onslaught of capitalist modernity, and they similarly both used charts formulated in the Confucian tradition to aid and understand that navigation. But they were different charts. Japan's modern politics of conservative liberalism and fascistic-inclined conservatism on the one hand, and China's modern politics of republicanism and revolutionary socialism on the other, resonated with differences in the respective modern crystallizations of Confucianism which emerged in each country. Crucially, looking from the perspective of the neo-liberal present, this different modern history informed very different approaches to liberalism. That modern historical difference around the currently hegemonic ideology of liberalism is related to the present discussion over Confucianism in China.

Contemporary China and Japanese history

The problem of liberalism as the hegemonic political ideology of capitalist modernity sits at the heart of the current Confucian revival in mainland China. Advocates of Confucianism like Kang Xiaoguang (1963–) see current politics as a choice between the increasingly corrupt Leninist party system and the perhaps equally corrupt global laissez faire neo-liberal capitalist order. For Kang, seeing the Leninist party state's days are clearly numbered, the only way to avoid conforming to the global hegemony of neo-liberal capitalism is a third option, and this for him is where Confucianism as a form of conservative Chinese cultural nationalism should find its place (Kang 2002: 7). This follows other, more politically influential mainland Chinese advocates for the revival of Confucianism like Jiang Qing (1953–), who has overtly presented his advocacy of a renewed Confucianism both as a counter to liberal democracy and as an alternative to the vision of Confucianism offered by the New Confucianism movement of ROC Taiwan, Hong Kong and US-based scholars like Mou Zongsan (1909–1995) and Tu Wei-ming (1940–) (Jiang 2003: 57–96; 250–350).

This Confucian revival, currently underway in China, is occurring in a socio-economic and political context very reminiscent of Japan in the mid-twentieth century. In early- and mid-twentieth century Japan, Confucianism was resuscitated through a state-encouraged cultural nationalist movement which prescribed Confucianism as an antidote for the excesses of industrial high modernity. As discussed in Chapter 6, the earlier late-nineteenth-century disestablishment of Confucianism and divorce from other social practices in the immediate post-Meiji Restoration period made it easy prey for later cooption by the powerful modern ideological forces of racial nationalism, radical conservatism, and later fascism that arose from within that cultural nationalist movement. The reason Confucianism was easily harnessed to these causes was not primarily related to any particular content in Confucian thought. It was rather because Confucianism's social disengagement allowed it to be easily monopolized by those in authority, thereby quashing Confucianism's capacities to promote diversity, critical thought, and critical activism. This despite the fact that, as the central chapters of this book argued, these capacities existed and were powerfully realized in many earlier historical manifestations of Confucianism.

Mainland China today is experiencing similar problems of industrial high modernity to Japan in the mid-twentieth century, including extreme wealth disparity, environmental degradation, and unequal development. As in Japan, the early phases of Chinese modernization, both under the KMT and the CCP, saw the destruction of most institutional nodes for the social integration of Confucianism. Just as in Japan, China in the modern period also saw Confucianism, its spaces and its practices, decimated (Yu 2004: 55). The Confucian revival in China today is thus occurring in a similar socio-political climate and in similar circumstances of Confucian social and institutional disconnection as Japan in the mid-twentieth century. Current attempts to resurrect Confucianism in China as a social movement need to start from scratch because most of the social frameworks which formerly supported Confucian activity were destroyed during modernization. As scholarship on this kind of revival in contemporary China indicates, resurrecting a tradition from scratch requires a particularly heavy subordination to the state and other institutions of power (Billioud 2015). As discussed in Chapter 6, it was revival under exactly these kinds of conditions which facilitated the rise of Confucian fascism in 1930s Japan.

Academic supporters of the contemporary Chinese Confucian revival, particularly those based in the United States, often compare the current Confucian revival with the slightly earlier revival in Buddhist practice and social engagement which occurred firstly in Taiwan, and then in China through the 1980s and thereafter (Yang and Tamney 2012; Madsen 2007). It is a commonly held opinion that the Buddhist revival in the Chinese-speaking world has contributed in some respects to education, social welfare, social engagement, and perhaps even the development of a more robust civil society. So it is no surprise that the Buddhist revival in Chinese-speaking countries serves as a naturally hopeful example to observers of the Confucian counterpart (Madsen 2007; Sun 2013). The Buddhist and Confucian revivals, however, must not be seen in parallel. Buddhist organizations have deep social roots, Confucians virtually none. Confucianism simply does not have the kind of social infrastructure Buddhism possesses. That is certainly the case in the modern period, where Confucian institutions, focused as they were on the fields of education and governance, were much worse savaged than those of the Buddhists during the processes of modernization. But even in the premodern periods Confucianism's institutional infrastructure was seldom as developed as that of the Buddhists. Throughout history, Confucianism has rarely if ever been able to function with the kind of social and political autonomy sometimes seen in Buddhism.

In contemporary China there are also other, specific problems likely to inhibit a successful modern resurrection of Confucianism. These problems can be seen most clearly in the nature of the current attempts at Confucian revival. There are two major streams discernable in the various attempts to resurrect Confucianism in the Chinese-speaking world today, each with its own historical and political problems. Firstly, there is the so-called New Confucianism movement, well represented in Taiwanese, Hong Kong, Singaporean, Chinese, and especially US-based English-language academic life. Since the 1990s this stream of Confucian advocacy has increasingly sought to promote Confucianism through linking it with allegedly positive cultural attributes of capitalism. New Confucianism scholar-advocates, despite on the one hand sometimes rhetorically claiming to be critical of capitalist modernity have on the other hand repeatedly associated Confucianism and "Confucian values" with "success" in capitalist development, competitiveness, and economic growth. The project of scholar-advocates like Wm. Theodore de Bary and Tu Weiming of positioning Confucianism in Weberian terms to represent the role of Protestantism in East Asian capitalism has thereby partially instrumentalized Confucianism and to an extent shackled it to one particular politicized socio-economic outlook: that of liberal-capitalist materialism (Tu 1996). New Confucianism, in some manifestations, has thus reduced Confucianism to being perceived in exactly the kind of instrumentalist terms that we saw damaged Confucianism so much through modern Japanese history. In Japan, as discussed in Chapter 6, Inoue Tetsujirō used late-nineteenth-century German social theory to instrumentalize Confucianism as a form of "national morality," thereby subordinating it to nationalism. In the United States and Singapore, Tu Weiming used early twentieth-century German social theory (Max Weber and Robert Bellah's 1950s US development of it) to instrumentalize Confucianism as a form of "capitalist ethic," thereby subordinating it to capitalism.

Secondly, we can discern a competing approach, based mainly in China, which advocates Confucianism as a form of conservative cultural nationalism. This tendency is linked historically with earlier modern attempts to rework Confucianism within Han ethnic nationalism, an approach attempted by republican historians like Yao Congwu (1894–1970), applied in Chiang Kai-shek's "New Life Movement" in the 1930s, and recently revived and developed by mainland political thinkers like Jiang Qing (Jiang 2003: 396–415; Liu 2013; Wang 2001: 183–5). Jiang Qing, Kang Xiaoguang, and other contemporary figures in this second trend promote Confucianism's role in Chinese society in almost the opposite terms of the New Confucians, seeing it as a bulwark of ethnic nationalism and conservatism against the intrusions of liberal capitalism and cosmopolitanism.

Thus, we can see that these two trends, on the one hand, appear to contradict and undercut each other. New Confucian advocates' utilization of Weberian theory to conceive of Confucianism in a manner which appears to acquiesce to the ideologies of liberal capitalism creates serious obstacles for any possible integration of Confucianism into contemporary China in the ways imagined by Jiang and Kang. Similarly, the image of Confucianism projected by Jiang and Kang directly undercuts the kind of liberal cosmopolitan support for the tradition that the New Confucianism movement has tried to harness. As argued in Chapter 7, in Japan the Confucian brand was damaged seemingly beyond repair through its association with fascism. In the Chinese-speaking context, Confucianism may have been similarly sullied through its recent association with capitalism and capitalism's current ideological handmaiden, neo-liberalism, *and* through an uncritical association with ethno-centric nationalism. Intriguingly, both these two main modern links which have been established for Confucianism in China over the past decades (to capitalism and ethnic nationalism) conform to the modern nationalist nature of the packaging which was created for Confucianism in the modern Japanese revival of the early twentieth century – a packaging which, as discussed in Chapter 6, was later directly used as a mobilizing tool of fascism.

In relation to these kinds of China–Japan parallels, it is also of great interest that the doctrinal approach of Jiang Qing breaks from the earlier modern Chinese tradition established by Kang Youwei and followed by most others. Jiang does not exclusively follow the Mencian individual moral development vision of Confucianism, and instead predominantly advocates a *Xunzi*-influenced vision of Confucianism which conforms much more to the pragmatic politically realist version of ancient learning scholarship traditionally favored in modern Japanese Confucianism (Jiang 2003: 40–57). His "constitutionalism," although read by his Western apologists as assent to a rule of law system in the modern sense, is in Confucian historical terms more directly related to the legalist tendencies in Confucianism. These tendencies were well exploited by fascist inclined political ideologues both in 1930s and 1940s imperial Japan, and in Chiang Kai-shek's "New Life Movement" of the Chinese Republic of the same decades (Wakeman 1997). Scholars who identify Jiang's position as "critical" or even "leftist" ignore the extent to which his political ideas rely upon the same nineteenth-century culturally essentialist conceptions of nation which informed many of the twentieth century's worst rightist excesses (Hammond 2015). Jiang's linking of political legitimacy to "blood lineage," and his nod toward a homophobic vision of "family morals" confirm the nineteenth-century social-Darwinian organic undercurrents of his thinking and in some ways take his radical conservatism even further than anything seen in 1930s or 1940s Japan (Jiang 2012: 36, 64 (note 38 on 220), 71–6, 80–5).[2] Crucially in the context of multi-ethnic China, this organic nature to Jiang's political Confucianism can only serve to reinforce ethnic hierarchies of domination, undercutting the side of traditional Confucianism which historically promoted interethnic "harmony." This resonates with the similarly imagined social-Darwinian influenced ideologies of imperialist Japan in the late nineteenth and early to mid-twentieth centuries. To be provocative, one could say that in all these different ways Jiang Qing's political Confucianism is, in the context of modern East Asian history, quintessentially Japanese.

At its roots, however, this kind of radical conservatism is of course neither essentially Japanese nor essentially Confucian. All around the globe twentieth-century history has thrown up examples of this kind of reactionary cultural politics, often in forms related to a religious tradition. As discussed in Chapter 6, Christian conservative groups in mid-twentieth-century Europe, most obviously Catholic-inspired conservative nationalist groups like *Action Française*, provide a clear comparative example.[3] In other words, this kind of manifestation of Confucianism is not indicative of any underlying character of Confucianism itself but rather has more to do with particular political patterns underlying modernity.

Confucianism need not be manifested in this way. All through this book I have provided examples of very different, often socially progressive manifestations of Confucianism from a range of earlier historical periods. Some of these positive premodern manifestations were facilitated by

Confucianism being practiced *through* other more socially embedded traditions – notably Buddhism. It is intriguing to note that most of the positive examples of Confucian revival which can be observed in East Asia today are similarly interlinked with Buddhism. For instance, in Taiwan there are currently a number of examples of successful Confucian revivals being facilitated, managed, and controlled by and within lay Buddhist organizations. This kind of Buddhist-managed Confucian revival presents none of the socially Darwinian, ethno-nationalist and other typically radical conservative features seen in the more influential metropolitan Chinese forms of Confucian revival discussed earlier. The social embeddedness enjoyed by Buddhist organizations in the community (as opposed to the non-existent social organization of Confucianism) allows them to present a much more humane and community-oriented vision of Confucianism – one which looks to facilitate social harmony rather than attack it. The relatively deep social penetration of Buddhist social organization gives Confucianism the capacity to be manifested in the diverse social reality of people's daily lives, a capacity not offered in stand-alone forms.[4] In fact, in modern East Asian history Confucianism only seems to have escaped an ultra-conservative political manifestation when deeply embedded in Buddhism. That the great Chinese political thinker Liang Qichao, one of the few reformist defenders of Confucianism in early Republican China, saw it as a form of Buddhism is an intriguing historical fragment when considering this aspect of the Confucian revival in the Chinese-speaking world today.[5]

This importance of community and social integration in determining the nature of contemporary Confucian revival returns us to the most crucial historical similarity in modern Chinese and Japanese experiences of Confucianism: the extent to which the social practices and settings of Confucianism were decimated during the early stages of modernization in both countries. Today, the lack of any substantial autonomous social infrastructure for Confucianism in modern Chinese-speaking countries, or in Japan, means that anyone who wants to claim "Confucian values" for themselves is relatively free to do so. Other than Buddhist organizations, there are no social groups capable of making counter-claims, offering alternatives, or indeed resisting in any way the kinds of radical rightist employments of Confucianism which have flourished thus far in modern politics. Just in the postwar twentieth century we can think of figures as diverse as Chiang Kai-shek, Park Chung-hee, Mishima Yukio, and Lee Kuan-Yew, all of whom were able to lay claim to "Confucian values" in representing hardline political positions, without facing sustained resistance from any alternative articulation of Confucianism from any "other" Confucians. Powerfully vested state and corporate interests and their anointed (and funded) cultural ambassadors enjoy relative freedom in their claims to "Confucian values." Because Confucianism in modernity was/is socially disengaged, with little but text behind it, anything that can be related to the text can be justified in Confucian terms. Of course, the Confucian textual canon, like that of any great religious tradition, is broad enough to accommodate a wide range of cynical cherry picking (Pines 2012: 610–13). This has led to Confucianism in modernity most often being manifested as an ideological instrument wielded by the powerful to justify authoritarianism. This is possible precisely because there are no Confucian movements anywhere in Asia organized or socially embedded enough to offer an alternative. This is not an inherent or essential nature of Confucianism; it is a function of its particular modern history and current manifestation, and thereby intimately related to modern global historical and social circumstances.

For that reason, Confucianism's long-term future in China cannot be predicted. It is impossible to say what role, if any, Confucianism may play in a post-industrial China decades from now. It may play a positive role in some form of distant post-capitalist, post-modern society. China today, however, is still very much in the grip of social, economic, environmental, and political problems that have gripped nearly every society which has endured high industrial capitalism. The most influential current attempts to revive Confucianism in China clearly also function within that paradigm, repeating already long established historical patterns of radical, reactionary conservatism. These are a politics the origins of which have much more to do with modernity than Confucianism. We have been able to observe that form of politics now in various different cultural manifestations across the globe for around a century, and the nature of *its* outcomes are depressingly easy to predict.

Notes

INTRODUCTION

1. The cover image, displaying the flags of Japan (centre) and the puppet states of Manchukuo (left) and the Provisional Government of the Republic of China (PGROC) (right), is a poster produced during the short-lived existence of the latter state in north China between 1937 and 1940. The building in the background appears to represent a Ming-period city gate – either of Beijing, where the PGROC was housed after the Japanese invasion, or of Shenyang (Mukden), the capital of Manchukuo (much of which had been built by the Qing on the Beijing model). The image thereby conflates the architectures and ideologies of the PGROC and the Manchukuo model upon which it was based. A slogan along the bottom of the poster (but not visible in the edited version on the cover) reads: "Japanese, Chinese and Manchu being mutually supportive, the whole realm is made tranquil and happy." The second half of this slogan thus resonates with one of the most famous parts of the *Greater Learning* (the first book in the Four Books canon of Neo-Confucianism): "The states being rightly governed; the whole realm was made tranquil and happy" (Legge 1983: 359). This conforms with both states' usages of Confucianism in official ideology and propaganda which, as discussed in Chapter 5, followed the Manchukuo model.
2. Lionel Jensen has influentially argued that the *term* "Confucianism" was an early modern invention (Jensen 1997). Others have challenged this analysis (Standaert 1999). Regardless of these debates about terms, however, there is little doubt that what we now call Confucianism did function as a meaningful and comparable *conceptual category* from at least the end of the Han dynasty, and particularly strongly after the Tang.
3. On late nineteenth- and early twentieth-century Japanese state-supported attempts to influence Western images of Japan, notably through disassociating them from China, see de Gruchy (2003).
4. Much of Kang's argument here builds on earlier work by Jiang Qing (Jiang 2003).

1. CONFUCIANISM AS CULTURAL CAPITAL

1. Confucian professors were transcribed into the Japanese of the time as "people who can read and write." A similar passage occurs in the *Kojiki* (712CE), which also mentions that Wani transmitted a ten-volume set of *Confucius Analects* (NKBT 1: 248–9).

2. The *Nihon Shoki* relates a number of instances of Confucian books and teachers being given as gifts to the Japanese sovereign by the Korean kingdom of Paekche. The first story, quoted earlier, is dated in the *Nihon Shoki* (using the traditional manner of calculating its dates) as having happened in 284. Peter Kornicki suggests this could possibly be recalculated to 405 (Kornicki 1998: 278–9). Delmer Brown in the *Cambridge History of Japan, vol. 1* instead emphasizes a later reference in the same text that speaks of another gift of Confucian scholarship in 513 (Hall and Brown 1993: 170). This reference can be found in NKBT 68: 28–35. Certainly by the eighth century when this source was written, Confucian ideas and texts were in Japan. Quotations from Confucian texts pepper the official Japanese writing of the period. The *Kojiki* (712) and *Nihon Shoki* (720) were the first official state histories and thereby key legitimizing devices of the early Japanese state. The idea of the emperor as descendant of the sun god, for instance, as well as other beliefs and practices commonly labeled today as Shinto, is usually explained using these texts, and these have been dated to the same general late seventh-century period (Breen and Teeuwen 2016, Chapter 1).

3. Even the core symbols of the Japanese emperors, the sword and mirror, were brought across to Japan as part of the transmission of Confucianism (NKBT 1: 248–9).

4. One of the most famous valorizations of the idea of harmony in Japanese culture came from Watsuji Tetsurō (1889–1960), an important mid-twentieth-century Japanese philosopher and ethicist. The revision of approach can be traced generationally through the work of his students, including Sagara Tōru (1921–2000). For a thought-provoking discussion of the idea of harmony in Japanese history and historiography, see Kurozumi 2006: 494–6.

5. This claim is most significantly recorded in the *Nihon Shoki*. The consensus in current historical writing is that Prince Shōtoku was probably an invention of seventh-century historical writers, constructed from a mix of real historical figures, most notably Prince Umayado.

6. For instance, the current prime minister of Japan, Shinzō Abe, has referred to it as part of his campaign to promote revision of the current post-World War II Japanese Constitution.

7. It is also important to note, however, that these points about relationships and trust, although presented primarily through Confucian terminology related to the sovereign–vassal relationship, are also backed up by reference to Buddhist ideas. For instance, in injunction fourteen, Buddhist ideas of trust are quoted to back up the points made in other injunctions (NST 2: 21). The position of Buddhism in Japanese society is also asserted in the second injunction that emphasizes the place of the Buddhist clergy and the role of Buddhist dharma as the underpinnings of all states (NST 2: 13). This is indeed the section of the *Seventeen Article Constitution* often quoted to demonstrate that early Japan by this stage was to some degree a "Buddhist state."

8. A repetition of the phrasing from the *Liji* (Book 3, section 3, para 14 in Legge's translation) occurs in Book 5 of the continued *Nihon Shoki* (NKBT 67: 248–9). Other examples linking military expeditions against *emishi* "barbarians" and culture can be found throughout, including in Book 26

(NKBT 68: 330–1). This last example is actually an interesting combination of both use of force and mediation between the state forces and the "barbarians."

9. On the role of ideas of culture and civilization in official "Japanese" court depictions of their campaign against the *emishi* "barbarians," see Friday 1997: 3–4. On domination and subordination in the Japan of this period, see Mizoguchi 2002: 29.

10. See for instance, the series edited by Amino Yoshihiko: Mori 1992; or for a general treatment of this problem, Amino 2000: 25–39.

11. On the importance of the Bohai state's relationship with Japan in the development of Japanese approaches to Chinese civilization, see Borgen 1986: 230–1.

12. There is also a Buddhist clergy chapter in the Japanese code that parallels the chapter on the officers of the Gods. This is not present in the Tang codes, and is actually taken from a Chinese monastic code (NST 3: 541, 529).

13. In the Tang version, the *Laozi* was also added to the end of this sentence, but interestingly not in the Japanese version (NST 3: 264).

14. Kornicki and McMullen 1996 give examples of several important exceptions.

15. All the state buildings burned down in this fire were reconstructed with the exception of the Confucian academy. Many of the objects necessary for conducting the *shidian* (Jp. *sekiten*) ceremony had already been stolen in the tenth century (Minamoto 1995: 77).

16. Collcutt 1981. For patronage under the Kamakura shogunate, see pp. 57–62, for patronage under Ashikaga shogunate see pp. 98–102. The Kamakura shogunal regent, Hōjō Tokiyori (1227–1263), is the most famous shogunal leader to have shown great interest in Zen.

17. Wang argues in Minamoto that Fujiwara Seika, the alleged originator of Tokugawa Confucianism, actually represents a continuation of the Zen Confucian tradition (Wang in Minamoto 1995: 127–8).

2. CONFUCIANISM AS RELIGION

1. As Richard Bowring and other scholars have shown, there was definitely awareness of Neo-Confucian commentaries in Japan as early as the thirteenth century. But few tried to adopt an independent Neo-Confucian posture until the late 1500s (Bowring 2006: 438–9).

2. Although seldom applied strictly in the historical reality of the Tokugawa period, these categories became reified by historians of the twentieth century, notably Inoue Tetsujirō and later Maruyama Masao, who used differences within these trends as the basis for their very intellectually based analyses of Tokugawa Confucianism (Inoue 1900, 1903, 1905; Maruyama 1974). However, we should be wary of the doctrinally centric approach inherent in this system of categorization, and especially wary of how the significance of these "schools" has been over-interpreted in modern history writing. Ogyū Sorai, for instance, although having much respect for certain ideas of Itō Jinsai, certainly did not see himself as part of a school originated by Jinsai – of whom he was also highly critical (NST 36: 165).

3. It's noteworthy that Zhu Xi and other Neo-Confucians also argued for such a view of historical rupture in order to facilitate a critical attitude to their own society.
4. As pointed out in the previous chapter, Neo-Confucian scholarship was present in Japan centuries before 1600, but mainly in nominally non-Neo-Confucian traditions: notably Buddhist monasteries and vestiges of the imperial academic structure like the Kiyohara family. Warrior schools like the Ashikaga Gakkō also used the Neo-Confucian Four Books canon, but combined it with Buddhist and other traditions, not identifying the school or themselves primarily with a holistic Neo-Confucian approach (Shirane 2000: 227).
5. This was a massive stipend, more than ten times as much as the Shogunate's Confucian scribe Hayashi Razan ever received.
6. For later rejection of the view that Hayashi Razan personally, or Confucianism in general, were core elements of early Tokugawa ideology, see Bitō (1961) and Watanabe (1985). Maruyama Masao, the scholar who first suggested Razan as a state ideologue, himself in the introduction to the translation in Maruyama (1974) rejected this perspective. For one of the clearest counter-theses see Kurozumi (1994).
7. Abe Yoshio (1965) famously argued that the effect of Korean Confucianism on Fujiwara Seika, through the transmission of Korean prisoners of war in the late 1500s, was instrumental in the rise of Neo-Confucianism in early 1600s Japan.
8. See the Ooms 1985 Epilogue. Others, however, have disputed Ooms' view. Pak Hong-gyu makes a convincing case that Yamazaki Ansai was principally highly critical of the Tokugawa regime, and actually saw it as society in a fallen state, in a similar way to how Zhu Xi saw Song China (Pak 2002: 66–70).
9. As had already been done in Yoshida Shinto (Teeuwen 2002).
10. Ogyū also questioned the provenance of both the *Greater Learning* and the *Doctrine of the Mean*.

3. CONFUCIANISM AS PUBLIC SPHERE

1. The rule was propagated in a 1635 revision of the Regulations for Samurai Households, drafted by Hayashi Razan and proclaimed by Tokugawa Iemitsu.
2. See also the list of acquaintances listed under twenty different fields of interest gleaned from the diary of just one person, Takayama Hikokurō, at http://www5.wind.ne.jp/hikokuro/koyuroku.htm (cited 6 August 2013).
3. As Kurozumi has pointed out, this ethics of "unlimited responsibility of the individual" actually often leads to an attitude of complete irresponsibility, as the act of suicide, or milder acts of, for instance, resignation from a position of responsibility, demonstrate (Kurozumi 2006: 467–8, footnote 16).
4. In fact, Kitō ryū jujitsu was one of the main elements Kanō Jigorō used to construct modern judo around 1880. In *shūkōroku*, however, Matsudaira is using the word *jūdō* in the contemporary vernacular sense to simply mean jujitsu.
5. On Zhu Xi's use of *kyorei*, see Shimada (1967: 47–8). Matsudaira Sadanobu confirms he is following Zhu Xi's interpretation of this term by this later use of the same allusion to a mirror made in the Zhu Xi commentary (Matsudaira 1942: 186).

6. Historical sources outlining the secret, or inner teachings of the tradition are even more heavily Confucian in nature, being made up predominantly of quotes from the Lunyu. The so-called secret teachings of this school of jujitsu can thus be seen to be ironically unoriginal and unmartial, primarily made up of quotes from publicly available Confucian classics (Imamura 1966: 375, 381).

7. See also Janine Sawada's relation of Sorai's invention of social reading to Jinsai's earlier use of *sakumon* (posing of problems) and Ishida Baigan's later organization of "support meetings" (Sawada 1993: 91–4).

8. See the quote from Bitō which opens this chapter.

9. On the difference between the meaning of publicness in late Tokugawa period Japan and today, see Watanabe (2012: 51–2).

10. Rawls's linkage of rationality and goodness in *A Theory of Justice* resonates with the particular articulation of Neo-Confucianism we see in the late Tokugawa shogunate (Rawls 1999: 347–90).

11. The link between this rebellion and nativism would later be used to try to portray Ōshio as a "loyalist" hero of pre-Restoration Japan by post-Meiji national ideologues, see for instance, Inoue and Kamie (1902). Research on this includes Kojima (2006) and Benesch (2009).

4. CONFUCIANISM AS KNOWLEDGE

1. The application of the concept of "useful knowledge" to the sociological sphere has been made by a number of STS and economic historians; for instance, Joel Mokyr has written: "technological creativity ... is the adoption of more efficient new production methods, widely defined to include organizational changes" (Mokyr 1994: 564).

2. The poverty of the fields of history of science and knowledge history of early modern Japan is particularly confronting when compared to the research done on China. The history of science for China is a huge and impressive field. There are research centers in Cambridge and Princeton devoted to the history of science in China, several major journals, and star scholars like Joseph Needham, whose multi-volume history of science in China is one of the great works of historical research of the mid-twentieth century (Needham 1956). Major China scholars like Benjamin Elman continue this tradition today (Elman 2005, 2006).

3. This outlook continued on in much liberal scholarship through the twentieth century, even by scholars in Asia (Maruyama 1974: 3). Through Hegel's influence on Marx, this outlook also permeated much leftist scholarship of the twentieth century. Marxism's strong influence in Japanese academia, and particularly in the discipline of history, also goes some way to explaining the endurance of this outlook in Japanese language scholarship. Conversely, the endurance of this outlook in English language scholarship on Japan is closely related to anti-Marxist (but also inherently anti-Chinese) ideology of American modernization theorists of the Cold War.

4. http://www.fjwh.gov.cn/html/10/76/20199_200910201041.html (cited 13 June 2014).

5. A more complete English translation of the title might be: *Complete Medical Book Demonstrating Famous Treatments of Various Kinds*. But because the book is also called *Yishu daquang* (literally *Complete Medical Book*), it has most often translated into English as "Encyclopedia of Medicine," for instance in Sugimoto (1989: 214).

6. This link may even hold for Chen Ziming, who was writing at the height of military conflict between the Southern Song and the Mongols, just before the ultimate liquidation of the former dynasty.

7. See for instance Kagawa's instructions for how to examine a patient (KISS 65: 25–7).

8. For the most recent English language research on shogunate engagement with medicine in the eighteenth century, see Hübner (2014).

9. Even as late as the 1850s and 1860s, the Dutch naval doctor Pompe van Meerdervoort's hospital in Nagasaki, sometimes described as the first Western medical hospital in Japan, was funded and integrated into government systems by the shogunate following the Koishikawa model and likewise called a *yōjōsho*.

10. This opening sentence is a quote from *Confucius Analects*, Wei Ling Gong, 10.

11. For instance, the scholars of the Kaitokudō. On Shibano as a later symbol of conservative orthodoxy, sometimes in contrast to the Kaitokudō, see Najita (1987: 182–5), and Screech (2000: 98–9, 258–9). I rebut that view in Paramore (2012a, 2012b).

12. Xue texts held by the Taki clan, with Seijukan markings and covers, can be found in the Waseda Kotenseki Database. For instance, gynecological texts similar to those recently reprinted as Xue (1976) and Chen (1985), *Furen Liangfang*: http://www.wul.waseda.ac.jp/kotenseki/html/ya09/ya09 _00584_0021/index.html (cited 18 March 2015).

13. *Oranda gen*, Manuscript with Igakukan seals dates 1843, Special Collection of Waseda University Library.

14. I follow Mikiso Hane's translation of this title as it appears in his translation of Maruyama (1974: 344).

15. Koga Tōan's *Kaibō okusoku* (1839) is usually cited as one of the major Tokugawa era works on coastal defence. On this work see Mitani (2006: 36–40).

16. Elliott (2001); Perdue (2005). The use of the word "imperialism" and the comparison with contemporary Western imperialism can be found in Larsen (2008: 1–10).

17. Makabe Jin notes the significant effect of Qing commentaries on the development of Koga Seiri's Confucianism, and the effect of Qing writings on both Seiri and Tōan's approach to foreign relations (Makabe, 2007: 232–81).

5. CONFUCIANISM AS LIBERALISM

1. See Fukuzawa's work of 1860 *Bankoku seihyō*, discussed in Ōkubo (2010: 77–9).

2. J.S. Mill's *On Liberty* was published in London the year before Nishi and Tsuda arrived in Leiden.

3. This book was later expanded the same year and reprinted with major contributions from two other major Japanese capitalist members of the Shibunkai, Yasuda

Zenjiro, and Morimura Ichizaemon. The new edition, titled "Complete Book of Self-Cultivation," *Shūyō Zensho* (Tokyo: Teikoku kyōiku gakkai, 1918).

4. This idea of *dokuritsu jison* was first articulated by Fukuzawa Yukichi in 1900 when giving the 404th Mita Lecture, which was entitled, "Outline of Self Cultivation."

5. Here in Shibusawa, as in much other Japanese scholarship of the period, the influence of Herbert Spencer's social organism theory can be felt. Herbert Spencer's ideas have also been related directly to the writing of Smiles, whose influence on Shibusawa seems clear (Kinmoth 1981: 10–11, 100).

6. Similarly uninspiring "concrete guides to self-cultivation practice" can be found in writings in this genre by other notable Japanese at the time. See for instance, Nitobe Inazo's advice to "wake up early" and such like in his "Self-Cultivation" *shūyō* (Nitobe 1969: 133–4).

7. The article this quote is taken from, "Tokugawa Confucianism and its Meiji Re-Release," *Tokugawa jukyō to meiji ni okeru sono saihen* (Kurozumi 2003: 165–90), is probably the most comprehensive academic writing on this issue. In English, the research of Matthew Fraleigh on Meiji period Sino-Japanese literature also develops many related themes (for instance, Narushima and Fraleigh 2010).

6. CONFUCIANISM AS FASCISM

1. On local resistance to the abolition of Confucian learning in place of modern schools, see Duke (2009: 169).

2. On the issue of the need for traditionalism to be repackaged in modern clothes to work in support of nationalism, see Duara (2003).

3. On Sakatani Shirushi's use of Confucianism in early Meiji intellectual and political debates, see Kōno (2011).

4. The article formed the basis of a quickly thereafter published book by Inoue of the same name (Inoue 1893). Many of the articles published during the first two years of the debate were collected at the time and published under the title "Dr. Inoue and the Christians," *Inoue hakase to kirisutokyōto* (Seki 1893).

5. On the complexities of Japanese sinology in this period, see Fogel (1984).

6. Indeed, it is exactly this issue which is highlighted in Prasenjit Duara's *Sovereignty and Authenticity*, Chapter 5 of which uses the history of occupied north China to explain how the Chinese Republic during this period created a new form of nationalism which had more in common with US than European models (Duara 2003: 179–208).

7. As pointed out by Duara, the nature of the Chinese Republic's use of Confucianism was different to Japan in that it underlay a vision of the nation which rather than being based on a homogenous ethnic model, rather saw it as the result of an "evolving history" or cultural interaction, or a "melting pot" as Chiang Kai-shek called it (Duara 2003: 195). Confucianism's role in this was as "The Central Plains Confucian Culture of the Great Unity," the cultural system which united differing ethnicities and histories into the Chinese nation (Duara 2003: 196).

8. How the ideology of Manchukuo subsequently evolved and influenced later developments in the Republic of China, the People's Republic of China, and

the rest of East and Southeast Asia is a larger and still intensely discussed academic question. See Duara 2003, Mitter 2000, and forthcoming publications from Jeremy Taylor.

9. Rana Mitter suggests that the Kingly Way ideology was also rather ineffective in Manchuria proper, mainly because it did not in any way interact with or develop local nationalist sentiment, having "little specifically northeastern about it" (Mitter 2000: 94). As both Smith and Duara point out, however, that was indeed what set the attempt to use Confucianism as ideology apart in Northern China, and made it interesting: it was ostensibly an attempt to sustain a state with an ideological alternative to standard nationalism.

10. On the social role of the sŏdang in the Chosŏn period, see Hatada (1969: 73).

11. Although I will not look beyond East Asian examples, the effect of the Japanese fascist occupation on propaganda and ideology in the later transwar period across other parts of Asia, notably South and South east Asia, has been written about by a number or scholars, for instance Mark (2006).

12. Opening statement of Japanese Defense Council at International Military Tribunal for the Far East, Presented by Kiyose Ichiro on 24 February 1947 (Session 166), Tokyo.

7. CONFUCIANISM AS TABOO

1. Yasuoka was asked to edit the surrender speech of Emperor Hirohito, the radio broadcast to the nation on August 15, 1945, being seen as the beginning of the secularization of the imperial family and end of the imperial cult. The insertion of the quote from the Song Confucian Zhang Zai (1020–1077) at the end of the second last paragraph of the speech, "we resolve to pave the way for a grand peace for all the generations to come," is attributed to Yasuoka (Kojima 2006: 158). On Yasuoka, see also Brown (2009, 2012).

2. This phenomenon is comparable to the prevalence of "scientism" among the elite of modern and contemporary China, especially the contemporary Chinese Communist Party (Callahan 2001; Yi 2011).

3. The most famous representative of this stream being Yanagita Kunio (1875–1962), whose work was also later associated with fascism (Kawada 1993; Koschmann 1985; Masuda 1965).

4. Eliminating words of Chinese origin from Japanese would mean removing around 50% of the words from the language (Shibatani 1990: 142–3).

5. Minamoto Ryōen influenced many of the new generation of predominantly progressive and pro-Asian scholars of the 1980s, notably including scholars like Ogyū Shigehiro and Kojima Yasunori, as well as Kurozumi Makoto, who was a student of Sagara. Importantly, however, these scholars were all also heavily influenced by the work of Maruyama Masao and by important reformist Sinologists in Japan like Yoshikawa Kōjirō.

6. Multiple personal communications. As I will expand upon below, these anti-Shibunkai sentiments seem to me unfair.

7. Including an award-winning book on the politics of the cultural integration of the Ryūkyū Islands into modern Japan published by Iwanami shoten (Yonaha

2009) and a string of scholarly articles in some of the most prestigious history, intellectual history, and ethnology journals in Japanese academia.

8. This field is nothing like the remnant "intellectual history" field in Europe. It rather resembles more English-language academia conceptions of "cultural history." In Taiwan, *sixiang* (the Chinese language version of *shisō* (thought)) is also used in a similar manner to indicate a much broader conception of culture than catered for in most Western conceptions of intellectual history. Maruyama began using this term in contrast to Inoue's preferred nomenclature of "philosophy" and "the history of philosophy," the politics of which was discussed in the last chapter.

9. Recently, Yasuoka Sadako, the granddaughter of Yasuoka Masahiro, also began giving seminars in the series. Her seminars aim to attract children and parents rather than retirees. She formerly gave these seminars at her own private school in Ginza but closed that school and moved to Yushima, seemingly due to a lack of sufficient student numbers to sustain an independent school. See Shibunkai (2015) and Yasuoka (2013).

10. Like most leaders of the Church of England, they have no belief in, or even wish for, any kind of "revival" of their religion. They just want to preserve it as heritage. Like the Church of England, they keep good cordial relations with related organizations abroad (Confucian organizations in Taiwan, and the traditional Kong "house" of Confucius in both Taiwan and China). Like the leaders of the Church of England their historically problematic relationship with imperialist violence leads them to adopt basically decent and preferably neutral political positions today. And like the Church of England, they are regarded as completely irrelevant by the vast majority of people in their country. The main difference is of course that the Shibunkai possesses only one property at Yushima, whereas the Church of England has thousands of properties, institutions, schools, and so on, which embed it in English cultural life and resource it financially.

EPILOGUE

1. In Liang Qichao represented through his readings of both Buddhism and Confucianism in Song-Ming terms, and in Sun Yat-sen through his references to Wang Yangming and others.

2. For his referral to legal enforcement of sexual mores, including in relation to homosexuality, see Footnote 38 on p. 220 in Jiang (2013).

3. Although Jiang's interpretation of Confucianism resembles mid-twentieth-century Japanese models very closely, his politics itself is more reminiscent of extreme European versions of 1930s radical conservatism. In fact, his political program resembles that of the early 1930s *Action Française* to a remarkable extent. Jiang Qing could therefore perhaps best be characterized politically as a contemporary Charles Maurras.

4. My more positive view of Confucianism when embedded in a Buddhist organizational form is deeply affected by my experience of fieldwork observing the use of Confucian pedagogy in Buddhist schools in Taipei between 2013 and 2015.

5. See quote which opens this epilogue.

Works Cited

Primary Source Collection Abbreviations

Nihon Shisō Taikei (NST) [Compendium of Japanese Thought],
Tokyo: Iwanami Shoten

NST 1
Aoki, Kazuo, ed. 1982. *Kojiki.* Nihon Shisō Taikei 1. Tokyo: Iwanami
Shoten.

NST 2
Ienaga, Saburō, ed. 1975. *Shōtoku Taishi Shū.* Nihon Shisō Taikei 2.
Tokyo: Iwanami Shoten.

NST 3
Inoue, Mitsusada, ed. 1976. *Ritsuryō.* Nihon Shisō Taikei 3. Tokyo:
Iwanami Shoten.

NST 5
Kawasaki, Tsuneyuki, ed. 1975. *Kūkai.* Nihon Shisō Taikei 5. Tokyo:
Iwanami Shoten.

NST 25
Ebisawa Arimichi, ed. 1970. *Kirishitan sho: Haiya sho.* Nihon Shisō
Taikei 25. Tokyo: Iwanami shoten.

NST 28
Ishida, Ichirō, ed. 1975. *Fujiwara Seika, Hayashi Razan.* Nihon Shisō
Taikei 28. Tokyo: Iwanami shoten.

NST 29
Yamanoi, Yū, ed. 1974. *Nakae Tōju.* Nihon Shisō Taikei 29. Tokyo:
Iwanami shoten.

NST 30
Gotō, Yōichi and Ryūtarō Tomoeda, eds. 1971. *Kumazawa Banzan.*
Nihon Shisō Taikei 30. Tokyo: Iwanami Shoten.

NST 31
Nishi, Junzō, Ryūichi Abe and Masao Maruyama, eds. 1980. *Yamazaki*
Ansai Gakuha. Nihon Shisō Taikei 31. Tokyo: Iwanami Shoten.

NST 32
Tahara, Tsuguo, ed. 1970. *Yamaga Sokō.* Nihon Shisō Taikei 32.
Tokyo: Iwanami shoten.

NST 33
Yoshikawa, Kōjirō, ed. 1971. *Itō Jinsai, Itō Tōgai*. Nihon Shisō Taikei 33.
Tokyo: Iwanami shoten.
NST 34
Araki, Kengo and Tadashi Inoue, eds. 1970. *Kaibara Ekiken, Muro
Kyūsō*. Nihon Shisō Taikei 34. Tokyo: Iwanami Shoten.
NST 35
Matsumura, Akira, ed. 1975. *Arai Hakuseki*. Nihon Shisō Taikei 35.
Tokyo: Iwanami shoten.
NST 36
Yoshikawa, Kōjirō, ed. 1973. *Ogyū Sorai*. Nihon Shisō Taikei 36. Tokyo:
Iwanami shoten.
NST 47
Nakamura, Yukihiko and Takehiko Okada, eds. 1972. *Kinsei Kōki
Jukashū*. Nihon Shisō Taikei 47. Tokyo: Iwanami Shoten.
NST 49
Uete, Michiari, ed. 1977. *Rai San'yō*. Nihon Shisō Taikei 49. Tokyo:
Iwanami Shoten.
NST 53
Imai, Usaburō, Yoshihiko Seya, and Masahide Bitō, eds. 1973.
Mitogaku. Nihon Shisō Taikei 53. Tokyo: Iwanami Shoten.
NST 55
Satō, Shōsuke, Michiari Uete and Muneyuki Yamaguchi, eds. 1971.
*Watanabe Kazan, Takano Chōei, Sakuma Shōzan, Yokoi Shōnan,
Hashimoto Sanai*. Nihon Shisō Taikei 55. Tokyo: Iwanami Shoten.
NST 64
Hirose, Hideo, Shigeru Nakayama, and Teizō Ogawa. 1972. *Yōgaku*.
Nihon Shisō Taikei 64–65. Tokyo: Iwanami Shoten.
NST 66
Numata, Jirō, Hiroaki Matsuzawa, Sadayū Tamamushi,
Takenaka Shibata, and Sakutarō Fukuda, eds. 1974. *Seiyō
Kenbunshū*. Nihon Shisō Taikei 66. Tokyo: Iwanami Shoten.

*Nihon Koten Bungaku Taikei (NKBT) [Compendium of Classical
Japanese Literature]*, Tokyo: Iwanami Shoten

NKBT 1
Ō, Yasumaro, Yūkichi Takeda, and Kenji Kurano, eds. 1965. *Kojiki;
Norito*. Nihon Koten Bungaku Taikei 1. Tokyo: Iwanami Shoten.
NKBT 67 NKBT 68
Sakamoto, Tarō, ed. 1965. *Nihon Shoki*. Nihon Koten Bungaku Taikei
67–68. Tokyo: Iwanami Shoten.
NKBT 71
Watanabe, Shōkō and Yūshō Miyasaka, eds. 1965. *Sangō Shiiki;
Shōryōshū*. Nihon Koten Bungaku Taikei 71. Tokyo: Iwanami Shoten.
NKBT 89

Yamagishi, Tokuhei, ed. 1966. *Gozan Bungaku Shū. Edo Kanshi Shū.*
Nihon Koten Bungaku Taikei 89. Tokyo: Iwanami Shoten.
NKBT 94
Nakamura, Yukihiko, ed. 1966. *Kinsei Bungaku Ronshū.* Nihon Koten
Bungaku Taikei 94. Tokyo: Iwanami Shoten.

*Kinsei Kanpō Igakusho Shūsei (KISS) [Collection of Early Modern
Japanese Chinese-Medicine Texts], Tokyo: Meicho Shuppan*

KISS 13
Ōtsuka Keisetsu and Yakazu Dōmei, eds. 1979. *Gotō Konzan,
Yamawaki Tōyō.* Kinsei kanpō igakusho shūsei 13. Tokyo: Meicho
Shuppan.
KISS 21
1979. *Honma Sōken. 1.* Kinsei kanpō igakusho shūsei 21. Tokyo:
Meicho Shuppan.
KISS 54
1981. *Fukui Fūtei.* Kinsei kanpō igakusho shūsei 54. Tokyo: Meicho
Shuppan.
KISS 66
1982. *Kagawa, Shūan. 2, Ippondō kōyo igen. kan 7–12.* Kinsei kanpō
igakusho shūsei 66. Tokyo: Meicho Shuppan.
KISS 67
1982. *Kagawa, Shūan. 3, Ippondō kōyo igen. kan 13–19.* Kinsei kanpō
igakusho shūsei 67. Tokyo: Meicho Shuppan.
KISS 68
1982. *Kagawa, Shūan. 4, Ippondō kōyo igen. kan 20–22.* Kinsei kanpō
igakusho shūsei 68. Tokyo: Meicho Shuppan.
KISS 69
1982. *Kagawa, Shūan. 5.* Kinsei kanpō igakusho shūsei 69. Tokyo:
Meicho Shuppan.
KISS 72
1983. *Tsuda gensen. 1.* Kinsei kanpō igakusho shūsei 72. Tokyo:
Meicho Shuppan.
KISS 73
1983. *Tsuda Gensen. 2.* Kinsei kanpō igakusho shūsei 73. Tokyo:
Meicho Shuppan.

*Nihon kyōikushi shiryō (NKSS) [Sources of Japanese Education
History]. Tokyo: Monbushō Sōmukyoku*

NKSS 6
Monbushō. 1891. *Nihon kyōikushi shiryō.* Vol. 6. Tokyo: Monbushō
Sōmukyoku.
NKSS 7
1890. *Nihon kyōikushi shiryō.* Vol. 7. Tokyo: Monbushō Sōmukyoku.

NKSS 9
1903. *Nihon kyōikushi shiryō.* Vol. 9. Tokyo: Tomiyama Shobō.

Chinese Text Project (ctext.org) (the title in italics below serves as the abbreviation) [all viewed 5 May 2015]

Book of Changes. 2015. Accessed May 5. http://ctext.org/book-of-changes.
Han Shu. 2015. Accessed May 5. http://ctext.org/han-shu.
Hou Han Shu. 2015. Accessed May 5. http://ctext.org/hou-han-shu.
Kongzi Jiayu. 2015. Accessed May 5. http://ctext.org/kongzi-jiayu.
Liji. 2015. Accessed May 5. http://ctext.org/liji. (including Legge's English translation)
Shang Han Lun. 2015. Accessed May 5. http://ctext.org/shang-han-lun.
The Analects. 2015. Accessed May 5. http://ctext.org/analects. (including Legge's English translation)
The Rites of Zhou. 2015. Accessed May 5. http://ctext.org/rites-of-zhou.
Xiao Jing. 2015. Accessed May 5. http://ctext.org/xiao-jing.
Xunzi. 2015. Accessed May 5. http://ctext.org/xunzi.

Other Works Cited

Abe, Yoshio. 1965. *Nihon Shushigaku to Chōsen.* Tokyo: Tōkyō Daigaku Shuppankai.
Aiso, Kazuhiro. 2003. *Ōshio Heihachirō Shokan No Kenkyū.* Osaka. Seibundō Shuppan.
Alavi, Seema. 2008. "Medical Culture in Transition: Mughal Gentleman Physician and the Native Doctor in Early Colonial India." *Modern Asian Studies* 42 (05): 853–97.
Amino, Yoshihiko. 2000. *"Nihon" to Wa Nani Ka.* Tokyo: Kōdansha.
Anderl, Christoph (ed.). 2012. *Zen Buddhist Rhetoric in China, Korea, and Japan.* Leiden; Boston: Brill.
Anderson, Perry. 1974. *Passages from Antiquity to Feudalism.* London: NLB.
2013. *Lineages of the Absolutist State.* London, New York: Verso Books.
Andō, Yūichirō. 2005. *Edo no Yōjōsho.* Tokyo: PHP.
Aoki, Toshiyuki. 2012. *Edo Jidai No Igaku: Meiitachi No 300-Nen.* Tokyo: Yoshikawa Kōbunkan.
Arai, Hakuseki. 1907. *Arai Hakuseki zenshū.* Vol. 6. Tokyo: Yoshikawa Hanshichi.
Yasunori, Arano, Ishii Masatoshi, and Murai Shōsuke. 1992. *Kaijō No Michi.* Tokyo: Tōkyō Daigaku Shuppankai.
Arano, Yasunori. 1988. *Kinsei Nihon to Higashi Ajia.* Tokyo: Tōkyō daigaku shuppankai.
Asad, Talal. 1993. *Genealogies of Religion: Discipline and Reasons of Power in Christianity and Islam.* Baltimore, MD etc: The Johns Hopkins University Press.

2003. *Formations of the Secular: Christianity, Islam, Modernity.* Stanford, CA: Stanford University Press.

Backus, Robert L. 1974. "The Relationship of Confucianism to the Tokugawa Bakufu as Revealed in the Kansei Educational Reform." *Harvard Journal of Asiatic Studies* 34: 97–162.

Barnes, Gina Lee. 2006. *State Formation in Japan: Emergence of a 4th-Century Ruling Elite.* London; New York, NY: Routledge.

Batten, Bruce Loyd. 2003. *To the Ends of Japan: Premodern Frontiers, Boundaries, and Interactions.* Honolulu: University of Hawai'i Press.

Beerens, Anna Maria Josephina Josephus. 2006. "Friends, Acquaintances, Pupils and Patrons: Japanese Intellectual Life in the Late Eighteenth Century: A Prosopographical Approach." Doctoral thesis. May 22. https://openaccess .leidenuniv.nl/handle/1887/4389.

Befu, Harumi. 2001. *Hegemony of Homogeneity: An Anthropological Analysis of "Nihonjinron."* Melbourne: Trans Pacific Press.

Bellah, Robert N. 1985. *Tokugawa Religion: The Cultural Roots of Modern Japan.* New York; London: Free Press; Collier Macmillan Publishers.

2005. "Civil Religion in America." *Daedalus* 134 (4): 40–55.

Bell, Daniel A. 2008. *China's New Confucianism: Politics and Everyday Life in a Changing Society.* Princeton, NJ etc: Princeton University Press.

Benesch, Oleg. 2009. "Wang Yangming and Bushidō: Japanese Nativization and Its Influences in Modern China." *Journal of Chinese Philosophy* 36 (3): 439–54.

2014. *Inventing the Way of the Samurai: Nationalism, Internationalism, and Bushidō in Modern Japan.* Oxford: Oxford University Press.

Bernstein, Andrew. 2006. *Modern Passings: Death Rites, Politics, and Social Change in Imperial Japan.* Honolulu: University of Hawaii Press.

Berry, Mary Elizabeth. 1994. *The Culture of Civil War in Kyoto.* Berkeley etc: University of California Press.

2006. *Japan in Print: Information and Nation in the Early Modern Period.* Berkeley, CA etc: University of California Press.

Billioud, Sébastien. 2015. "A Revival of Confucianism in China Today?" *Réseau Asie.* Accessed July 24. http://www.reseau-asie.com/edito-en/revival-confu ciasnim-china-billioud/revival-confuciasnim-china-billioud/revival-confu ciasnim-china-billioud/.

Bitō, Masahide. 1961. *Nihon Hōken Shisōshi Kenkyū: Bakuhan Taisei No Genri to Shushigaku-Teki Shii.* Tokyo: Aoki Shoten.

1993. "'Chūsei No Shūkyō to Gakumon' [Medieval Religion and Learning]." In Kimura Shōsan (ed.), *Chūseishi Kōza* [*Medieval History: A Reader*]. Tokyo: Gakuseisha.

Blacker, Carmen. 1964. *The Japanese Enlightenment: A Study of the Writings of Fukuzawa Yukichi.* Cambridge: University Press.

Bodart-Bailey, Beatrice. 1993. "The Persecution of Confucianism in Early Tokugawa Japan." *Monumenta Nipponica* 48 (3): 293–314.

Bodiford, William M. 1993. *Sōtō Zen in Medieval Japan.* Honolulu: University of Hawaii Press.

Boot, W.J. 1983. *The Adoption and Adaptation of Neo-Confucianism in Japan: The Role of Fujiwara Seika and Hayashi Razan*. Ph.D. dissertation, Leiden University.

Borgen, Robert. 1986. *Sugawara No Michizane and the Early Heian Court*. Cambridge, MA: Council on East Asian Studies, Harvard University.

Bowring, Richard John. 2006. "Fujiwara Seika and the Great Learning." *Monumenta Nipponica* 61 (4): 437–57.

Breen, John and Mark Teeuwen. 2016. *Capital of the Gods: A Social History of the Ise Shrines*. (Chapter 1) (manuscript forthcoming from Bloomsbury).

2010. *A New History of Shinto*. Chichester; Malden, MA: Wiley-Blackwell.

2000. *Shinto in History*. Richmond: Curzon.

Brown, Frederick. 2014. *The Embrace of Unreason: France, 1914–1940*. New York: Alfred A. Knopf.

Brown, Roger H. 2012a. "(The Other) Yoshida Shigeru and the Expansion of Bureaucratic Power in Prewar Japan." *Monumenta Nipponica* 67 (2): 283–327.

2012b. "Yasuoka Masahiro's 'New Discourse on Bushidō Philosophy': Cultivating Samurai Spirit and Men of Character for Imperial Japan." *Social Science Japan Journal* 16 (1): 107-129.

2009. "Shepherds of the People: Yasuoka Masahiro and the New Bureaucrats in Early Showa Japan." *The Journal of Japanese Studies* 35 (2): 285–319.

Burns, Susan L. 2003. *Before the Nation: Kokugaku and the Imagining of Community in Early Modern Japan*. Durham, NC: Duke University Press.

Buzo, Adrian. 2007. *The Making of Modern Korea*. London etc: Routledge.

Callahan, William. 2001. "China and the Globalisation of IR Theory: Discussion of 'Building International Relations Theory with Chinese Characteristics.'" *Journal of Contemporary China* 10 (26): 75–88.

2012. "Sino-Speak: Chinese Exceptionalism and the Politics of History." *The Journal of Asian Studies* 71 (01): 33–55.

2015. "History, Tradition and the China Dream: Socialist Modernization in the World of Great Harmony." *Journal of Contemporary China* April: 1–19.

Carlebach, Julius. 1978. *Karl Marx and the Radical Critique of Judaism*. London etc: Routledge and Kegan Paul.

Casanova, José. 1994. *Public Religions in the Modern World*. Chicago, IL: University of Chicago Press.

Chen, Weigang. 2014. *Confucian Marxism a Reflection on Religion and Global Justice*. Leiden etc: Brill.

Chen, Yong. 2013. *Confucianism as a Religion Controversies and Consequences*. Leiden etc: Brill.

Chen, Ziming. 1985. *Fu Ren Da Quan Liang Fang*. Beijing: Ren min wei sheng chu ban she.

Chikamatsu, Monzaemon. 1961. *Major Plays of Chikamatsu*. New York etc: Columbia University Press.

Chow, Kai-wing. 1994. *The Rise of Confucian Ritualism in Late Imperial China: Ethics, Classics, and Lineage Discourse.* Stanford, CA: Stanford University Press.

Cohen, Paul. 1985. "The Quest for Liberalism in the Chinese Past: Stepping Stone to a Cosmopolitan World or the Last Stand of Western Parochialism?: A Review of 'The Liberal Tradition in China.'" *Philosophy East and West* 35 (3): 305–10.

Collcutt, Martin. 1981. *Five Mountains: The Rinzai Zen Monastic Institution in Medieval Japan.* Cambridge, MA: Published by Council on East Asian Studies, Harvard University.

Como, Michael I. 2008. *Shōtoku: Ethnicity, Ritual, and Violence in the Japanese Buddhist Tradition.* New York etc: Oxford University Press.

Conrad, Sebastian. 1999. "What Time Is Japan? Problems of Comparative (Intercultural) Historiography." *History and Theory* 38 (1): 67–83.

De Bary, William Theodore. 2009. *Zhongguo de zi you chuan tong.* Guiyang Shi: Guizhou renmin chubanshe.

  1981. *Neo-Confucian Orthodoxy and the Learning of the Mind-and-Heart.* New York: Columbia University Press.

  1983. *The Liberal Tradition in China.* Hong Kong: New York: Chinese University Press; Columbia University Press.

  1989. *The Message of the Mind in Neo-Confucianism.* New York, NY: Columbia University Press.

  1993. *Waiting for the Dawn: A Plan for the Prince: Huang Tsung-Hsi's Ming-I Tai-Fang Lu.* New York: Columbia University Press.

  2013. *The Great Civilized Conversation: Education for a World Community.* New York: Columbia University Press.

De Bary, Wm Theodore, Carol Gluck, Andrew E. Barshay, and William M. Bodiford. 2005. *Sources of Japanese Tradition. Vol. 2: 1600 to 2000.* 2nd ed. New York: Columbia University Press.

De Gruchy, John Walter. 2003. Orienting Arthur Waley: Japonism, Orientalism, and the Creation of Japanese Literature in English. Hawaii: University of Hawaii Press.

De Vries, Jan. 2008. *The Industrious Revolution: Consumer Behavior and the Household Economy, 1650 to the Present.* Cambridge; New York: Cambridge University Press.

Dickinson, Frederick R. 1999. *War and National Reinvention: Japan in the Great War, 1914–1919.* Cambridge, MA: Harvard University Asia Center.

Dirlik, Arif. 2004. "Spectres of the Third World: Global Modernity and the End of the Three Worlds." *Third World Quarterly* 25 (1): 131–48.

  2005. "Performing the World: Reality and Representation in the Making of World Histor(ies)." *Journal of World History* 16 (4).

  2011a. "Revisioning Modernity: Modernity in Eurasian Perspectives." *Inter-Asia Cultural Studies* 12 (2): 284–305.

  2011b. "Guoxue/National Learning in the Age of Global Modernity." *China Perspectives* 2011 (1): 4–13.

  2012. "Transnationalization and the University: The Perspective of Global Modernity." *Boundary 2* 39 (3): 47–73.

Douglas, Mary. 2002. *Purity and Danger: An Analysis of Concept of Pollution and Taboo*. London etc: Routledge.

Duara, Prasenjit. 1988. *Culture, Power, and the State: Rural North China, 1900–1942*. Stanford, CA: Stanford University Press.

2003. *Sovereignty and Authenticity: Manchukuo and the East Asian Modern*. Lanham, MD etc: Rowman & Littlefield.

Dubois, Thomas David. 2005. "Hegemony, Imperialism, and the Construction of Religion in East and Southeast Asia." *History and Theory* 44 (4): 113–31.

2011. *Religion and the Making of Modern East Asia*. Cambridge; New York: Cambridge University Press.

Duke, Benjamin. 1989. *Ten Great Educators of Modern Japan: A Japanese Perspective*. Tokyo: University of Tokyo Press.

2009. *The History of Modern Japanese Education: Constructing the National School System, 1872–1890*. New Brunswick, NJ etc: Rutgers University Press.

Duus, Peter and Wan-yao Chou. 1996. *The Japanese Wartime Empire, 1931–1945*. Princeton, NJ: Princeton University Press.

Eisenstadt, S.N. 2003. *Comparative Civilizations and Multiple Modernities*. Leiden etc: Brill.

Elliott, Mark C. 2001. *The Manchu Way; the Eight Banners and Ethnic Identity in Late Imperial China*. Stanford, CA: Stanford University Press.

Elman, Benjamin A. 2000. *A Cultural History of Civil Examinations in Late Imperial China*. Berkeley: University of California Press.

2005. *On Their Own Terms: Science in China, 1550–1900*. Cambridge, MA etc: Harvard University Press.

2006. *A Cultural History of Modern Science in China*. Cambridge, MA etc: Harvard University Press.

Elman, Benjamin A. and Martin Kern. 2010. *Statecraft and Classical Learning: The Rituals of Zhou in East Asian History*. Leiden; Boston: Brill.

Fan, Ruiping. 1999. *Confucian Bioethics*. Dordrecht etc: Kluwer Academic Publishers.

2010. *Reconstructionist Confucianism: Rethinking Morality after the West*. Dordrecht etc: Springer.

Fan, Ruiping and Erika Yu. 2011. *The Renaissance of Confucianism in Contemporary China*. Dordrecht etc: Springer.

Fan, Ye. 1985. *Xin Jiao Ben Hou Han Shu Bing Fu Bian Shi San Zhong*. Taibei Shi: Ding wen shu ju.

Faure, Bernard. 1993. *Chan Insights and Oversights: An Epistemological Critique of the Chan Tradition*. Princeton, NJ: Princeton University Press.

Feng, Youlan and Derk Bodde. 1966. *A Short History of Chinese Philosophy*. New York: Free Press.

Finlayson, James Gordon and Fabian Freyenhagen. 2011. *Habermas and Rawls: Disputing the Political*. New York: Rouledge.

Fitzgerald, John. 1996. *Awakening China: Politics, Culture, and Class in the Nationalist Revolution*. Stanford, CA: Stanford University Press.

2004. *Huan Xing Zhongguo: Guo Min Ge Ming Zhong de Zheng Zhi, Wen Hua Yu Jie Ji*. Beijing: Sheng huo, du shu, xin zhi san lian shu dian.

Flueckiger, Peter. 2008. "Reflections on the Meaning of Our Country: Kamo No Mabuchi's Kokuikō." *Monumenta Nipponica* 63 (2): 211–38.

2011. *Imagining Harmony: Poetry, Empathy, and Community in Mid-Tokugawa Confucianism and Nativism*. Stanford, CA: Stanford University Press.

Fogel, Joshua A. 1984. *Politics and Sinology: The Case of Naitō Konan (1866–1934)*. Cambridge, MA etc: Council on East Asian Studies, Harvard University.

2004. *The Role of Japan in Liang Qichao's Introduction of Modern Western Civilization to China*. Berkeley, CA: Institute of East Asian Studies, University of California Berkeley, Center for Chinese Studies.

2009. *Articulating the Sinosphere: Sino-Japanese Relations in Space and Time*. Cambridge, MA etc: Harvard University Press.

Fogel, Joshua A. and S. Yamamuro. 2007. "Chimera: A Portrait of Manzhouguo. Harmony and Conflict." March. http://japanfocus.org/-S-Yamamuro/2384/article.html. [cited 5 May 2015].

Friday, Karl F. 1997. "Pushing Beyond the Pale: The Yamato Conquest of the Emishi and Northern Japan." *Journal of Japanese Studies* 23 (1): 1–21.

2012. *Japan Emerging: Premodern History to 1850*. Boulder, CO: Westview Press.

Fujikawa, Yū. 1941. *Nihon Igakushi*. Tokyo: Nisshin Shoin.

1980. *Fujikawa Yū chosakushū*. Kyoto: Shibunkaku Shuppan.

Fujiwara, Noboru. 1986. *Nihon ni okeru shominteki jiritsuron no keisei to tenkai*. Tokyo: Perikansha.

Fukuoka, Maki. 2006. *Between Knowing and Seeing: Shifting Standards of Accuracy and the Concept of Shashin in Japan, 1832–1872*. Ann Arbor: UMI.

Fukushima, Kashizō, Tokugawa Iesato, and Tokugawa-kō keishū shichijūnen shukuga kinenkai. 1939. *Kinsei Nihon no jugaku: Tokugawa-kō keishū shichijūnen shukuga kinen*. Tokyo: Iwanami shoten.

Fukuyama, Francis. 1992. *The End of History and the Last Man*. New York: Toronto: New York: Free Press; Maxwell Macmillan Canada; Maxwell Macmillan International.

Fukuzawa, Yukichi. 1966. *The Autobiography of Yukichi Fukuzawa*. New York etc: Columbia University Press.

1969. *Fukuzawa Yukichi's An Encouragement of Learning*. Tokyo: Sophia University.

1973. *An Outline of a Theory of Civilization*. Tokyo: Sophia University.

Gerhart, Karen M. 2009. *The Material Culture of Death in Medieval Japan*. Honolulu: University of Hawai'i Press.

Gilley, Sheridan and Brian Stanley. 2006. *The Cambridge History of Christianity. Vol. 8: World Christianities C. 1815-C. 1914*. Cambridge etc: Cambridge University Press.

Girardot, N.J. 2002. *The Victorian Translation of China: James Legge's Oriental Pilgrimage*. Berkeley etc: University of California Press.

Goble, Andrew. 1995. "Social Change, Knowledge, and History: Hanazono's Admonitions to The Crown Prince." *Harvard Journal of Asiatic Studies* 55 (1): 61–128.

Gonoi, Takashi. 2002. *Nihon Kirishitan Shi No Kenkyū*. Tokyo: Yoshikawa Kōbunkan.

Goossaert, Vincent. 2011. *The Religious Question in Modern China*. Chicago, IL, etc: The University of Chicago Press.

Görlitz, Axel. 1970. *Handlexikon zur Politikwissenschaft*. München: Ehrenwirth.

Gramlich-Oka, Bettina. 2011. "Neo-Confucianism Reconsidered: Family Rituals in the Rai Household." *U.S.-Japan-Women's Journal* 39: 7–37.

Grapard, Allan G. 1992. "The Shinto of Yoshida Kanetomo." *Monumenta Nipponica* 47 (1): 27–58.

Grayson, James Huntley. 2002. *Korea – a Religious History*. Abingdon etc: RoutledgeCurzon.

Habermas, Jürgen. 1991. *The Structural Transformation of the Public Sphere: An Inquiry into a Category of Bourgeois Society*. Cambridge, MA: MIT Press.

Habermas, Jürgen and Ciaran Cronin. 2008. *Between Naturalism and Religion: Philosophical Essays*. Cambridge, UK; Malden, MA: Polity Press.

Habermas, Jürgen and Eduardo Mendieta. 2002. *Religion and Rationality: Essays on Reason, God, and Modernity*. Cambridge, MA: MIT Press.

Halliday, Jon. 1975. *A Political History of Japanese Capitalism*. New York: Pantheon Books.

Hall, John Whitney. 1955. *Tanuma Okitsugu, 1719–1788, Forerunner of Modern Japan*. Cambridge: Harvard University Press.

Hall, John Whitney and Delmer M. Brown. 1993. *The Cambridge History of Japan. Vol. 1: Ancient Japan*. Cambridge etc: Cambridge University Press.

Hall, John Whitney and James L. MacClain. 1991. *The Cambridge History of Japan. Vol. 4: Early Modern Japan*. Cambridge etc: Cambridge University Press.

Hall, John Whitney, Donald H. Shively, and William H. MacCullough. 1999. *The Cambridge History of Japan. Vol. 2: Heian Japan*. Cambridge etc: Cambridge University Press.

Hall, John Whitney and Kozo Yamamura. 1990. *The Cambridge History of Japan. Vol. 3: Medieval Japan*. Cambridge etc: Cambridge University Press.

Hammond, Kenneth. J. 2015. "The Return of the Repressed: The New Left and 'Left' Confucianism in Contemporary China." In Kenneth. J. Hammond and Jeffrey L. Richey. *The Sage Returns: Confucian Revival in Contemporary China*. Albany: SUNY Press.

Han Sŏk-hŭi. 1988. *Nihon no Chōsen shihai to shūkyō seisaku*. Tokyo: Miraisha.

Hardacre, Helen. 1989. *Shintô and the State, 1868–1988*. Princeton, NJ: Princeton University Press.

Hare, Thomas Blenman. 1990. "Reading Writing and Cooking: Kūkai's Interpretive Strategies." *The Journal of Asian Studies* 49 (2): 253–73.

Harrell, Paula. 2012. *Asia for the Asians: China in the Lives of Five Meiji Japanese*. Portland, ME: MerwinAsia.

Hashimoto, Akihiko. 1994. *Edo Bakufu Shiken Seidoshi No Kenkyū*. Tokyo: Kazama Shobō.

Hashimoto Akihiko (ed.). 2007. *Shōheizaka Gakumonjo Nikki*. Tokyo: Shibunkai.

Hatada, Takashi. 1969. *A History of Korea*. Santa Barbara, CA: ABC-clio Press.

Hayami, Akira. 2003. *Kinsei Nihon No Keizai Shakai*. Tokyo: Reitaku Daigaku Shuppankai.

Hayami, Akira and Saitō, Osamu. 2009. *Population, Family and Society in Pre-Modern Japan: Collected Papers of Akira Hayami*. Vol. v. 4. Folkestone, UK: Global Oriental.

Hayami, Akira and Saitō, Osamu. 2004. *Emergence of Economic Society in Japan, 1600–1859*. Oxford etc: Oxford University Press.

Hayashi, Fukusai. 1912. *Tsūkō Ichiran*. Tokyo: Kokusho Kankōkai.

Hayashi, Razan. 1977–9. *Hayashi Razan bunshū*. Tokyo: Perikansha.

Hayek, Matthias and Annick Horiuchi. 2014. *Listen, Copy, Read: Popular Learning in Early Modern Japan*. Leiden; Boston: Brill.

Higashijima, Makoto. 2013. *Nihon No Kigen*. Tokyo: Kabushiki Kaisha Ōta Shuppan.

Sadao, Honma. 2009. "Motogi Shōhei." In Wolfgang Michel, Yumiko Torii, and Mahito Kawashima (eds.), *Kyūshū No Rangaku: Ekkyō to Kōryū*. Kyoto: Shibunkaku Shuppan.

Horiuchi, Annick. 2003. "When Science Develops Outside State Patronage: Dutch Studies in Japan at the Turn of the Nineteenth Century." *Early Science and Medicine* 8 (2): 148–72.

Huang, Zongxi. 1987. *The Records of Ming Scholars*. Honolulu: University of Hawaii Press.

Hübner, Regina Beate. 2014. "State Medicine and the State of Medicine in Tokugawa Japan: *Kōkei saikyūhō* (1791), an emergency handbook initiated by the Bakufu." (Ph.D. Dissertation, Clare Hall, Cambridge University, July 2014)

Ikeda, Nobuo. 2012. *Kawaru Sekai, Kawarenai Nihonjin, "Nihon Shi" No Owari*. Tōkyō: PHP.

Ikegami, Eiko. 2005. *Bonds of Civility: Aesthetic Networks and the Political Origins of Japanese Culture*. Cambridge; New York: Cambridge University Press.

Imai Jun, and Yamamoto Shinkō. 2006. *Sekimon shingaku no shisō*. Tokyo: Perikansha.

Imamura, Yoshio. 1966. *Nihon budō zenshū. 5: dai gokan: jūjutsu, karate, kenpō, aikijutsu*. Vol. 5. Tokyo: Jinbutsu ōraisha.

Inoguchi, Atsushi. 1982. *Fujiwara Seika; Matsunaga Sekigo*. Tokyo: Meitoku shuppansha.

Inoue, Atsushi. 2010. "Kindai Nihon Ni Okeru Yi Toegye Kenkyū No Keifugaku – Abe Yoshio, Takahashi Susumu No Gakusetu No Kentō wo Chūshin ni." *Sōgō Seisaku Ronsō*, Shimane Kenritsu Daigaku Sōgō Seisaku Gakkai 18 (February): 61–83.

Inoue, Shōichi. 2008. *Nihon Ni Kodai Wa Atta No Ka*. Tokyo: Kadokawa Gakugei Shuppan.

Inoue, Tetsujirō. 1912. *Kokumin Dōtoku Gairon*. Tokyo: Sanseidō.

1944. "Jukyō no chōsho to tansho (tetsugakkaikōen)." In *Nihon shushigakuha no tetsugaku*. Tokyo: Fuzanbō, 745–807.

1900. *Nihon Yōmeigakuha no Tetsugaku*. Tokyo: Fuzanbō.

1903. *Nihon Kogakuha no Tetsugaku*. Tokyo: Fuzanbō.

1905. *Nihon Shushigakuha no Tetsugaku.* Tokyo: Fuzanbō.

1890. *Chokugo engi.* Tokyo: Keigyōsha.

1893. *Kyōiku to shūkyō no shōtotsu.* Tokyo: Tetsugaku shoin.

1942. *Shakumei Kyōiku Chokugo Engi.* Tokyo: Kōbundō Shoten.

1944. *Nihon Shushigaku-Ha No Tetsugaku,* [Teiseiban]. Tōkyō: Fuzanbō.

2003. *Inoue Tetsujirō shū. *Dai nanakan* Tōyō bunka to Shina no shōrai.* Tokyo: Kuresu Shuppan.

Inoue Tetsujirō, and Kanie Yoshimaru (eds.) 1902. *Nihon rinri ihen.* Vol. 3. Tokyo: Ikuseikai.

Ishida, Ichirō. 1975. *Fujiwara Seika, Hayashi Razan.* Tokyo: Iwanami shoten.

Ishikawa, Ken. 1960. *Nihon Gakkoshi No Kenkyu.* Tokyo: Aoki shoten.

Ishin, Sūden. 1989. *Ikoku nikki: Konchiin Sūden gaikō monjo shūsei: eiinbon.* Tokyo: Tōkyō bijutsu.

Ishioka, Hisao. 1967. *Nihon heihō zenshū.* Tokyo: Jinbutsu ōraisha.

Jannetta, Ann. 2007. *The Vaccinators: Smallpox, Medical Knowledge, and the "Opening" of Japan.* Stanford, CA: Stanford University Press.

1987. *Epidemics and Mortality in Early Modern Japan.* Princeton, NJ: Princeton University Press.

Jensen, Lionel M. 1997. *Manufacturing Confucianism: Chinese Traditions & Universal Civilization.* Durham: Duke University Press.

Jiang, Qing. 2012. *A Confucian Constitutional Order: How China's Ancient Past Can Shape Its Political Future.* Princeton, NJ: Princeton University Press.

Jiang, Qing. 2003. *Zheng zhi ru xue: dang dai ru xue de zhuan xiang, te zhi yu fa zhan.* Beijing: Shenghuo, dushu, xinzhisanguan shudian.

2009. *Ru xue de shi dai jia zhi.* Chengdu: Sichuan renmin chubanshe.

Josephson, Jason Ānanda. 2012. *The Invention of Religion in Japan.* Chicago; London: The University of Chicago Press.

Kanetomo, Yoshida. 1992. "Yuiitsu Shintō Myōbō Yōshū." *Monumenta Nipponica* 47 (2): 137–61.

Kang, David C. 2007. *China Rising: Peace, Power, and Order in East Asia.* New York: Columbia University Press.

2010. *East Asia before the West: Five Centuries of Trade and Tribute.* Contemporary Asia in the World. New York: Columbia University Press.

Kang, Etsuko Hae-jin. 1997. *Diplomacy and Ideology in Japanese–Korean Relations: From the Fifteenth to the Eighteenth Century.* Houndmills, Basingstoke, Hampshire; New York, NY: Macmillan Press; St. Martin's Press.

Kang, Xiaoguang. 2002. *Xin bao shou zhu yi zheng lun ji.* Beijing: s.n.

2003. *Zhongguo de dao lu.* Beijing: s.n.

2005. *Ren zheng: Zhongguo zheng zhi fa zhan de di san tiao dao lu.* Singapore: Global Publishing.

2008. *Zhongguo gui lai: dang dai Zhongguo da lu wen hua min zu zhu yi yun dong yan jiu.* Singapore: Global Publishing.

Kang, Xiaoguang, Liu Shilin Liu, and Wang Jin. 2010a. *Zhen di zhan: guan yu Zhonghua wen hua fu xing de ge lan xi shi fen xi = Struggle for Cultural Hegemony: Gramscian Perspectives of Revitalizing Chinese Traditional Culture.* Beijing: Shehui kexue wenjian chupanshe.

Kant, Immanuel. 1996. *The Metaphysics of Morals.* Cambridge, MA etc: Cambridge University Press.

2002. *Immanuel Kant: Groundwork of the Metaphysics of Morals: In Focus.* London etc: Routledge.

Karaki, Junzō. 2001. *Gendaishi e no kokoromi.* Kyoto: Tōeisha.

Karube, Tadashi. 2008. *Maruyama Masao and the Fate of Liberalism in Twentieth-Century Japan.* Tokyo: International House of Japan.

Katayama Sen. 1904. "Sangyō Rieki No Bunhai." *Shakai Shugi* 8 (8): 2–12.

1931. *Jiden.* Kaizō Bunko. Tokyo: Kaizōsha.

Kaviraj, Sudipta and Sunil Khilnani. 2001. *Civil Society: History and Possibilities.* Cambridge, UK; New York: Cambridge University Press.

Kawada, Minoru. 1993. *The Origin of Ethnography in Japan: Yanagita Kunio and His Times.* London etc: Kegan Paul International.

Keane, Webb. 2007. *Christian Moderns: Freedom and Fetish in the Mission Encounter.* Berkeley: University of California Press.

Kersten, Rikki. 1996. *Democracy in Postwar Japan: Maruyama Masao and the Search for Autonomy.* London etc: Routledge.

Ketelaar, James Edward. 1990. *Of Heretics and Martyrs in Meiji Japan: Buddhism and Its Persecution.* Princeton, NJ: Princeton University Press.

Kim, Hwansoo Ilmee. 2012. *Empire of the Dharma: Korean and Japanese Buddhism, 1877–1912.* Cambridge, MA etc: Harvard University Asia Center.

Kinmonth, Earl H. 1981. *The Self-Made Man in Meiji Japanese Thought: From Samurai to Salary Man.* Berkeley; London: University of California Press.

Kitanaka, Junko. 2012. *Depression in Japan: Psychiatric Cures for a Society in Distress.* Princeton, NJ: Princeton University Press.

Kiyowara, Sadao. 1944. "Japanization of Oriental Thoughts." *Contemporary Japan* 13 (7): 720–31.

Kobori, Keiichirō (ed.). 1995. *Tōkyō Saiban Nihon No Benmei: "Kyakka Miteishutsu Bengogawa Shiryō" Bassui.* Kōdansha Gakujutsu Bunko 1189. Tokyo: Kōdansha.

Ko, Dorothy. 1994. *Teachers of the Inner Chambers: Women and Culture in Seventeenth-Century China.* Stanford, CA: Stanford University Press.

Ko, Dorothy, JaHyun Kim Haboush, and Joan R. Piggott. 2003. *Women and Confucian Cultures in Premodern China, Korea, and Japan.* Berkeley, CA etc: University of California Press.

Kohn, Livia. 2000. *Daoism Handbook.* Leiden etc: Brill.

Koizumi, Junichiro. 2005. "Statement by Prime Minister Junichiro Koizumi." August 15. http://www.mofa.go.jp/announce/announce/2005/8/0815.html. (viewed 5th May 2015)

Kojima, Tsuyoshi. 2006. *Kindai Nihon No Yōmeigaku.* Kōdansha Sensho Mechie 369. Tokyo: Kōdansha.

2005. *Chūgoku Shisō to Shūkyō No Honryū: Sōchō.* Tokyo: Kōdansha.

2007. *Yasukuni shikan: Bakumatsu Ishin to iu shin'en.* Tokyo: Chikuma shinsho.

2013. *Higashi ajia no jukyō to rei.* Tokyo: Libretto.

Kokuritsu Kōbunshokan. 1984. *Sūmitsuin Kaigi Gijiroku: Kokuritsu Kōbunshokan Shozō.* Tokyo: Tōkyō Daigaku Shuppankai.

Komai, Norimura. n.d. *Uguisu Yado Zakki* 鶯宿雑記. Manuscript in National Diet Library.

Konishi, Sho. 2014. "The Emergence of an International Humanitarian Organization in Japan: The Tokugawa Origins of the Japanese Red Cross." *The American Historical Review* 119 (4): 1129–53. doi:10.1093/ahr/119.4.1129.

Kōno, Yūri. 2011. *Meiroku zasshi no seiji shisō: Sakatani Shiroshi to "dōri" no chōsen.* Tokyo: Tōkyō Daigaku Shuppankai.

Kornicki, Peter F. 1998. *The Book in Japan: A Cultural History from the Beginnings to the Nineteenth Century.* Leiden; Boston: Brill.

Kornicki, Peter and James McMullen. 1996. *Religion in Japan: Arrows to Heaven and Earth.* Cambridge; New York: Cambridge University Press.

Kosato, Hiroshi. 2014. *Kanpō no rekishi: chūgoku, nihon no dentō igaku.* Tokyo: Taishūkan.

Koschmann, J. Victor. 1987. *The Mito Ideology: Discourse, Reform, and Insurrection in Late Tokugawa Japan, 1790–1864.* Berkeley: University of California Press.

Koschmann, J. Victor, Keibō Ōiwa, and Shinji Yamashita. 1985. *International Perspectives on Yanagita Kunio and Japanese Folklore Studies.* Ithaca, NY: China-Japan Program, Cornell University.

Koyasu Nobukuni. 1995. *Edo no shiso.* Tokyo: Perikansha.

2002. *"Ajia" wa dō katararete kita ka: kindai Nihon no Orientarizumu.* Tokyo: Fujiwara Shoten.

2003. *Nihon kindai shisō hihan: ikkokuchi no seiritsu.* Iwanami gendai bunko. Tokyo: Iwanmi shoten.

2004. *Kokka to saishi: kokka Shintō no genzai.* Tokyo: Seidosha.

2007. *Nihon nashonarizumu no kaidoku.* Tokyo: Hakutakusha.

Kriechbaum, Maximiliane. 1996. *Actio, ius und dominium in den Rechtslehren des 13. und 14. Jahrhunderts.* Ebelsbach: Aktiv.

Kublin, Hyman. 1964. *Asian Revolutionary: The Life of Sen Katayama.* Princeton, NJ: Princeton University Press.

Kūkai. 1972. *Kūkai: Major Works.* New York: Columbia University Press.

Kuo, Ya-Pei. 2013. "'Christian Civilization' and the Confucian Church: The Origin of Secularist Politics in Modern China." *Past & Present* 218 (1): 235–64.

Kuroda, Toshio. 1975. *"Chusei kokka to tenno,"* in *Iwanami kōza Nihon rekishi. 6: Chūsei 2.* Tokyo: Iwanami Shoten.

Kurokawa, Mamichi. 1977. *Nihon Kyōiku Bunko / Kurokawa Mamichi Hensan.* Tokyo: Nihon Tosho Sentā.

Kurozumi, Makoto. 2003. *Kinsei Nihon Shakai to Jukyō.* Shohan. Tokyo: Perikansha.

2006. *Fukusūsei no Nihon shisō.* Tokyo: Perikansha.

Kurozumi, Makoto and Herman Ooms. 1994. "The Nature of Early Tokugawa Confucianism." *Journal of Japanese Studies* 20 (2): 331–76.

Larsen, Kirk W. 2008. *Tradition, Treaties, and Trade: Qing Imperialism and Chosŏn Korea, 1850–1910.* Cambridge, MA: Harvard University Asia Center.

Lau, D.C. (trans.). 1979. *The Analects = (Lun Yü).* New York: Penguin Books.

Legge, James. 1983. *The Chinese classics. I-II: Confucian Analects, the Great Learning, the Doctrine of the Mean, the Works of Mencius.* Taipei: Southern Materials Center, SMC.

Liang, Qichao. 1985. *Liang Qichao lun Qing xue shi er zhong.* Shanghai: Fudan daxue chubanshe.

Liu, Lydia H., Rebecca E. Karl, and Dorothy Ko. 2013. *The Birth of Chinese Feminism: Essential Texts in Transnational Theory.* New York etc: Columbia University Press.

Liu, Wennan. 2013. "Redefining the Moral and Legal Roles of the State in Everyday Life: The New Life Movement in China in the Mid-1930s." *Cross-Currents: East Asian History and Culture Review,* 7: 30–59. https://cross -currents.berkeley.edu/e-journal/issue-7/liu.

Machi, Senjuro. 1999. "The Development of Scholarship in the Igakkan (1): The Founding of the Igakkan." *Journal of the Japan Society of Medical History* 45 (3): 339–72.

Machi Senjuro, Kosoto Hiroshi, and Hanawa Toshihiko. 2003. "The Background of Taki Motoyasu's Fall: Regarding the Circumstances of the Nationalization of the Igakkan." *Journal of the Japan Society of Medical History* 49 (2): 205–21.

MacMahon, Keith. 2013. *Women Shall Not Rule: Imperial Wives and Concubines in China from Han to Liao.* Lanham, MD etc: Rowman & Littlefield.

Madsen, Richard. 2007. *Democracy's Dharma: Religious Renaissance and Political Development in Taiwan.* Berkeley: University of California Press.

Maeda, Tsutomu. 1996. *Kinsei Nihon No Jugaku to Heigaku.* Tōkyō: Perikansha.

2009. *Edo kōki no shisō kūkan.* Tokyo: Perikansha.

2012. *Edo No Dokushokai: Kaidoku No Shisōshi.* Tokyo: Heibonsha.

Makabe, Jin. 2007. *Tokugawa Kōki No Gakumon to Seiji; Shōheizaka Gakumonjo Jusha to Bakumatsu Gaikō Hen'yō.* Nagoya: Nagoya Daigaku Shuppankai.

Makeham, John. 2008. *Lost Soul: "Confucianism" in Contemporary Chinese Academic Discourse.* Cambridge, MA: Published by the Harvard University Asia Center for the Harvard-Yenching Institute.

Manase, Yōan'in. *Kani Kafu.* Manuscript held in University of Tokyo Historiographical Documents Insititute.

Manchoukuo Dept. of Foreign Affairs. 1932. *Proclamations, Statements and Communications of the Manchoukuo Government.* Dept. of Foreign Affairs. Publications, Series no. 1. Hsinking, Manchuria: s.n.

Marchand, Suzanne L. 2009. *German Orientalism in the Age of Empire: Religion, Race, and Scholarship.* Cambridge: Cambridge University Press.

Mark, Ethan. 2006. "'Asia's' Transwar Lineage: Nationalism, Marxism, and 'Greater Asia' in an Indonesian Inflection." *The Journal of Asian Studies* 65 (3): 461–93.

Maruyama, Masao. 1963. *Thought and Behaviour in Modern Japanese Politics.* London etc: Oxford University Press.

1974. *Studies in the Intellectual History of Tokugawa Japan.* Princeton, NJ: Princeton University Press.

Marx, Karl. 1968. *Selected Essays.* Freeport, NY: Books for Libraries Press.

Masuda, Katsumi. 1965. *Yanagita Kunio.* Tōkyō: Chikuma shobō.

Matsudaira, Sadanobu. 1942. *Uge No Hitokoto, Shugyōroku*. Tōkyō: Iwanami Shoten.

Matsudaira, Sadanobu and Kodera Jūjirō. 1928. *Haru no kokoro: Rakuō kō gochosakushū*. Rakuō hyakunen kinen taisai kyōsankai.

Matsuda, Kōichirō. 2008. *Edo No Chishiki Kara Meiji No Seiji E*. Tokyo: Perikansha.

McBride, Richard D. 2010. *State and Society in Middle and Late Silla*. Cambridge, MA: Korea Institute, Harvard University.

McMullen, James. 1999. *Idealism, Protest, and the "Tale of Genji": The Confucianism of Kumazawa Banzan (1619–91)*. Oxford etc: Clarendon.

McNally, Mark. 2005. *Proving the Way: Conflict and Practice in the History of Japanese Nativism*. Cambridge, MA: Harvard University Asia Center; Distributed by Harvard University Press.

Meissner, Kurt. 1934. *Grundlagen der nationalen Erziehung in Japan: Vortrag*. Tokyo.

Mill, John Stuart. 1989. *On Liberty; with The Subjection of Women; and Chapters on Socialism*. Cambridge etc: Cambridge University Press.

Mill, John Stuart and Masanao Nakamura (eds.). 1872. *Jiyū no ri*. Shizuoka: Kihei Kenichirō.

Minamoto, Ryōen. 1969. *Giri to Ninjō: Nihonteki Shinjō No Ichikōsatsu*. Tokyo: Chūō Kōronsha.

Minamoto, Ryōen. 1995. *Shisō*. Tokyo: Taishūkan Shoten.

Minear, Richard H. 1976. "Ogyū Sorai's Instructions for Students: A Translation and Commentary." *Harvard Journal of Asiatic Studies* 36: 5–81.

Mishima, Yukio. 2005. *Mishima Yukio zenshū ketteiban*. Tokyo: Shinchōsha.

Mitani, Hiroshi. 2004. *Higashi Ajia No Kōron Keisei*. Tokyo: Tōkyō Daigaku Shuppankai.

2003. *Perii raikō*. Tokyo: Yoshikawa kōbunkan.

2006. *Escape from Impasse: The Decision to Open Japan*. Tokyo: International House of Japan.

Mitter, Rana. 2000. *The Manchurian Myth: Nationalism, Resistance and Collaboration in Modern China*. Berkeley CA etc: Univeristy of California Press.

Miyamoto, Tsuneichi. 2008. *Shibusawa keizō*. Tokyo: Miraisha.

Miyata, Setsuko. 1985. *Chōsen minshū to "kōminka" seisaku*. Tokyo: Miraisha.

Miyoshi, Masao and H.D. Harootunian. 1989. *Postmodernism and Japan*. Durham etc: Duke University Press.

2002. *Learning Places: The Afterlives of Area Studies*. Durham etc: Duke University Press.

Mizoguchi, Kōji. 2002. *An Archaeological History of Japan: 30,000 B.C. to A.D. 700*. Philadelphia, PA: University of Pennsylvania Press.

Mokyr, Joel. 1994. "Cardwell's Law and the Political Economy of Technological Progress." *Research Policy* 23 (5): 561–74.

2002. *The Gifts of Athena: Historical Origins of the Knowledge Economy*. Princeton, NJ etc: Princeton University Press.

Mori Kōichi. 1992. *Umi to rettō bunka*. Tokyo: Shōgakkan.

Mori, Saburō. 1933. *Takishi no jiseki*. Tokyo: Ōzorasha.

Mori, Shikazō. 1977. *Naitō Konan: Nihon bunkaron; Uno Enkū: Inasaku to shinkō.* Tōkyō: Kōdansha.

Motoda, Eifu. 1939. *Yōgaku Kōyō.* Tokyo: Iwanami Shoten.

Mungello, D.E. 1994. *The Chinese Rites Controversy: Its History and Meaning.* Nettetal: Steyler Verlag.

Murakami, Naojirō. 1929. *Ikoku ōfuku shokanshū; Zōtei Ikoku nikkishō.* Tokyo: Shunnansha.

Murray, Julia K. 2009. "'Idols' in the Temple: Icons and the Cult of Confucius." *The Journal of Asian Studies* 68 (02): 371–411.

Naitō, Torajirō. 1972. *Naitō Konan Zenshū.* Vol. 5. Tokyo: Chikuma Shobō.

Najita, Tetsuo. 1987. *Visions of Virtue in Tokugawa Japan: The Kaitokudō Merchant Academy of Osaka.* Chicago: University of Chicago Press.

Nakai, Kate Wildman. 1988. *Shogunal Politics: Arai Hakuseki and the Premises of Tokugawa Rule.* Cambridge: Council on East Asian Studies, Harvard University: Distributed by Harvard University Press.

Nakamura, Ellen Gardner. 2005. *Practical Pursuits: Takano Chōei, Takahashi Keisaku, and Western Medicine in Nineteenth-Century Japan.* Cambridge, MA: Harvard University Asia Center; Distributed by Harvard University Press.

Nakasone, Yasuhiro. 1999. *The Making of the New Japan: Reclaiming the Political Mainstream.* Richmond: Curzon.

Naoki, Kōjirō (ed.). 1988. *Shoku Nihongi.* Tōyō Bunko 489. Tōkyō: Heibonsha.

Narushima, Ryūhoku. 2010. *New Chronicles of Yanagibashi and Diary of a Journey to the West: Narushima Ryūhoku Reports from Home and Abroad.* Ithaca, NY: East Asia Program, Cornell University.

Needham, Joseph. 1956. *Science and Civilisation in China. Vol. 2: History of Scientific Thought.* Cambridge etc: Cambridge University Press.

Neville, Robert C. 2000. *Boston Confucianism: Portable Tradition in the Late-Modern World.* Albany, NY: State University of New York Press.

Newmark, Jeffrey. 2014. "Yamadaya Daisuke's 1837 Nose Movement." http://hdl.handle.net/1811/65305 [cited 5 May 2015].

Nihon Jukyō Sen'yōkai 1934. *Nihon No Jukyō.* Tokyo: Nihon Jukyō Sen'yōkai.

Niijima, Jō. 1977. *Niijima Jō, Uemura Masahisa, Kiyozawa Manshi, Tsunashima Ryōsen shū.* Tokyo: Chikuma shobō.

Niijima, Jō. 2005. *Niijima Jō No Tegami.* Iwanami Bunko. Tōkyō: Iwanami Shoten.

Nirenberg, David. 2013. *Anti-Judaism: The Western Tradition.* New York, NY etc: WWNorton & Company.

Nishi Amane. 1879. *Seihō Setsuyaku.* Ōtsu: Takada Yoshitoshi.

——— 1962. *Nishi Amane zenshū.* Tokyo: Munetaka shobō.

Nitobe, Inazō. 1969. *Nitobe Inazō Zenshū. Vol. 7: Shuyo.* Tokyo: Kyōbunkan.

Nosco, Peter (ed.). 1984. *Confucianism and Tokugawa Culture.* Princeton, NJ: Princeton University Press.

Numata, Jirō. 1992. *Western Learning: A Short History of the Study of Western Science in Early Modern Japan.* Tokyo: Japan-Netherlands Institute.

Ōba Osamu. 1967. *Edo Jidai Ni Okeru Tōsen Mochiwatarisho No Kenkyū.* Suita: Kansai Daigaku Shuppanbu.

1996. *Kodai chūsei ni okeru Nitchū kankeishi no kenkyū.* Kyōto: Dōhōsha shuppan.

Obata, Kyugoro. 1938. *An Interpretation of the Life of Viscount Shibusawa.* Tokyo: Tokyo Insatsu Kabushiki Kaisha (Tokyo Printing Company, Ltd.).

Ogyū, Sorai and Samuel Hideo Yamashita. 1994. *Master Sorai's Responsals: An Annotated Translation of Sorai Sensei Tōmonsho.* Honolulu: University of Hawaii Press.

Ogyū, Shigehiro. 2008. *Kindai, Ajia, yōmeigaku.* Tokyo: Perikansha.

Ogyū, Sorai. [Tetsuo Najita (trans.)] 1998. *Tokugawa Political Writings.* Cambridge etc: Cambridge University Press.

[John Allen Tucker (trans.)]. 2006. *Ogyū Sorai's Philosophical Masterworks: The Bendō and Benmei.* Honolulu: Association for Asian Studies.

Ōishi, Manabu. 2003. *Kyōhō kaikaku to shakai henyō.* Tokyo: Yoshikawa kōbunkan.

Ōkubo, Takeharu. 2010. *Kindai Nihon no seiji kōsō to Oranda.* Tokyo: Tōkyō Daigaku Shuppankai.

Ōkuwa, Hitoshi. 1989. *Nihon Kinsei No Shisō to Bukkyō.* Kyōto: Hōzōkan.

2003. *Nihon Bukkyō No Kinsei.* Kyōto: Hōzōkan.

2012. "'Kinsei Kokka No Shūkyōsei' (the Religiosity of the Early Modern State)." *Nihonshi Kenkyū* 600 (August): 111–37.

Ōkuwa, Hitoshi and Maeda Ichirō. 2006. *Razan, Teitoku "jubutsu mondō": chūkai to kenkyū.* Tokyo: Perikansha.

Ooms, Herman. 1975. *Charismatic Bureaucrat: A Political Biography of Matsudaira Sadanobu, 1758–1829.* Chicago; London: University of Chicago Press.

1985. *Tokugawa Ideology: Early Constructs, 1570–1680.* Princeton, NJ: Princeton University Press.

2009. *Imperial Politics and Symbolics in Ancient Japan: The Tenmu Dynasty, 650–800.* Honolulu: University of Hawai'i Press.

Ōta Nanpo. 1985–1990. *Ōta Nanpo zenshū.* Tokyo: Iwanami Shoten.

Ōta Hideaki. 2013. *Nihon shakai minshu shugi no keisei: Katayama Sen to sono jidai.* Tokyo: Nihon hyōronsha.

Ōta Seikyū. 1985. *Fujiwara Seika.* Tokyo: Yoshikawa kōbunkan.

Pak, Hong-gyu. 2002. *Yamazaki Ansai no seiji rinen.* Tokyo: Tōkyō daigaku shuppankai.

Palmer, David A., Glenn Shive, and Philip Wickeri. 2011. *Chinese Religious Life.* New York etc: Oxford University Press.

Paramore, Kiri. 2006. "Hayashi Razan's Redeployment of Anti-Christian Discourse: The Fabrication of Haiyaso." *Japan Forum* 18 (2): 185–206.

2009. *Ideology and Christianity in Japan.* London etc: Routledge.

2012a. "Political Modernity and Secularization: Thoughts from the Japanese Eighteenth and Nineteenth Centuries." *Journal of Religious History* 36 (1): 19–30.

2012b. "Confucianism versus Feudalism: The Shoheizaka Academy and Late Tokugawa Reform." In Mark Teeuwen and Anna Beerens (eds.), *Uncharted Waters: Intellectual Life in the Edo Period.* Leiden: Brill.

2012c. "The Nationalization of Confucianism: Academism, Examinations, and Bureaucratic Governance in the Late Tokugawa State." *The Journal of Japanese Studies* 38 (1): 25–53.

2015. "'Civil Religion' and Confucianism: Japan's Past, China's Present, and the Current Scholarly Boom on Confucianism." *Journal of Asian Studies* 74 (2): 269–82.

Passin, Herbert. 1965. *Society and Education in Japan*. New York: Teachers College Press; New York.

Perdue, Peter C. 2005. *China Marches West: The Qing Conquest of Central Eurasia*. Cambridge, MA: Belknap Press of Harvard University Press.

Piggott, Joan R. 1997. *The Emergence of Japanese Kingship*. Stanford, CA: Stanford University Press.

Piketty, Thomas. 2014. *Capital in the Twenty-First Century*. Cambridge MA: The Belknap Press of Harvard University Press.

Pines, Yuri. 2012. "A Confucian Constitutional Order: How China's Ancient Past Can Shape Its Political Future by Jiang Qing (review)." *China Review International* 19 (4): 608–14.

Pollack, David. 1985. *Zen Poems of the Five Mountains*. New York, NY; Decatur, GA: Crossroad Pub.; Scholars Press.

1986. *The Fracture of Meaning: Japan's Synthesis of China From the Eighth Through the Eighteenth Centuries*. Princeton, NJ: Princeton University Press.

Puett, Michael. 2010. "Theodicies of Discontinuity: Domesticating Energies and Dispositions in Early China." *Journal of Chinese Philosophy* 37 (Supplement 1): 51–66.

2013. "Critical Approaches to Religion in China." *Critical Research on Religion* 1 (1): 95–101.

2014. *The Ground Between: Anthropologists Engage Philosophy*. Durham: Duke University Press.

Rangen. Anonymous manuscript held by Waseda University Library with Igakukan stamps and dated 1843.

Rawls, John. 1999. *A Theory of Justice*. Cambridge, MA: Belknap Press of Harvard University Press.

Rosenblum, Nancy L. and Robert Post (eds.). 2002. *Civil Society and Government*. Princeton, NJ: Princeton University Press.

Rotschild, Norman Harry. 2003. *Rhetoric, Ritual, and Support Constituencies in the Political Authority of Wu Zhao, Woman Emperor of China*. Ann Arbor: UMI.

Rozman, Gilbert. 2014. *The East Asian Region: Confucian Heritage and Its Modern Adaptation*. Princeton: Princeton University Press.

Rubinger, Richard. 1982. *Private Academies of Tokugawa Japan*. Princeton, NJ: Princeton University Press.

2007. *Popular Literacy in Early Modern Japan*. Honolulu: University of Hawai'i Press.

Sagers, John H. 2006. *Origins of Japanese Wealth and Power: Reconciling Confucianism and Capitalism, 1830–1885*. New York: Palgrave Macmillan.

Saigusa, Hiroto. 1956. *Nihon tetsugaku shisō zensho. dai jūrokkan: shūyō hen, chadō hen*. Vol. 16. Tokyo: Heibonsha.

Sakurai, Eiji. 1996. *Nihon Chūsei No Keizai Kōzo*. Tōkyō: Iwanami Shoten.

Sassa, Mitsuaki. n.d. "Higashi Ajia Kindai Ni Okeru Kōkyō Undō no tenkai – Kang Youwei to Chōsenjin Jugakusha to no kōryū wo chūshin ni." *Ritsumeikan Bungaku* 626: 1484–897.

Sassen, Saskia. 2006. *Territory, Authority, Rights: From Medieval to Global Assemblages.* Princeton, NJ etc: Princeton University Press.

Sawada, Janine Anderson. 1993. *Confucian Values and Popular Zen: Sekimon Shingaku in Eighteenth-Century Japan.* Honolulu: University of Hawaii Press.

1998. "Mind and Morality in Nineteenth-Century Japanese Religions: Misogi-Kyō and Maruyama-Kyō." *Philosophy East and West* 48 (1): 108–41. doi:10.2307/1399927.

2004. *Practical Pursuits: Religion, Politics, and Personal Cultivation in Nineteenth-Century Japan.* Honolulu: University of Hawai'i Press.

Scalapino, Robert A. 1983. *The Early Japanese Labor Movement: Labor and Politics in a Developing Society.* Berkeley, CA: Institute of East Asian Studies, University of California, Berkeley, Center for Japanese Studies.

Schwab, Raymond. 1984. *The Oriental Renaissance: Europe's Rediscovery of India and the East, 1680–1880.* New York: Columbia University Press.

Schwartz, Benjamin I. and Charlotte Furth. 1972. *Reflections on the May Fourth Movement: A Symposium.* Cambridge: East Asian Research Center, Harvard University; distributed by Harvard University Press.

Screech, Timon. 1996. *The Western Scientific Gaze and Popular Imagery in Later Edo Japan: The Lens within the Heart.* Cambridge etc: Cambridge University Press.

2000. *The Shogun's Painted Culture: Fear and Creativity in the Japanese States, 1760–1829.* Envisioning Asia. London: Reaktion.

Seki, Kōsaku. 1893. *Inoue Hakase to kirisutokyōto: kyōiku to shūkyō no shōtotsu ronsō.* Tokyo: Tetsugaku shoin.

Seth, Michael J. 2002. *Education Fever: Society, Politics, and the Pursuit of Schooling in South Korea.* Honolulu: University of Hawaii Press.

2010. *A Concise History of Modern Korea: From the Late Nineteenth Century to the Present.* Lanham, MD: Rowman & Littlefield.

Shibatani, Masayoshi. 1990. *The Languages of Japan.* Cambridge etc: Cambridge University Press.

Shibunkai (ed.). 1999. *Shibunkai 80 Nen Shushi.* Tokyo: Shibunkai.

2015. "Yushima Seidō no Shōgai Gakushū." [pamphlet] Tokyo: Shibunkai.

Shinbunkai. 1999. *Nihon Jugaku nenpyō.* Tokyo: Shinbunkai.

Shibusawa, Eiichi. 1918. *Shisei Doryoku Shūyō Kōwa.* Tokyo: Tachikawa bunmeidou.

1937. *Rakuōkō den.* Tokyo: Iwanami shoten.

1994. *The Autobiography of Shibusawa Eiichi: From Peasant to Entrepreneur.* Tokyo: University of Tokyo Press.

Shibusawa, Eiichi, Yasuda Zenjiro, Morimura Ichizaemon. 1918. *Shūyō Zensho.* Tokyo: Teikoku kyōiku gakkai.

Shimada, Kenji. 1967. *Daigaku Chūyō.* Tokyo: Asahi shinbunsha.

Shimao, Arata and Kojima Tsuyoshi. 2014. *Higashi Ajia no naka no Gozan bunka.* Tokyo: Tokyo University Press.

Shin, Doh Chull. 2012. *Confucianism and Democratization in East Asia*. New York: Cambridge University Press.

Shirane, Haruo and Suzuki Tomi. 2000. *Inventing the Classics: Modernity, National Identity, and Japanese Literature*. Stanford, CA: Stanford University Press.

Smith, Warren W. 1959. *Confucianism in Modern Japan: A Study of Conservatism in Japanese Intellectual History*. Tokyo: Hokuseido Press.

Smith, Wilfred Cantwell. 1963. *The Meaning and End of Religion; a New Approach to the Religious Traditions of Mankind*. New York: Macmillan.

Smits, Ivo. 1995. *The Pursuit of Loneliness: Chinese and Japanese Nature Poetry in Medieval Japan, Ca. 1050–1150*. Stuttgart: Franz Steiner Verlag.

Snodgrass, Judith. 2003. *Presenting Japanese Buddhism to the West: Orientalism, Occidentalism, and the Columbian Exposition*. Chapel Hill: University of North Carolina Press.

Souyri, Pierre François. 2001. *The World Turned Upside Down: Medieval Japanese Society*. New York: Columbia University Press.

Standaert, Nicolas. 1999. "The Jesuits Did NOT Manufacture 'Confucianism.'" *East Asian Science, Technology, and Medicine* 16 (January): 105–32.

Stanley, Brian. 1990. *The Bible and the Flag: Protestant Missions and British Imperialism in the Nineteenth and Twentieth Centuries*. Leicester, England: Apollos.

Starrs, Roy. 1994. *Deadly Dialectics: Sex, Violence, and Nihilism in the World of Yukio Mishima*. Honolulu: University of Hawaii Press.

2011. *Politics and Religion in Modern Japan: Red Sun, White Lotus*. Houndmills etc: Palgrave Macmillan.

Strathern, Alan. 2007. "Transcendentalist Intransigence: Why Rulers Rejected Monotheism in Early Modern Southeast Asia and Beyond." *Comparative Studies in Society and History* 49 (2): 358–83.

Sueki, Fumihiko. 2004. *Kindai Nihon no shisō saikō*. Tokyo: Transview.

2012a. *Nihon no kosei: "rekishi" kara "genzai" o yomitoku tame no 9-shō*. Tokyo: Shinjinbutsu Ōraisha.

2012b. *Tetsugaku no genba: Nihon de kangaeru to iu koto*. Tokyo: Transiew.

Sugawara, Hikaru. 2009. *Nishi Amane no seiji shisō*. Tokyo: Perikansha.

Sugimoto, Masayoshi. 1989. *Science and Culture in Traditional Japan*. Rutland, VT: Charles E Tuttle Co.

Sun, Anna. 2013. *Confucianism as a World Religion: Contested Histories and Contemporary Realities*. Princeton, NJ: Princeton University Press.

Tajiri, Yūichirō. 2006. *Yamazaki Ansai no sekai*. Tokyo: Perikansha.

Takazawa Noriharu. 2012. *Matsudaira Sadanobu*. Tokyo: Yoshikawa Kōbunkan.

Takeuchi Makoto. 2009. *Kansei kaikaku no kenkyū*. Tokyo: Yoshikawa Kōbunkan.

Takimoto, Seiichi (ed.). 1914. *Nihon Keizai Sōsho, Vol. 17*. Tokyo: Nihon keizai sosho kankokai.

Teeuwen, Mark. 2002. "From Jindō to Shinto: A Concept Takes Shape." *Japanese Journal of Religious Studies* 29 (3/4): 233–63.

2007. "Comparative Perspectives on the Emergence of Jindō and Shinto." *Bulletin of the School of Oriental and African Studies* 70 (2): 373–402.

Toby, Ronald P. 2008. *"Sakoku" to Iu Gaikō.* Tokyo: Shōgakkan.

Tsuda, Mamichi. 2001. *Tsuda Mamichi zenshū.* Tokyo: Misuzu Shobō.

Tsuda, Sōkichi. 1970. *Shina shisō to Nihon.* Tōkyō: Iwanami shoten.

Tsujimoto, Masashi. 1990. *Kinsei Kyōiku Shisōshi No Kenkyū: Nihon Ni Okeru "Kōkyōiku" Shisō No Genryū.* Kyōto: Shibunkaku Shuppan.

Tsūkō ichiran. 1913. Tokyo: Kokusho kankōkai.

Tsutsui, Kiyotada. 1999. *Ishibashi Tanzan: jiyū shugi seijika no kiseki.* Tokyo: Chūō Kōronsha.

Tu, Weiming. 1996. *Confucian Traditions in East Asian Modernity: Moral Education and Economic Culture in Japan and the Four Mini-Dragons.* Cambridge, MA: Harvard University Press.

Tu, Wei-ming, Milan Hejtmanek, and Alan Wachman. 1992. *The Confucian World Observed: A Contemporary Discussion of Confucian Humanism in East-Asia.* Honolulu: Institute of Culture and Communication, The East-West Center.

Tu, Weiming and Mary Evelyn Tucker. 2004. *Confucian Spirituality.* New York: Crossroad Publishing Company.

Tucker, John Allen. 2013. "Japanese Confucian Philosophy." In Edward N. Zalta (ed.), *The Stanford Encyclopedia of Philosophy.* Fall.

2013. *Critical Readings on Japanese Confucianism.* Leiden etc: Brill.

1988. "Religious Aspects of Japanese Neo-Confucianism: The Thought of Nakae Tōju and Kaibara Ekken." *Japanese Journal of Religious Studies* 15 (1): 55–69.

Tucker, Mary Evelyn. 1998. "Religious Dimensions of Confucianism: Cosmology and cultivation (The Religious Dimension of Confucianism in Japan)." *Philosophy East and West* 48 (1).

Tsuji, Tetsuo. 2013. *Nihon no kagaku shiso; sono jiritsu eno mosaku.* Tokyo: Kobushi Shobō.

Umihara Ryō. 2007. *Kinsei iryō no shakaishi: chishiki, gijutsu, jōhō.* Tokyo: Yoshikawa Kōbunkan.

Umihara Tōru. 1983. *Kinsei shijuku no kenkyū.* Kyōto: Shibunkaku shuppan.

Vaporis, Constantine Nomikos. 2008. *Tour of Duty: Samurai, Military Service in Edo, and the Culture of Early Modern Japan.* Honolulu: University of Hawai'i Press.

Veer, Peter van der. 2001. *Imperial Encounters: Religion and Modernity in India and Britain.* Princeton, NJ: Princeton University Press.

Victoria, Daizen. 1997. *Zen at War.* New York: Weatherhill.

Wajima, Yoshio. 1965. *Chūsei No Jugaku.* Tokyo: Yoshikawa Kōbunkan.

Wakabayashi, Bob Tadashi. 1986. *Anti-Foreignism and Western Learning in Early-Modern Japan: The New Theses of 1825.* Cambridge, MA: Council on East Asian Studies, Harvard University.

Wakeman, Frederic, Jr. 1997. "A Revisionist View of the Nanjing Decade: Confucian Fascism." *The China Quarterly* 150: 395–432.

Waldron, Jeremy J. 1984. *Theories of Rights.* Oxford etc: Oxford University Press.

Wang, Jiahua. 1988. *Nitchū Jugaku No Hikaku.* Tokyo: Rokkō Shuppan.

Wang, Qingjia. 2001. *Inventing China through History: The May Fourth Approach to Historiography.* Albany, NY: State University of New York Press.

Wang, Yuan-Kang. 2011. *Harmony and War: Confucian Culture and Chinese Power Politics*. New York: Columbia University Press.

Watanabe, Hiroshi. 1985. *Kinsei Nihon shakai to Sōgaku*. Tōkyō: Tōkyō Daigaku Shuppankai.

1997. *Higashi Ajia No Ōken to Shisō*. Tōkyō: Tōkyō Daigaku Shuppankai.

2000. "Fūfu Yūbetu to Fūfu Aiyawarashi." *Chuugoku – Shakai to Bunka* 15.

2010. *Nihon seiji shisōshi: jūshichi–jūkuseiki*. Tōkyō: Tōkyō Daigaku Shuppankai.

2012. *A History of Japanese Political Thought, 1600–1901*. Tokyo: International House of Japan.

Watanabe, Hiroshi and Ch'ung-sŎk Pak, eds. 2005. *Kankoku Nihon "Seiyō": Sono Kōsaku to Shisō Hen'yō*. Tokyo: Keiō Gijuku Daigaku Shuppankai.

Watanabe, Yogorō. 1985. *Shimon Fisseringu kenkyū*. Tokyo: Bunka shobō hakubunsha.

Weller, Robert P. 2005. *Civil Life, Globalization, and Political Change in Asia: Organizing between Family and State*. London; New York: Routledge.

Xiong, Zongli. 1988. *Ming Fang Lei Zheng Yi Shu Da Quan*. Shanghai: Shanghai ke xue ji shu chu ban she.

Xue, Ji. 1976. *Jiao Zhu Fu Ren Liang Fang: (quan)*. Hancheng: Jin Yong chu ban she.

Xu, Changzhi. 1855. *Po xie ji. [8 zhuan]*. Mito: Kōdōkan.

Xu, Jiyu. 2000. *Ying Huan Zhi Lüe*. Beijing: Zhonghua quan guo tu shu guan wen xian suo wei fu zhi zhong xin.

Yamamoto, Shinkō. 1985. *Shingaku Gorinsho No Kisoteki Kenkyū*. Tokyo: Gakushūin Daigaku.

Yamazaki, Ansai. 1978. *Yamazaki Ansai zenshū*. Vol. 3. Tokyo: Perikansha.

Yamazaki, Tasuku. 1953. *Edo-Ki Zen Nihon Iji Hōsei No Kenkyū*. Tōkyō: Chūgai Igakusha.

Yamazumi, Masami (ed.). 1990. *Nihon Kindai Shisō Taikei*. Vol. 6, Kyoiku no taikei. Tokyo: Iwanami Shoten.

Yang, C.K. 1967. *Religion in Chinese Society*. Berkeley: University of California Press.

Yang, Daqing. 2012. *Toward a History beyond Borders: Contentious Issues in Sino-Japanese Relations*. Cambridge, MA etc: Harvard University Press.

Yang, Fenggang and Joseph B. Tamney. 2012. *Confucianism and Spiritual Traditions in Modern China and Beyond*. Leiden etc: Brill.

Yao, Xinzhong. 2000. *An Introduction to Confucianism*. Cambridge etc: Cambridge University Press.

Yonaha, Jun. 2009. *Hon'yaku No Seijigaku: Kindai Higashi Ajia Sekai No Keisei to Nichi-Ryū Kankei No Hen'yō*. Tokyo: Iwanami Shoten.

2011. *Chūgokuka Suru Nihon: Nitchū Bunmei No Shōtotsu Issennenshi*. Tokyo: Bungei Shunjū.

2013. *Zhongguo Hua de Riben: Ri Zhong "Wen Ming Chong Tu" Qian Nian Shi*. Guilin Shi: Guangxi shi fan da xue chu ban she.

2012–13. "One Step Ahead of History." *2012–2013*, Nihon Keizai Shinbun edition. http://toyokeizai.net/category/j-yonaha [viewed 5 May 2015].

Yonemoto, Marcia. 2003. *Mapping Early Modern Japan: Space, Place, and Culture in the Tokugawa Period, 1603–1868*. Berkeley: University of California Press.

Yoshikawa, Kōjirō. 1983. *Jinsai, Sorai, Norinaga: Three Classical Philologists of Mid-Tokugawa Japan*. Tokyo: Tōhō Gakkai.

Yoshimi, Yoshiaki. 1987. *Kusa No Ne No Fashizumu: Nihon Minshū No Sensō Taiken*. Tokyo: Tōkyō Daigaku Shuppankai.

Yu, Anthony C. 2005. *State and Religion in China: Historical and Textual Perspectives*. Chicago: Open Court.

Yu, Ying-shih. 2004. *Xian dai ru xue de hui gu yu zhan wang*. Beijing: ShenhuoDushu, Xinzhisanlianshudian.

Zhu, Xi. 1983. *Si Shu Zhang Ju Ji Zhu*. Beijing: Zhonghua shu ju.

1985. *Zhuzi Yu Lei: [140 Juan]*. Beijing: Zhonghua shu ju.

Zürcher, Erik 2000. "China and the West: The Image of Europe and Its Impact." In Uhalley Stephen, Jr. and Xiaoxin Wu (eds.), *China and Christianity: Burdened Past, Hopeful Future*. Armonk, NY: Sharpe.

Index